IMAGES
of America

PORT ISABEL

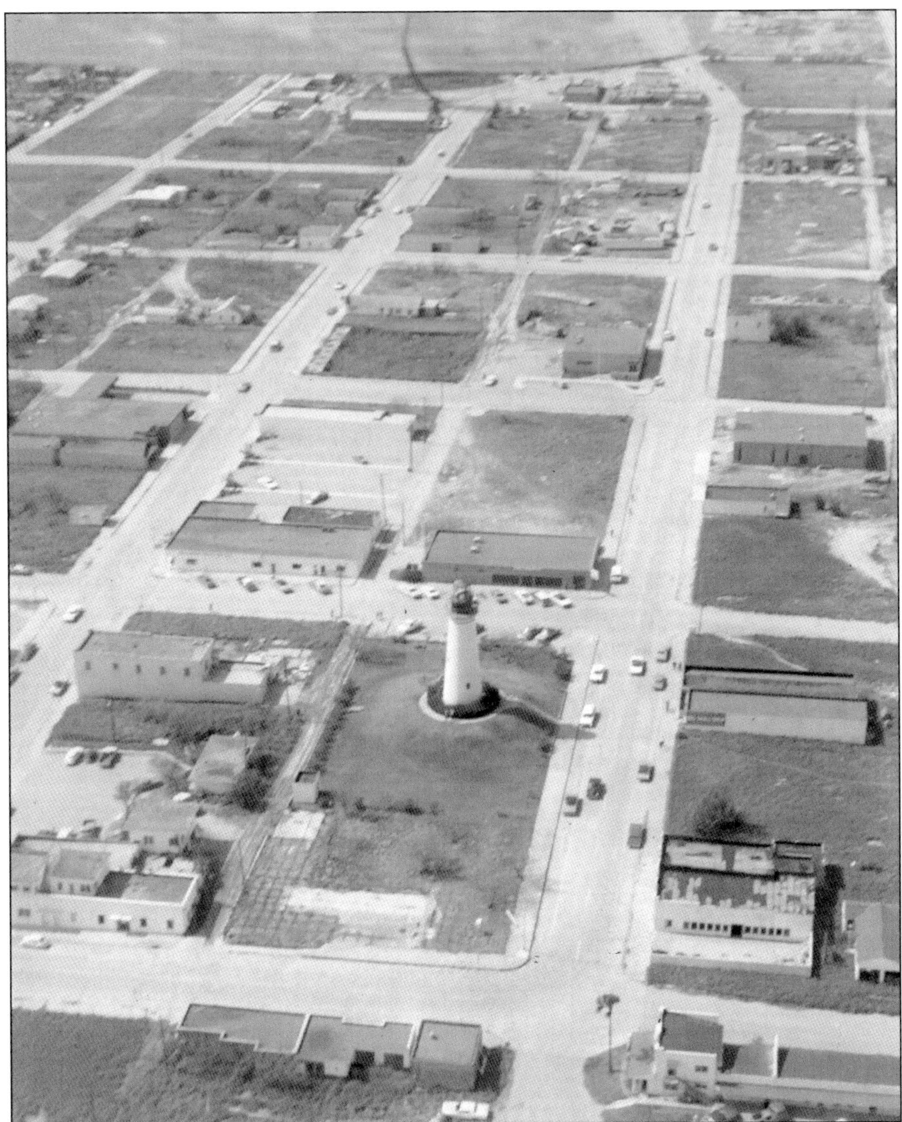

Taken between 1968 and prior to the construction of the 1974 Queen Isabella Causeway, the lighthouse sat on a city block bordered by Powers (left), Tarnava (top), Maxan (right), and Garcia Streets (bottom). At this time, Purdy's Courts was still housing visitors. There were the new post office and new city hall on Maxan Street and a new Merchants Marine Bank on Powers Street. The lighthouse was still open to the public at this time, and its stairway was located on the north side. The half block between the north alley and Powers Street and Garcia Street and Yturria Street was entirely razed to make way for a four-lane State Highway 100 with a median.

On the Cover: Port Isabel is poised for the future. Less than 200,000 vehicles were registered in Texas around the time this photograph was taken in the early 1920s, and the road between San Benito and Port Isabel was not an all-weather affair, but the lure of the coast for both the tourist and pioneer was hard to resist. Plans were underway for a complete overhaul of the town, and when rebuilding began, the Champion Building, the lighthouse, and a few residential and commercial buildings were all that remained. (Courtesy Museums of Port Isabel.)

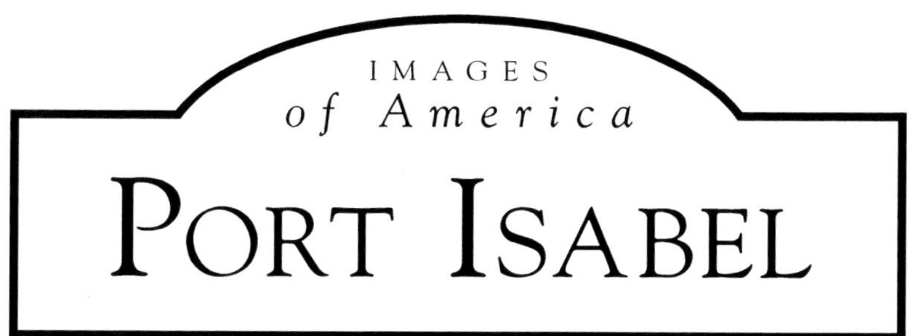

Valerie D. Bates

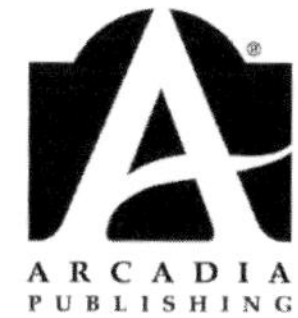

ISBN 978-0-7385-9687-7

Published by Arcadia Publishing
Charleston, South Carolina

Printed in the United States of America

Library of Congress Control Number: 2012954200

For all general information, please contact Arcadia Publishing:
Telephone 843-853-2070
Fax 843-853-0044
E-mail sales@arcadiapublishing.com
For customer service and orders:
Toll-Free 1-888-313-2665

Visit us on the Internet at www.arcadiapublishing.com

To my dear Port Isabellian, my daughter Amber,
who loves this history as much as I do

Contents

Acknowledgments

As 2012 marks the 15th anniversary of the Museums of Port Isabel, I wish to acknowledge the museums and Edward Meza for their tireless pursuit of the vision to protect the history of the Lower Laguna Madre and to the community of Port Isabel for making it impossible not to love our history.

I also wish to acknowledge the Harlingen Public Library Archives and Norman Rozeff for the fantastic "building a city where a city belongs" bond material.

Unless otherwise noted, all images appear courtesy of the Museums of Port Isabel Archives, private collections, or the Harlingen Public Library Archives.

The Museums of Port Isabel consists of three sites: the Port Isabel lighthouse and keeper's cottage, Port Isabel Historical Museum (housed in the Champion Building), and the Treasures of the Gulf Museum. They are all situated within walking distance of each other. For hours and ticket information, visit www.portisabelmuseums.com or www.portisabellighthouse.com.

Museums of Port Isabel
317 East Railroad Avenue
Port Isabel, Texas, 78578
956/943-7602

INTRODUCTION

Port Isabel is an indelible community located on the very southern tip of Texas, on the banks of the Laguna Madre Bay, just two miles from Brazos de Santiago Pass and the open waters of the Gulf of Mexico. Once known as a leading seaside resort for wealthy Mexican families, it was in those days known as El Fronton de Santa Isabella. A split in ideals resulted in a name change, and the town on the northern beaches was called El Fronton and the southern part of the town Punta Isabella, later Point Isabel. When Port Isabel was incorporated on March 13, 1928, the name was changed to Port Isabel.

Port Isabel's storied past begins in the sea breezes. As an outlet to the coast, Port Isabel became a natural attraction for the wealthy, adventurous, and mobile in the area of south Texas and northern Mexico. Locals made a living fishing and servicing the fishing and tourism industry. By the early 1800s, ranching had become important, and Don Rafael Garcia made the first land claim. Granted on January 24, 1829, it served as the first of the roots that would become a townsite. Property boundaries were marked with cabbage and ebony trees and posts and rocks.

Gen. Zachary Taylor arrived in 1846 with troops following either overland from Corpus Christi or by water. An earthen bastion he named Fort Polk was carved out of the clay, which was used as a supply base for the Mexican-American War. The strategic location choice for Fort Polk was not only important to the successful outcome of the Mexican-American War, but it also fostered Port Isabel's development.

By 1850, funding had been secured for the beacon to be built at Point Isabel. In 1853, the Point Isabel Lighthouse was lit and offered a 16-mile view in all directions. The year 1855 brought an addition of a keeper's house. A combination of the natural harbor, 30-foot bluffs, and its location within the barrier island of South Padre made Port Isabel a vital shelter for seagoing vessels.

The Civil War came to south Texas, and the lighthouse became a lookout for both Union and Confederate troops. Its lens was removed and hidden. It sustained a Confederate blast, which succeeded in only slightly damaging the top of the brick structure and blowing out the glass in the lantern.

A series of storms and hurricanes brought with them challenges, including loss of life and extensive property damage. In spite of the difficulties, a rail line from Port Isabel to Brownsville was constructed in 1872. The route selected, as the crow flies, bore the brunt of tides and storms. Often a scout would be sent out to report the track's condition before a trip could be made. During a stretch of six weeks without rail service, the route was reengineered to more stable ground.

The Bandit Wars between 1910 and 1918 brought the US Army to south Texas and Port Isabel. It also served to create an interest in what would later become a winter Texan destination for some of those same retiring troops. The tradition still continues for many Midwesterners.

The 1920s was a roaring time in Port Isabel. On the heels of widespread irrigation in the Rio Grande Valley, a master plan was put into motion. Streets, utilities, dredging, mass marketing, and the incorporation of the city culminated in the fruition of "building a city where a city belongs."

Just five years later, in 1933, the area was hard hit by a series of storms, causing widespread damage. Port Isabel and the attention it had garnered as a "phoenix rising from the ashes" was again in the news statewide, and the word of Port Isabel's death was greatly exaggerated. Missouri Pacific Railroad and community leaders launched an aggressive campaign to show the country that fishing was still spectacular in Port Isabel, and thus the Texas International Fishing Tournament was born.

Newspaper headlines as early as 1919 reflect the tremendous effort of the Rio Grande Valley to bring a deepwater port to Port Isabel. As railroad lines lengthened to that region, irrigation grew the agricultural industry and quality of life in south Texas was undisputed, thus a deepwater port was of utmost necessity. At last, on the July 30, 1935, at the opening of the seaport, Gov. James Allred announced, "When the valley's ship goes out, her ship will come in." The goal of a seaport was demonstrative of a valley-wide collaboration, as many communities raised funds for the SOS (Save Our Seaport) program.

As Port Isabel entered mid-century, the shrimping industry took center stage with the community taking on the title of "Shrimping Capital of the World." The lighthouse celebrated its century mark in 1952 and, with much fanfare, became a state park. Improvements continued and paved the way for the opening of the first Queen Isabella Causeway in February 1954. Though Port Isabel and South Padre Island had been connected by ferries and barges, which shuttled people, automobiles, and supplies back and forth, the convenience of a causeway brought an increase of traffic and development on both sides of the bridge.

By 1968, and ahead of schedule, the toll for the Queen Isabella Causeway was removed, and Port Isabel saw an increase in tourist traffic again. Souvenir shops, motor courts, hotels, motels, and restaurants sprang up around the lighthouse and all along State Highway 100. Fresh sea breezes, freshly caught and prepared seafood, and the open waters of the Laguna Madre Bay and the Gulf of Mexico made the coastal Port Isabel experience a unique one for the traveler from northern Mexico, Brownsville, and the Rio Grande Valley as well as the visitors from the Midwest.

In 1974, a second Queen Isabella Causeway was constructed just to the north of the original bridge. The resulting bridge abutment brought drastic changes to the townsite, including the removal of Powers Street, the street just south of the lighthouse, and the widening of State Highway 100. A number of historic buildings were razed to make way for the four-lane highway and its median. The original bridge was turned over to the Texas Parks and Wildlife Department. Its center span was removed, and the eastern portion became known as the Queen Isabella State Fishing Pier.

Eagerly embarking on the future, Port Isabel was a townsite that would not be denied. A great many obstacles have changed her path but not her mission. Still, the coast offers a superior quality of life for visitors and residents, and Port Isabel has tenaciously held to her history and culture and place on the southern tip of Texas.

One

Beginnings on the Bluff

El Paso de Brazos de Saint Iago (Pass of the Arms of Saint James) was the second point of discovery in the United States by Alonzo Alvarez de Pineda, on July 15, 1523, St. James Day, and this is where Port Isabel's recorded history begins.

An offer of 500 pesos to an Escandon colonist during the mid-1700s was advertised throughout the northern Mexican states. Spots were quickly filled, and settlements in the region known as Nuevo Santander sprang up. Mexican settlers within 200 miles vacationed at the coast in Port Isabel.

El Fronton de Santa Isabel, a ranch settlement, was established on property known as the Santa Ysabel Grant, which was given to Don Rafael Garcia on January 24, 1829. The cattle ranch was worked by hired hands while Garcia resided in nearby Matamoros, Tamaulipas, Mexico. A 10-year-old boy named Don "Chencho" Rosales, who later became a Port Isabel icon, relocated to the point from Matamoros, perhaps as one of Garcia's hired hands.

Trade and travel came through Brazos Santiago, and in 1844, Port Isabel was declared a port of entry. By 1859, $10 million worth of goods was imported and exported through Port Isabel. Gold in California brought fortune-seekers arriving by steamer from New Orleans, who then traveled overland.

"Exposed frontier" was the two-word description that President Polk used to describe this area in 1846. As negotiations broke down with Mexico over the boundaries of the newly formed state of Texas, Gen. Zachary Taylor was granted authority to use any means necessary to protect the border. Arriving in March 1846, Taylor set about constructing a depot to occupy the point. Supplies brought in from New Orleans were shipped by lighter from Brazos Santiago to the mainland. The fort was abandoned in 1850 but was a vital component in the Mexican-American War.

In December 1849, four Oblate Fathers stepped on shore, known as the Pilgrim Fathers of the Valley, making Port Isabel the Plymouth Rock of the Padres. The first Mass was held on December 3, 1849, and by 1854, the first chapel was constructed.

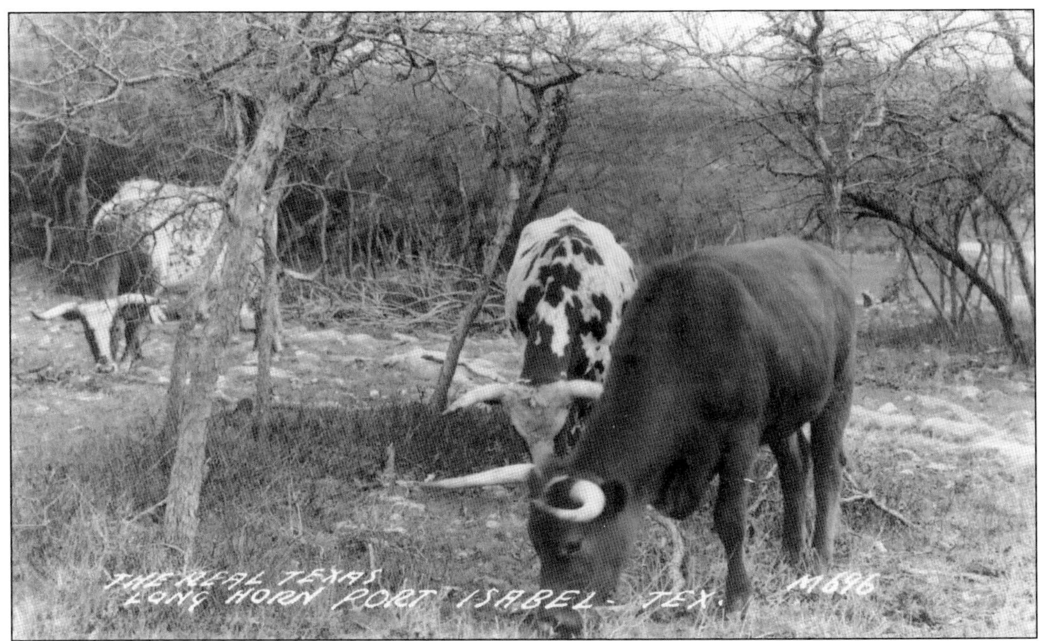

Don Rafael Garcia brought cattle ranching to Port Isabel during the early 1800s. Herds were shipped out through Brazos Santiago and also served several military encampments. Garcia's daughters would later be responsible for naming the streets on the 1875 plat of the townsite of Point Isabel.

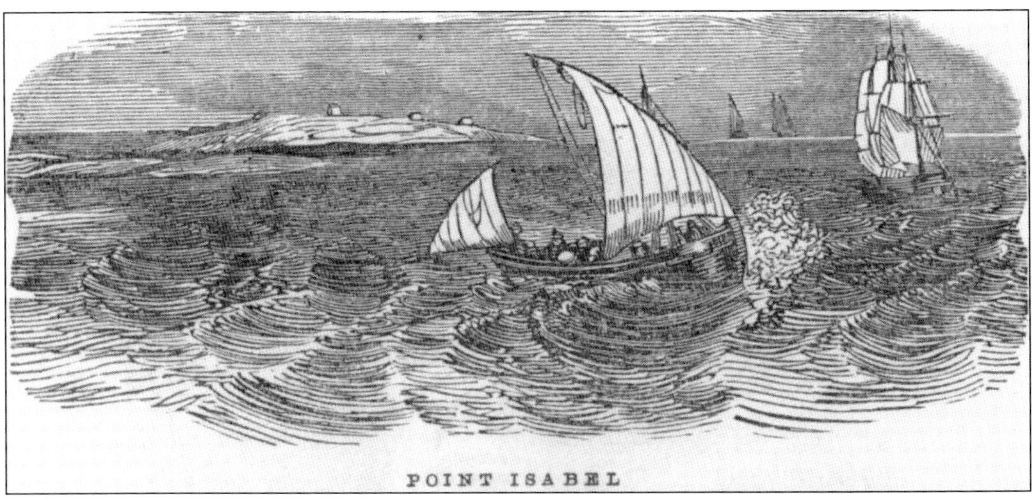

POINT ISABEL

Eyewitness accounts told of a variety of strange looking vessels around Port Isabel. Lesser drafting vessels able to make it over the bar at the pass and into the Laguna Madre Bay tied up in Port Isabel. Bluffs rising in the distant were inspiration for the earliest name of Port Isabel, El Fronton de Santa Ysabel; El Fronton meaning the "front," "bluff," or "pediment."

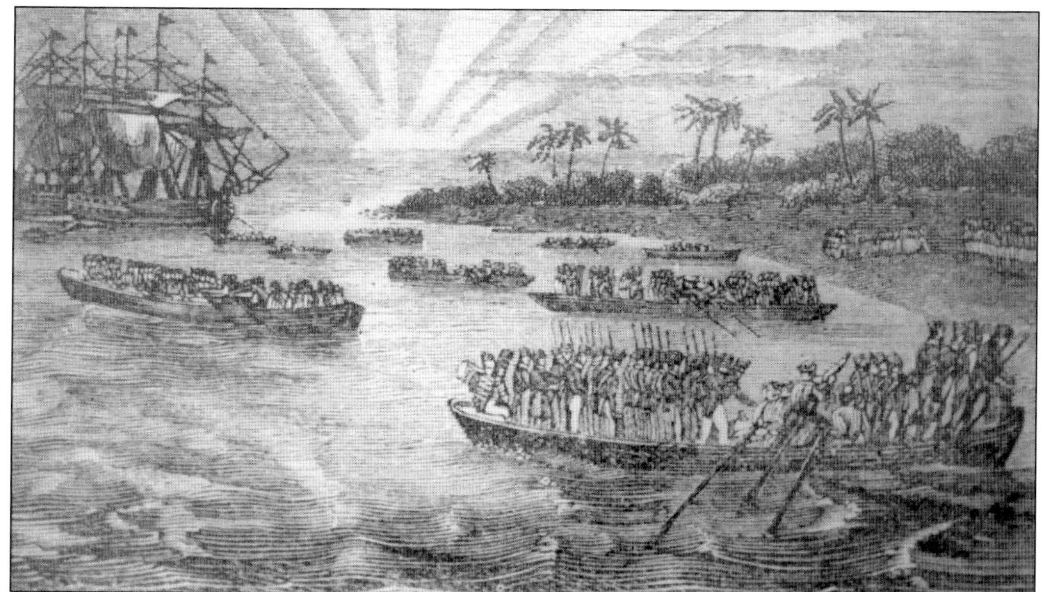

This old woodcut illustrates General Taylor's army making its way across the Laguna Madre Bay to the point to construct Fort Polk. It was thought to be extremely desolate by some, including a French war bride, who noted in a letter back home, "God give me the patience, to bear Point Isabel." Upon completion, Fort Polk became the home of the largest military hospital in the United States.

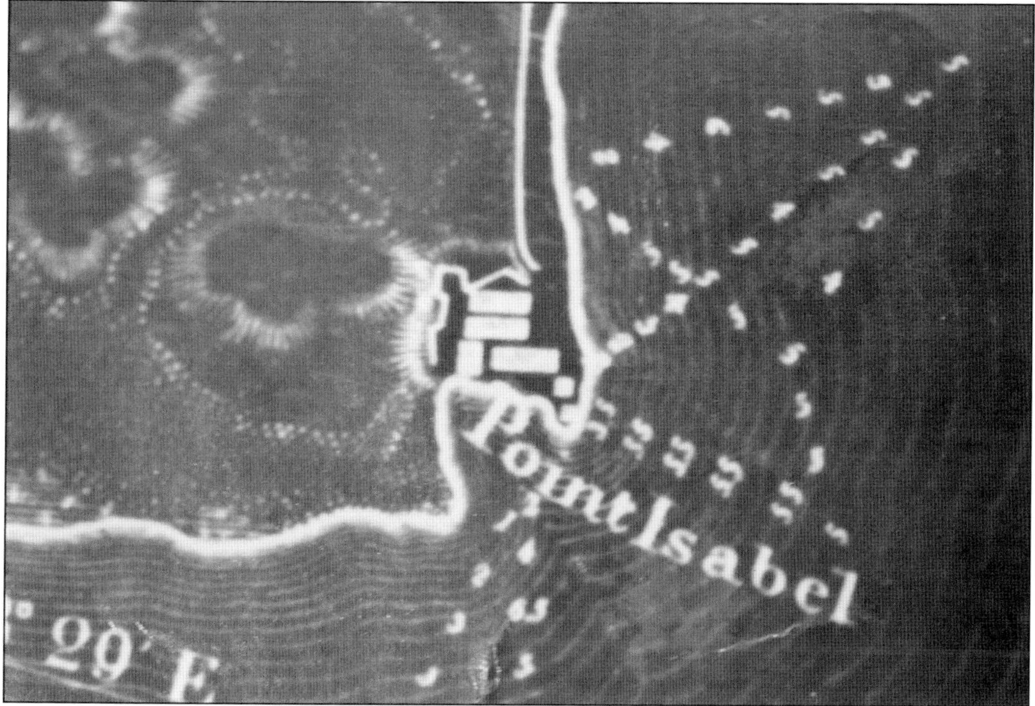

The site of Fort Polk on the point featured a six-sided fort, named for President Polk. It consisted of four sides of earthen embankments and two sides open to the shoreline. The fort was abandoned in 1850. Remnants of it were visible until the 1920s.

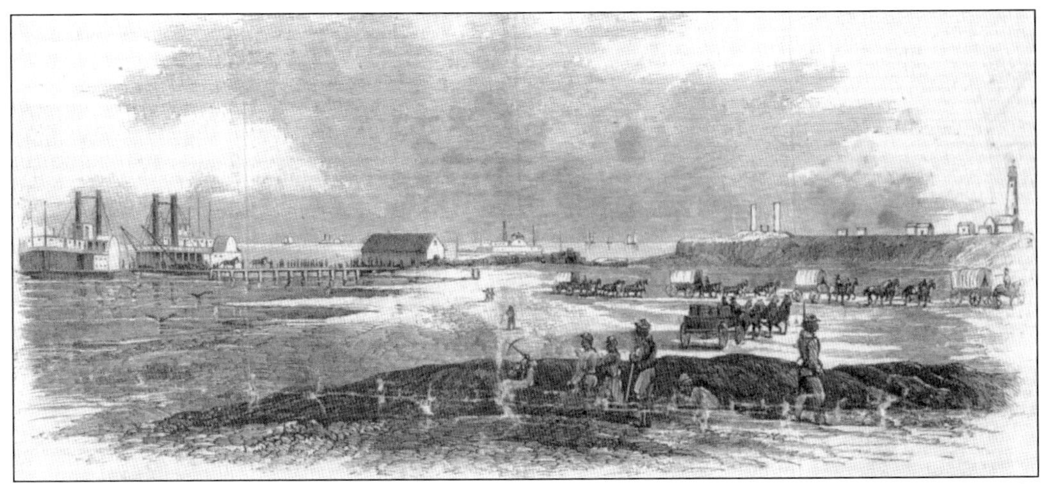

This *Frank Leslie's Illustrated Newspaper* sketch of Port Isabel shows a bustling 1864 seaside community, where the lighthouse and outlying buildings (right) tower over the shoreline of the bay. Soldiers are digging a trench in the foreground, center-wheel steamers and other watercraft dot the water, and men are using horses and wagons to unload provisions at the dock.

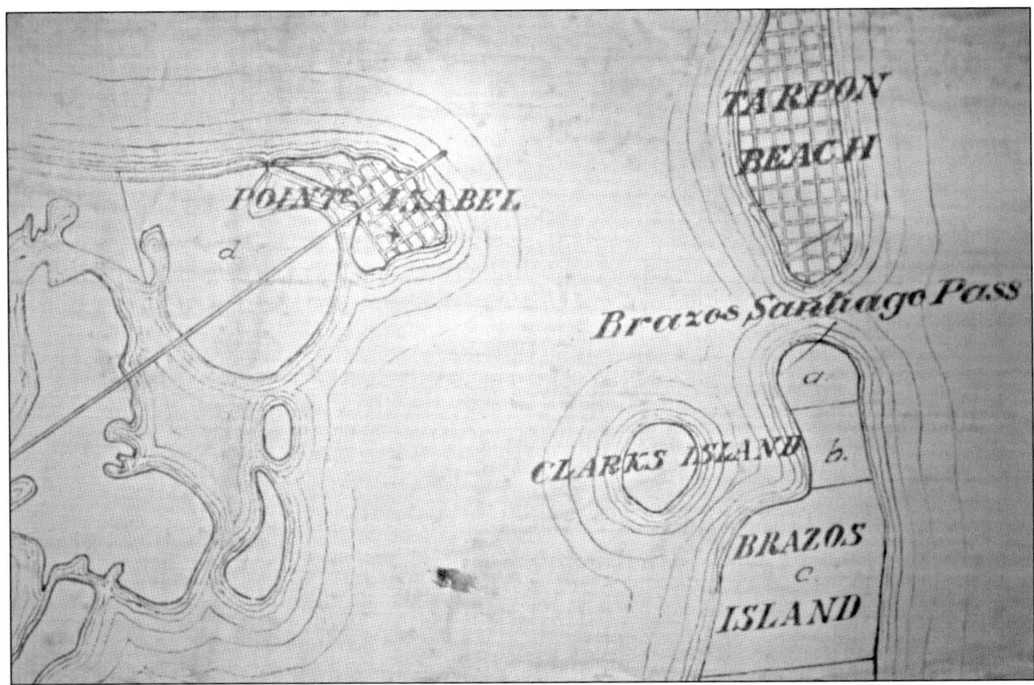

This portion of a 1917 map of Cameron County illustrates the proximity of Point Isabel to Tarpon Beach (South Padre Island), Brazos Santiago Pass, Clarks Island, and Brazos Island. With the open waters of the Gulf of Mexico just beyond the pass, the natural break in the barrier island at Brazos was a welcomed shelter to seagoing vessels.

Two

BUILDING A LIGHTHOUSE

It was determined in 1850 that there was a need for a navigational beacon in the Laguna Madre area. When Fort Polk was abandoned after the Mexican-American War, the site was transferred to the Treasury Department. On September 28, 1850, Congress appropriated $15,000 for a lighthouse and beacon light at Brazos Santiago. Upon completion in 1852, four lamps illuminated the lantern, and the structure stood 57 feet above the ground and 82 feet above sea level. In 1854, the lantern was fixed with 15 lamps and 21 reflectors. Three years later, a third-order lens was installed, and the fixed light was varied by flashes one minute apart.

At the conclusion of the Civil War, the light station was overhauled, refitted, and relit on February 22, 1866. In 1879, the lighthouse board's inspection discovered the poor condition of the tower. It was impossible to keep the lens and lamps dry in a rain, as the lantern leaked in every direction. In 1881, a new iron lantern was installed. The new octagon-shaped lantern now contained just 10 glass panes.

Property ownership came into question in 1887. It was found that the United States had no title to the land though it had been occupied by Gen. Zachary Taylor as a camp and depot at the start of the Mexican-American War. The light was extinguished on May 15, 1888, and the station abandoned pending settlement.

As the area was still in need of a navigational beacon, it was determined that $8,000 was needed to purchase land for a site. Owners of the Point Isabel Lighthouse site offered to sell it for $6,000. Congress appropriated $8,000 to purchase the land in 1889. As adversity was found on the title, with a debate about ownership of the property, the case was called for trial in 1891 in an effort to have the site condemned. Sale for $5,000 was finalized after the attorney general approved the title. The deed for the site was officially now in the government's possession. On July 15, 1895, the light was re-exhibited. Just 10 years later, in 1905, it was discontinued for the last time. In 1927, the site was again sold; the highest bidder paid $2,760.

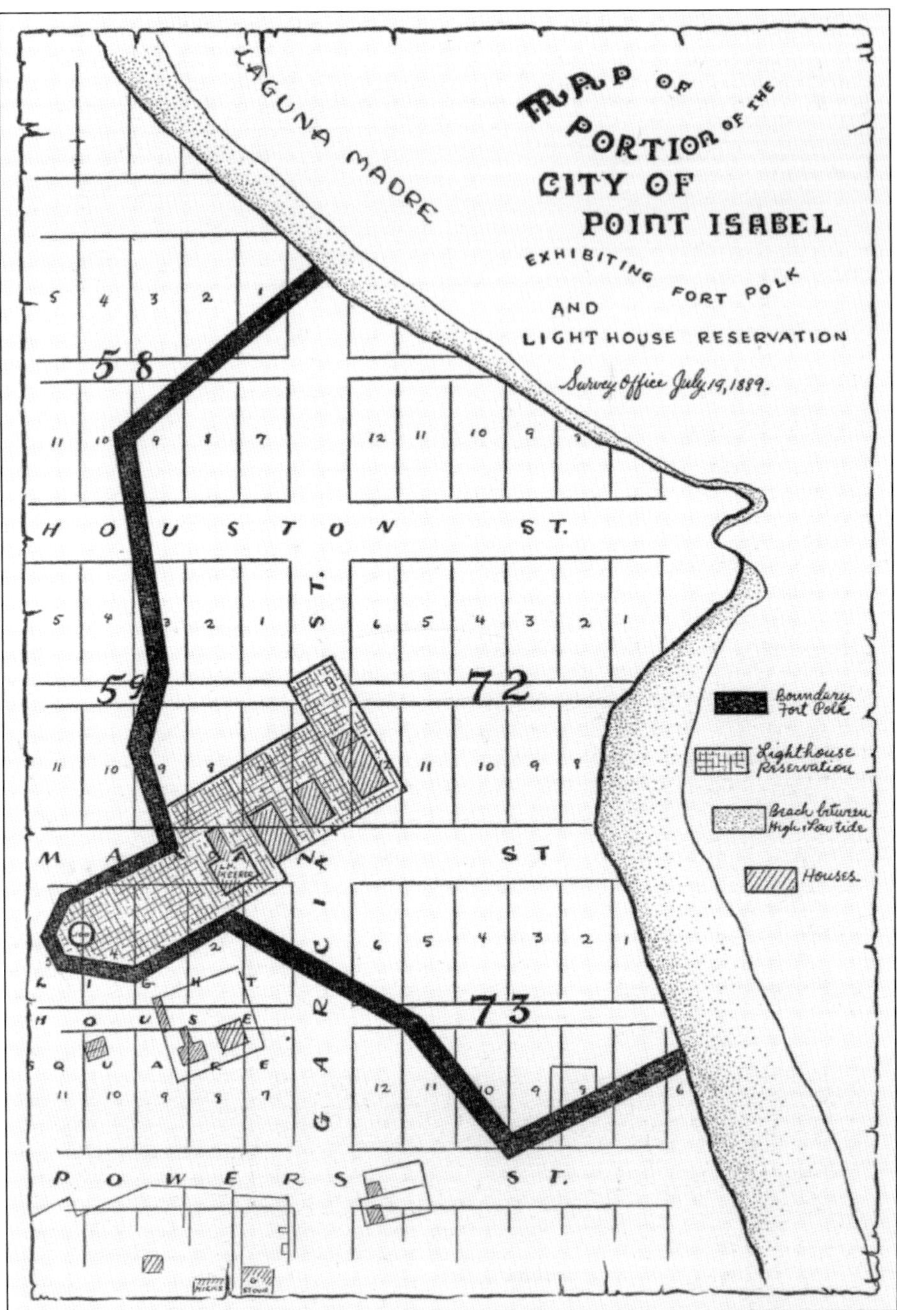

Located at 26º 04' 36" N and 97º 12' 24 W, between Maxan, Garcia, Powers, and Tarnava Streets, the site for the lighthouse fell within the boundaries of Fort Polk. The keeper's house, constructed three years after the lighthouse was completed, was in the middle of Maxan Street. The remaining outlying buildings were positioned northeast of the keeper's house, all within the boundaries of Gen. Zachary Taylor's Fort Polk. The elevation of the point, which originally attracted the construction of an earthen bastion, would also serve the lighthouse. The height of the tower was 50 feet, and the elevation of the lighthouse was 117 feet. It was declared a National Historic Site in 1976.

Two of the three 12-light windows are visible in this 1910s photograph of the tower. They were glazed with 8-inch-by-10-inch glass. Two of them were fixed, and the middle one was hinged to allow light in on the stairway. The photograph was taken before the hill it sits on was carved out of the terrain. The keeper's house and other outlying buildings are visible in the background.

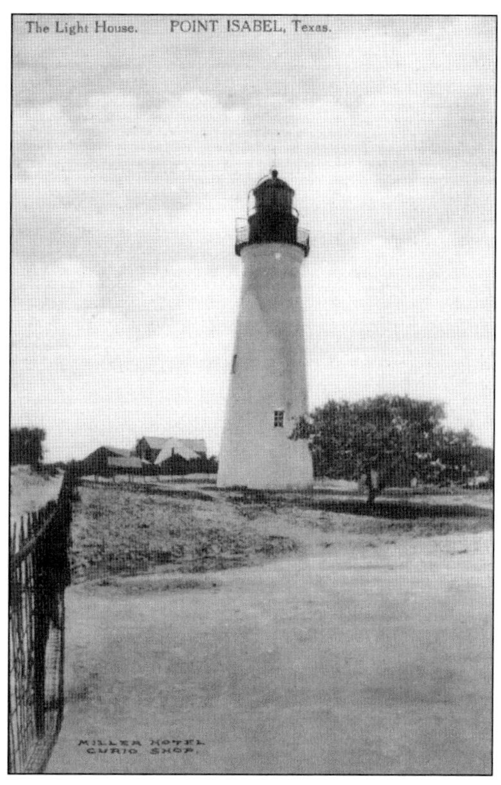

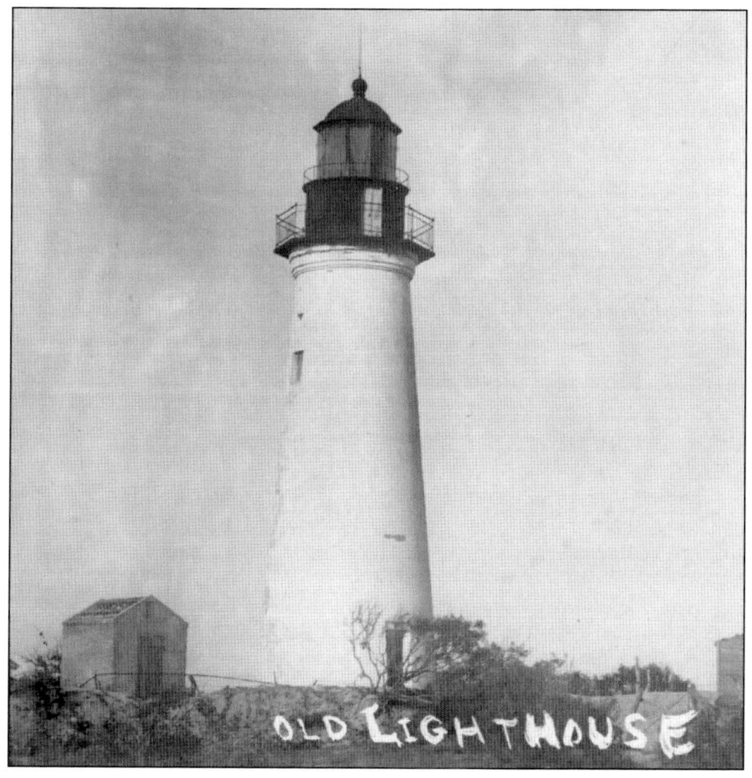

Shown around 1900 is the northwest side of the lighthouse with fencing and a brick oil house with roof damage. Note that the curtains are drawn, which occurred daily during daylight hours as part of the keeper's duties. The glass in the lantern room had to be replaced multiple times when birds crashed into the panes; removal of the birds was also a task to be attended to.

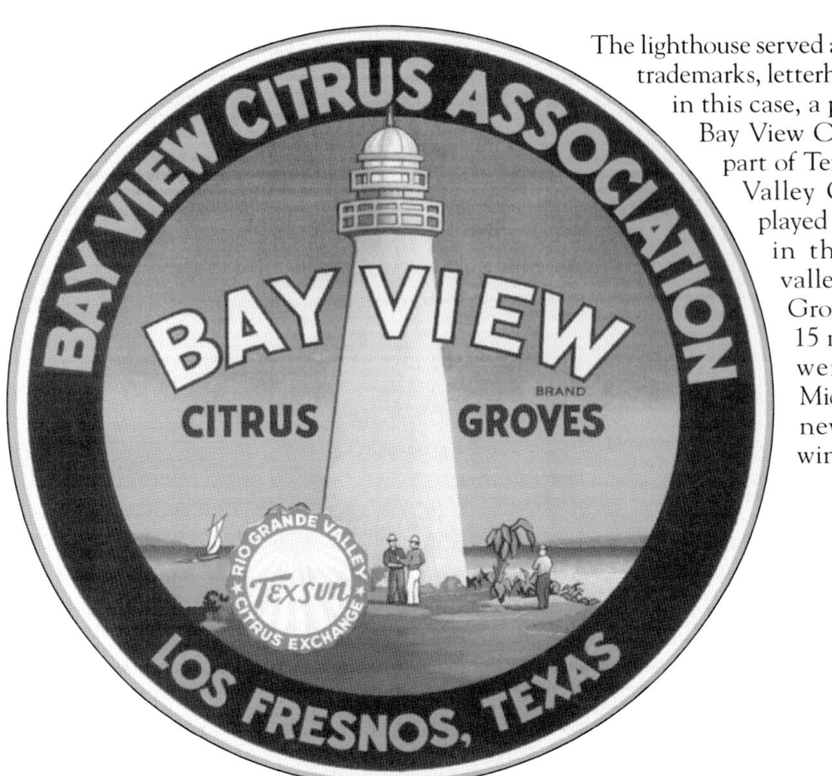

The lighthouse served as an icon for many trademarks, letterheads, signage, and, in this case, a produce label. The Bay View Citrus Association, part of Texsun's Rio Grande Valley Citrus Exchange, played an important role in the growth of the valley and Port Isabel. Groves planted within 15 miles of Port Isabel were used to lure Midwesterners to their new self-sustaining winter homesite.

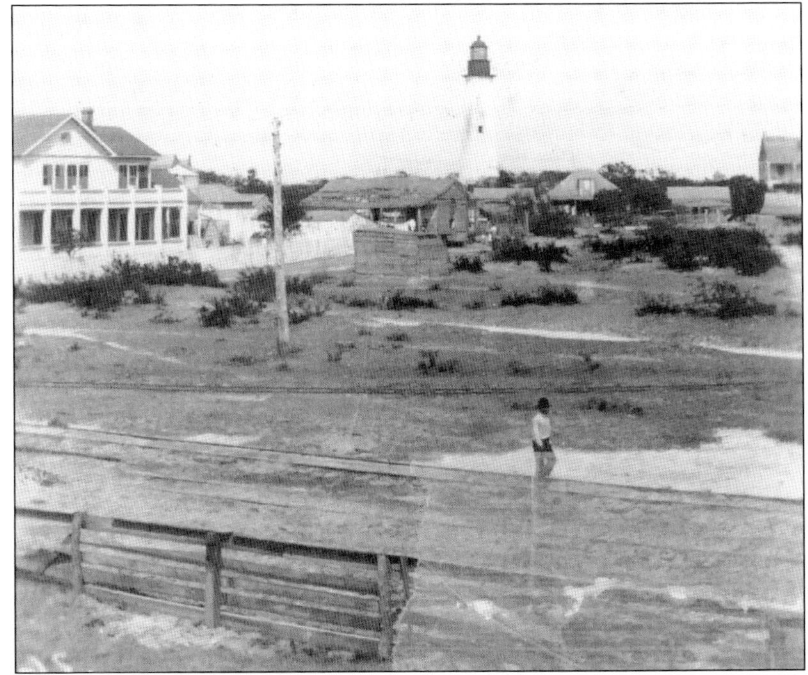

The lighthouse is operational in this pre-1905 photograph. Taken from south of the railroad tracks on the south side of the lighthouse, the image shows a town of contrasts. Buildings heavily damaged by storms are nestled among white picket-fenced, two-story houses with surrounding galleys. On the far right-hand side, a portion of the keeper's house is visible.

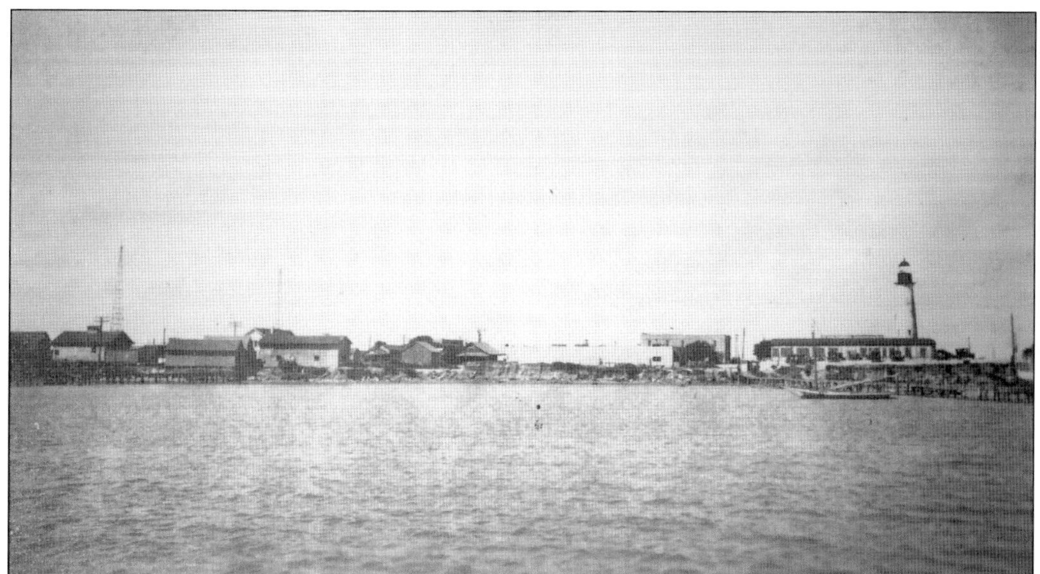

Here is an early-1920s skyline view of Port Isabel from the Laguna Madre Bay, which is where the lighthouse (right) sits behind the Port Isabel Company Administration Building. In this photograph, the new drugstore (left of the Administration Building) had just been completed. The Champion Building is about in the center with its windmill. Both wireless towers still stand at this time.

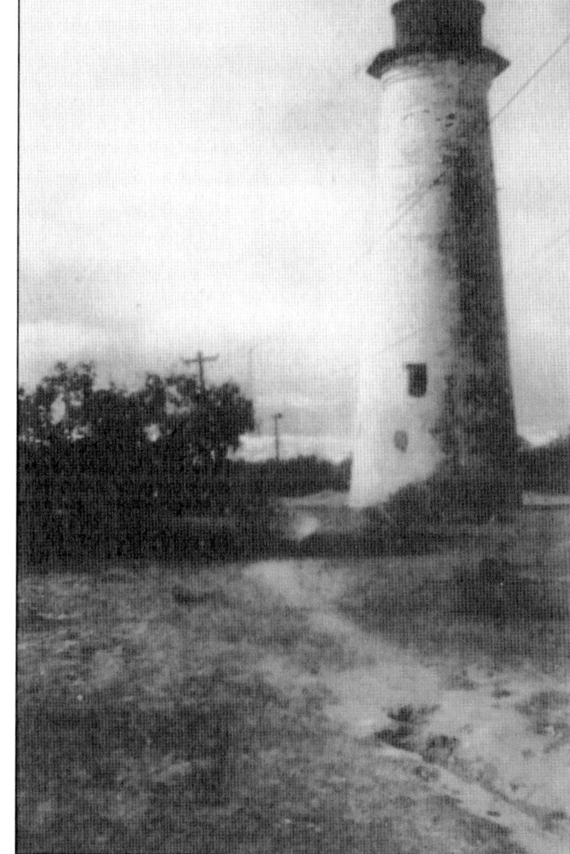

The lens is missing, and several of the panes in the lantern room and the railing on the catwalk suggest that the lighthouse is out of commission at the time of this photograph. A ravine has begun to form next to the lighthouse. In a 1943 interview, Don Chencho was convinced that the lighthouse would be torn down and the bricks used for another project.

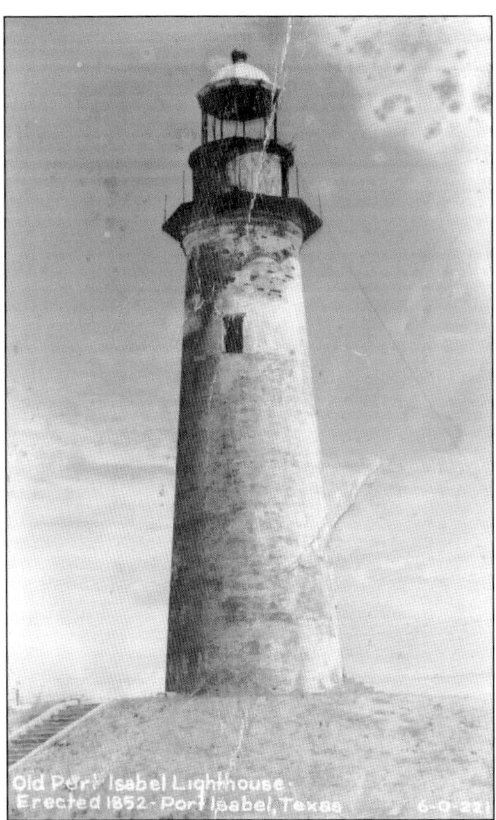

On December 6, 1851, the contract to construct the lighthouse was let by the US government. Despite it being about 90 years old and looking pretty rough, the lighthouse was still a popular tourist draw at the time of this photograph. It was the most photographed structure in the Rio Grande Valley.

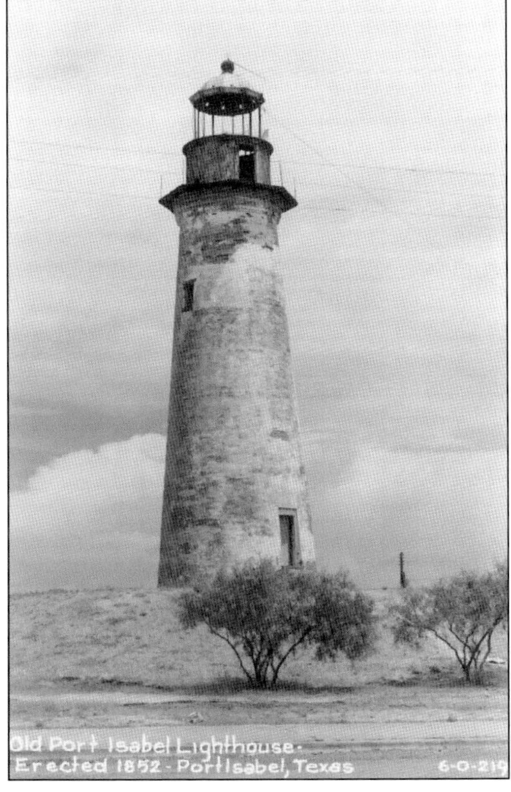

The mesquite trees in this photograph are still in existence on the northwest side of the property. A great deal of the stucco is missing on the outside of the tower, which was locked for about 10 years prior to the 1952 renovation. It had been struck twice by lightening, and bricks were crumbling away.

The iconic lighthouse serves as a brand for the City of Port Isabel and a wide variety of events and organizations. It functions as a beacon and a lure to the Port Isabel charm and mystique. Of the 16 lighthouses in existence on the Texas Gulf Coast, it is the only one open to the public.

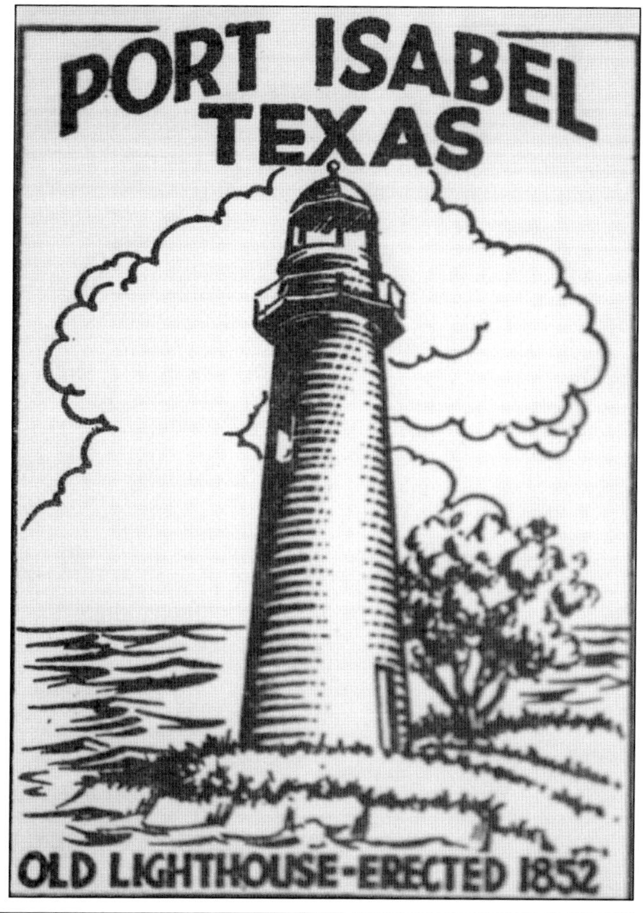

The late-1940s Port Isabel skyline demonstrates the height of the bluff that first made this such an important location for Fort Polk. Purdy's Courts is the tall building to the left of the lighthouse. Purdy's offered its guests use of this private pier extending out into the Laguna Madre Bay, complete with railing. The location is the present-day Pirates Landing parking lot.

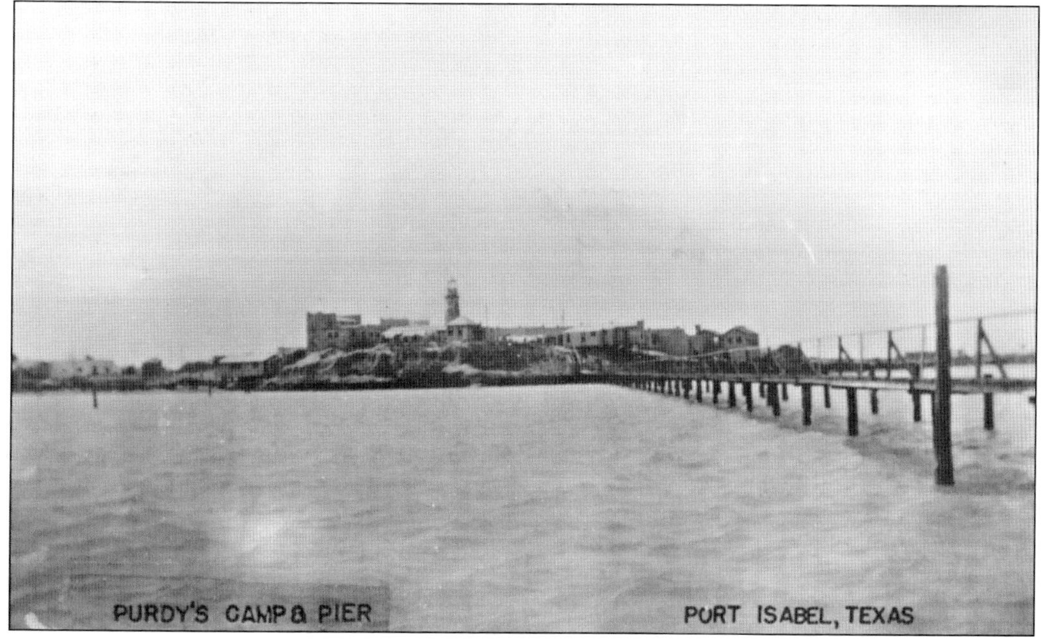

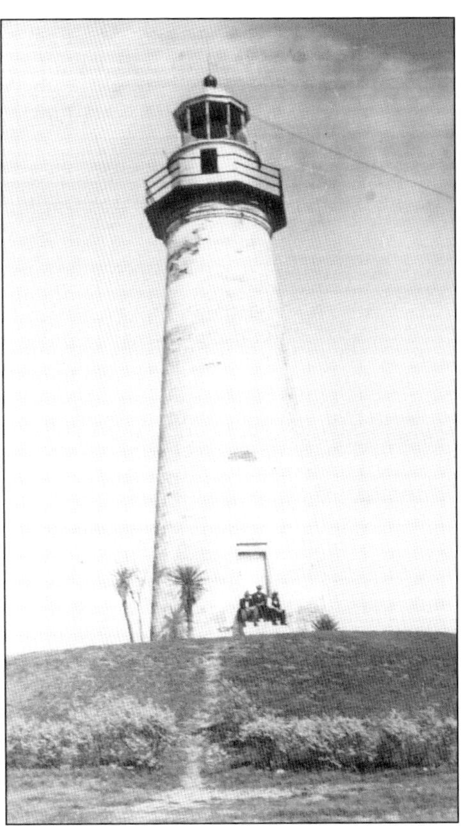

Seen in 1927, these three visitors have arrived to find the heavy door barred. Even though it suffered from a lack of regular hours, staffing, and maintenance through the years, the lighthouse was still a tourist attraction. Some repairs have been made to the railing around the catwalk on the top of the lighthouse. The trail leading to the door would suggest that the sidewalk on the north side has not been added yet.

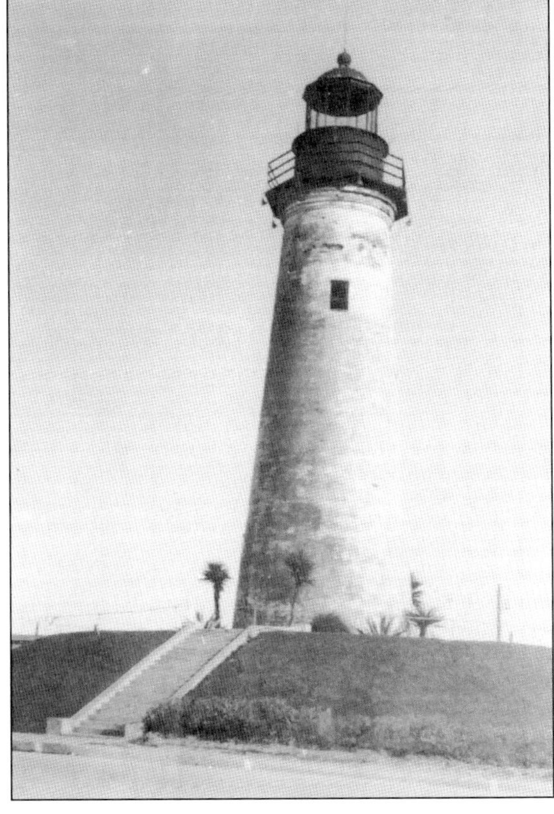

The Port Isabel Company made a number of modifications to the lighthouse in 1928, including the addition of floodlights on the underside of the catwalk meant to illuminate the tower at night. While tourists were welcome to climb the winding stairs, caution was recommended, "As slips may be experienced."

On the back of this photograph, a visitor wrote back home rather tepidly, "Well, here I am at Port Isabel." The lighthouse was open on this day, and visitors are seen at the top on the catwalk. Since neon was popular at this time, the top of the copper dome has been decorated with red neon symbolizing a flame.

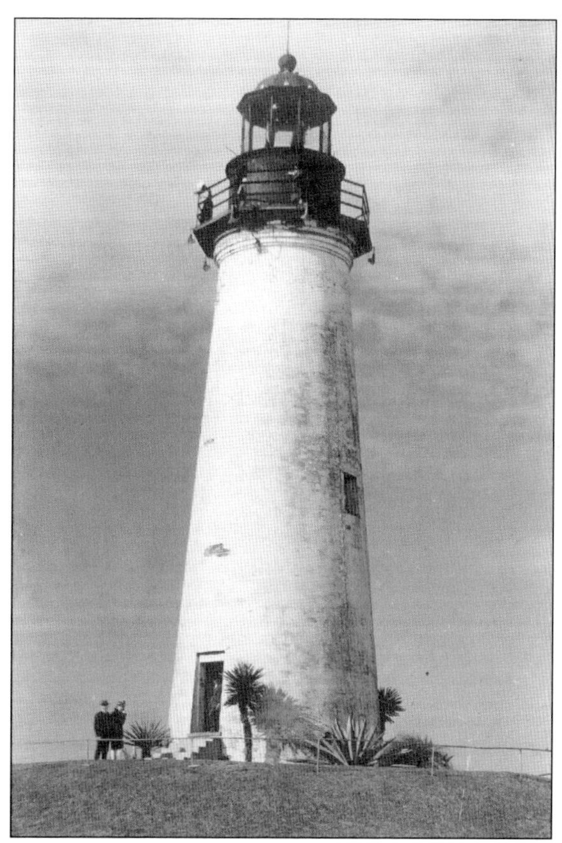

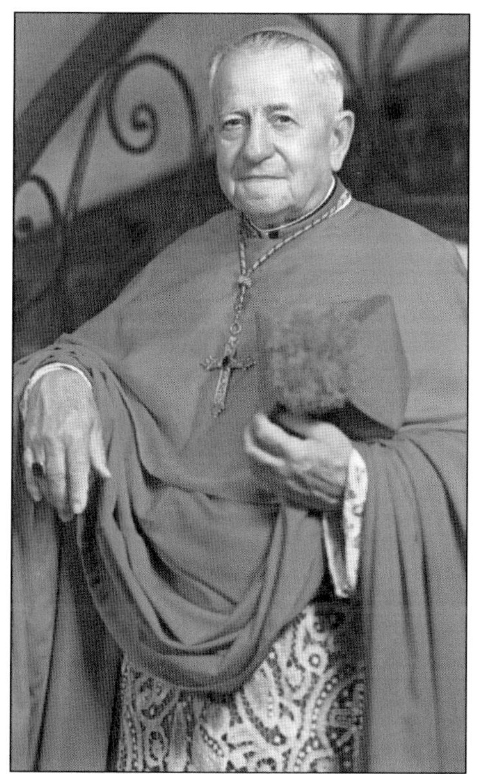

The Most Reverend Mariano S. Garriga was the bishop of Corpus Christi and a Port Isabel native. Garriga's father served as acting assistant lighthouse keeper from May 10, 1895, to February of the following year. On the occasion of the centennial celebration of the lighthouse, Garriga stated in the dedication address, "Teaching our younger generation to revere the traditions and history of America, we must also preserve the buildings and objects associated with those traditions."

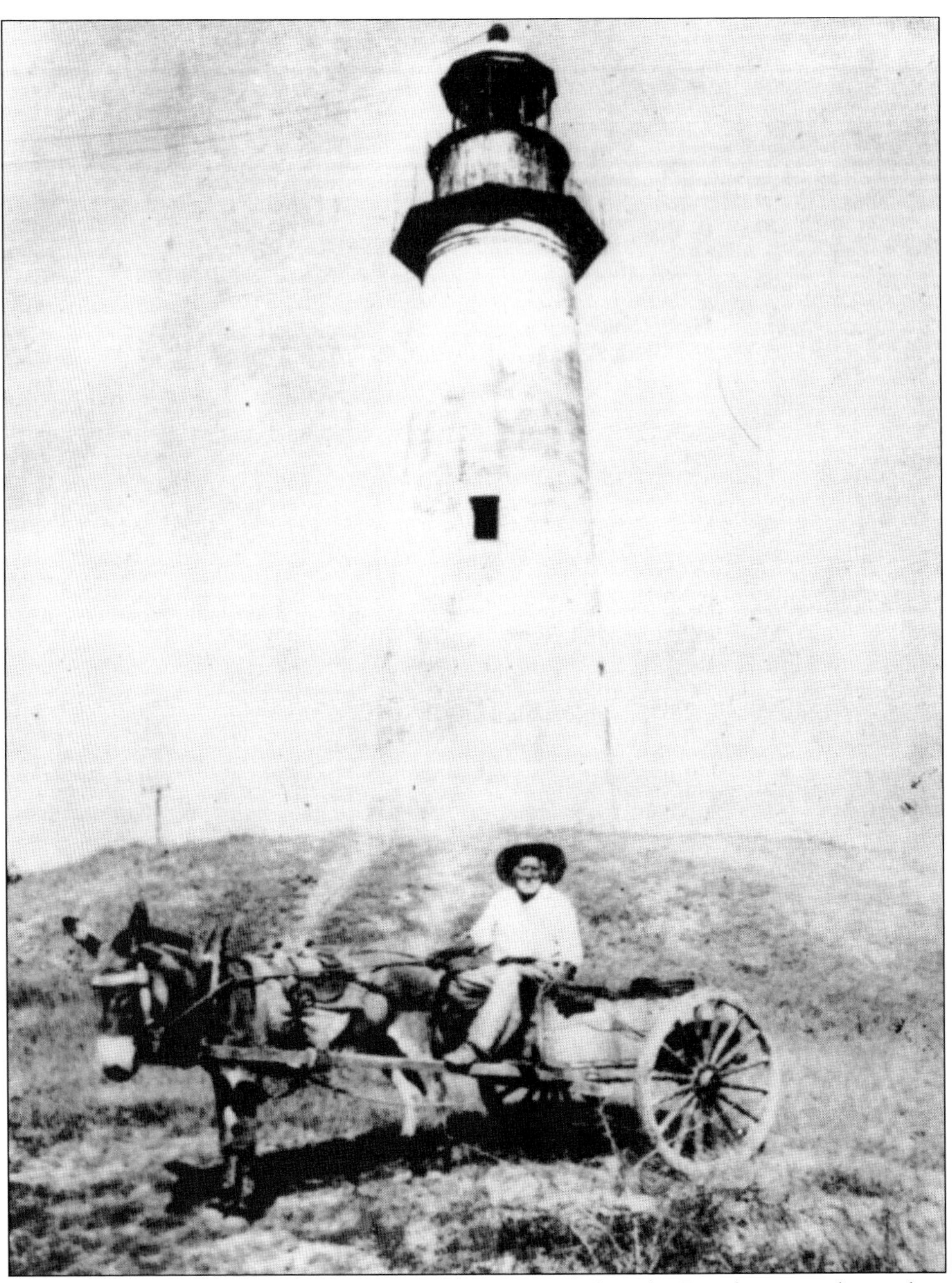

In 1851, when construction began on the lighthouse, Don Chencho Rosales was in his mid-teens. An 1849 epidemic of cholera hit the area and was said to have swept away most of the population. Two years later, there was just sufficient enough help to construct the lighthouse. Rosales was born in San Luis Potosi, Mexico, came to Matamoros, and had been in Port Isabel for perhaps five or six years when construction started. He helped build the lighthouse and stayed in the area until his death in 1950. His age was said to be anywhere from 115 to 128 years at the time of his passing. Rosales was the most photographed man in Port Isabel as it was inscribed on some postcards. It was said that he had no concept of money and did not want to accept paper money in payment.

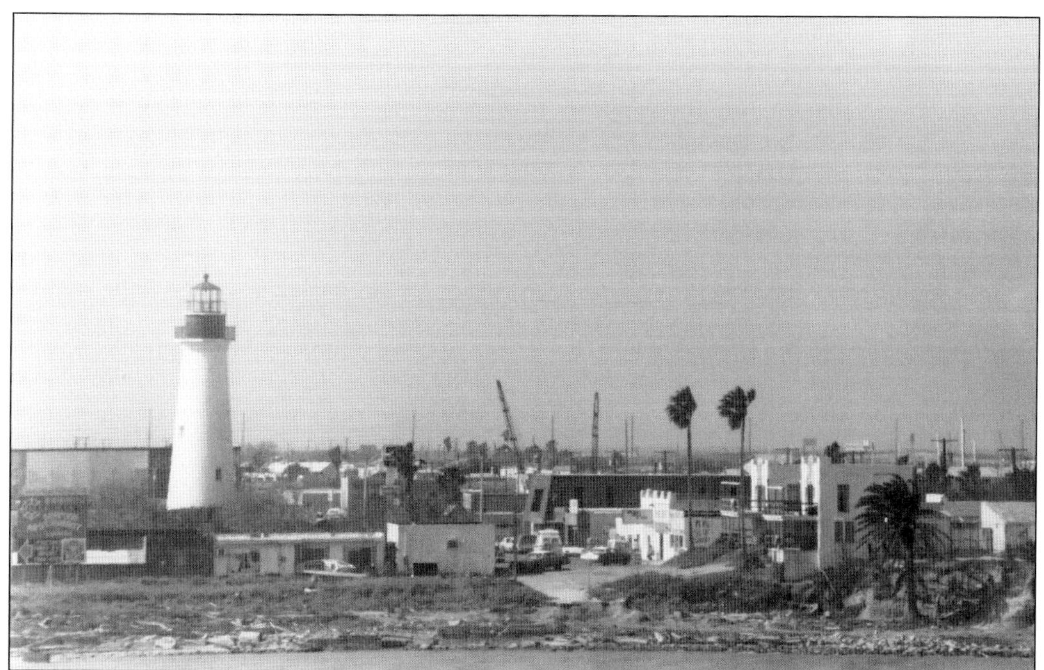

Taken in the morning, the wind is blowing from the north in this late-1970s photograph. To the right is Purdy's Courts, which was razed in 1984. It was a popular tourist spot but had been abandoned for some time. The lighthouse once again underwent renovations in 1970. A concrete floor was installed around the lantern, the lantern glass was replaced with Plexiglas, part of the brickwork was replaced near the top, and the tension band was replaced.

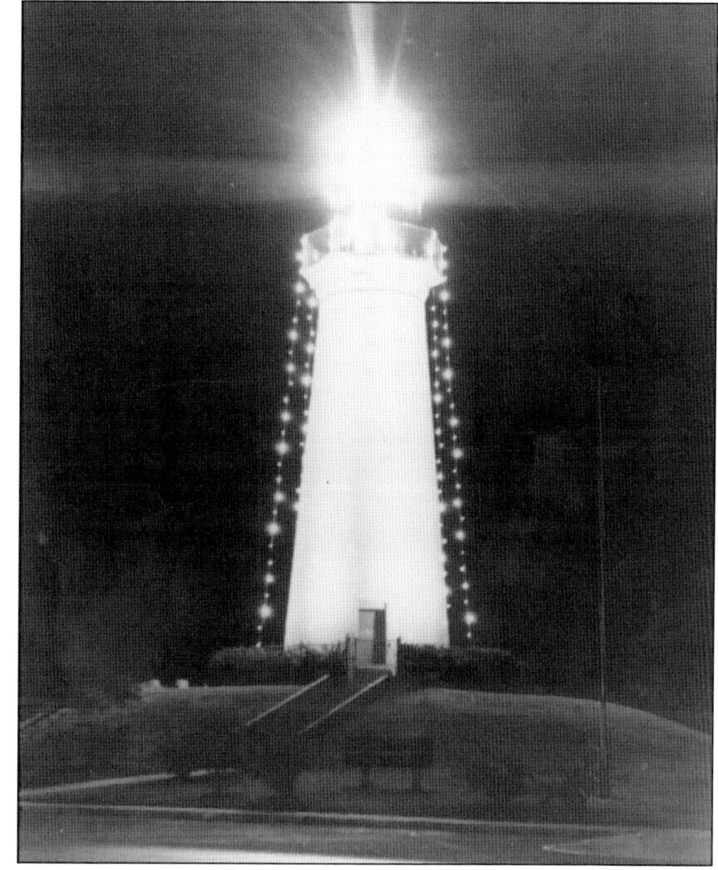

In 1968, the Port Isabel Lighthouse became a kind of a Christmas tree. The first weekend in December, lines were strung up from eyes on the ground to the catwalk above, and Christmas lights were then added. It has been an annual tradition since.

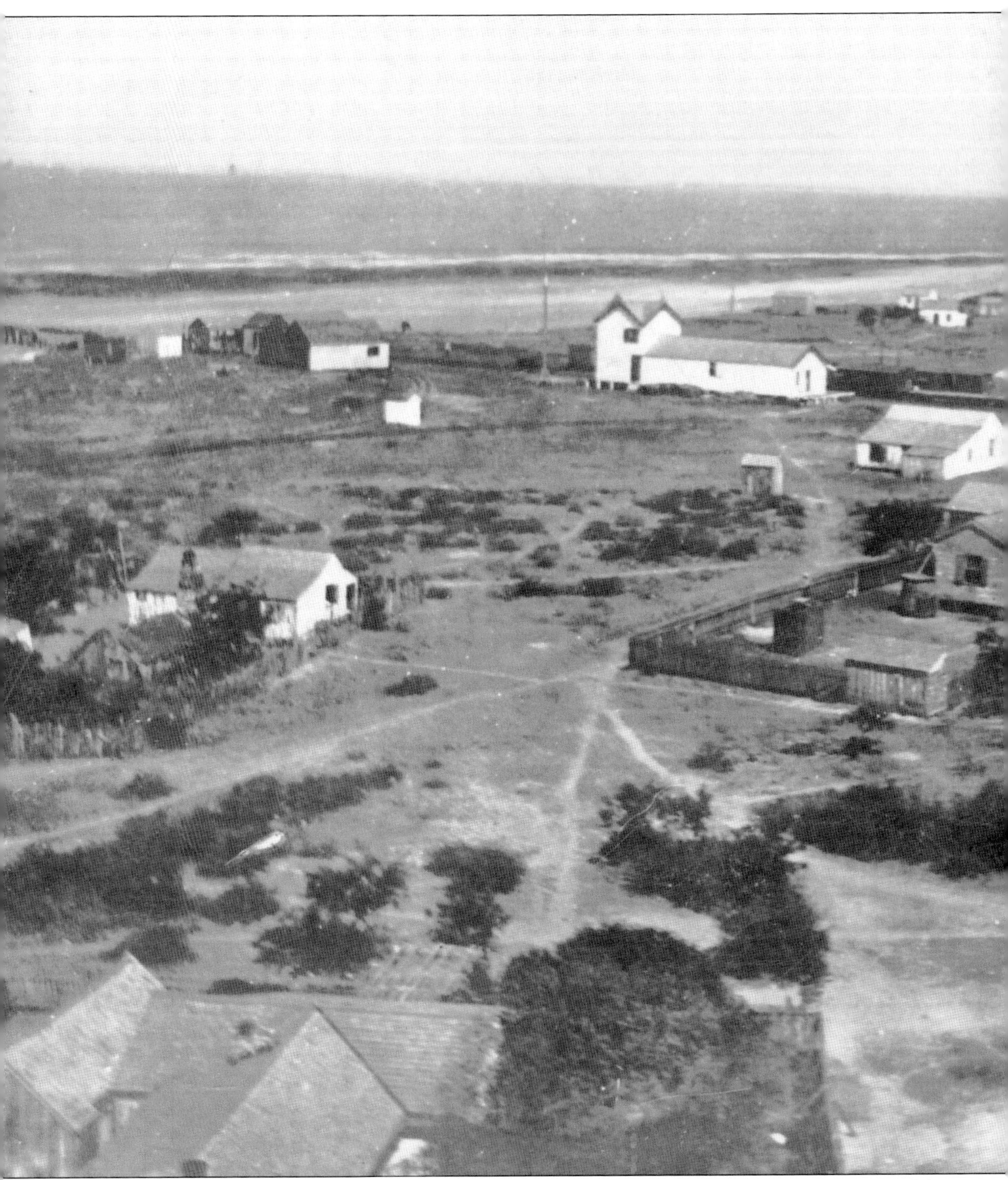

This view from the top of the lighthouse, looking southeast, shows Port Isabel at the turn of the century. Diagonal footpaths connect common destinations before graded, paved, or oiled roads and sidewalks existed. The white building with the Gingerbread Carpenter Gothic roofline is the railroad depot. Don Chencho helped build the depot in the 1870s. A passenger train waits on the tracks in front of it. Farther west down the tracks, more cars wait cargo processing. A

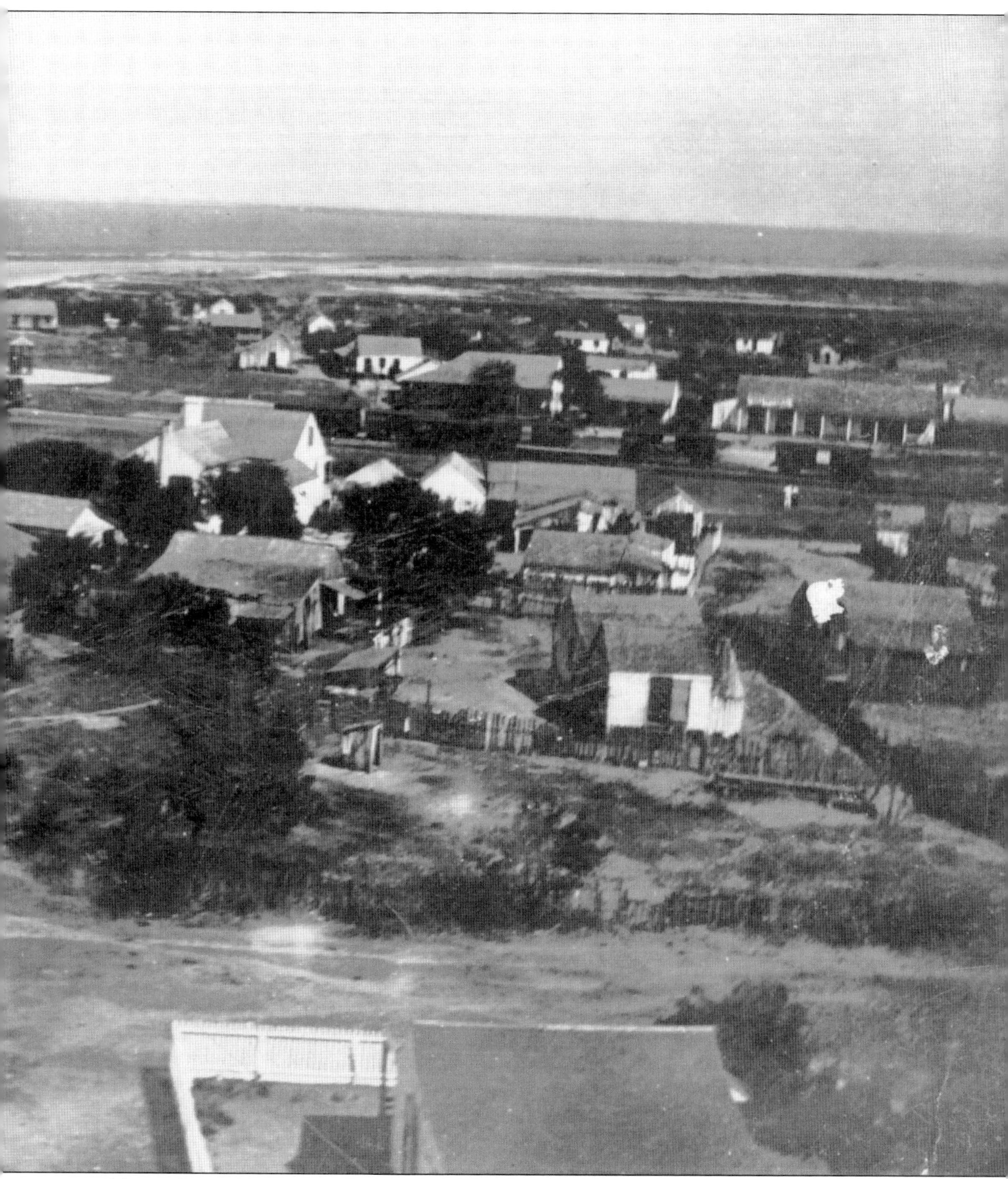

sprinkling of commercial buildings appears on the coastline along the track as it extended into the bay. A plaza with a bandstand is just southwest of the depot. On the horizon (left) is the Brazos Santiago Pass Lighthouse. The passage of time and several harsh hurricane seasons took their toll on many of the buildings in this photograph. During the mid-1920s, many more were razed and empty lots were offered for sale.

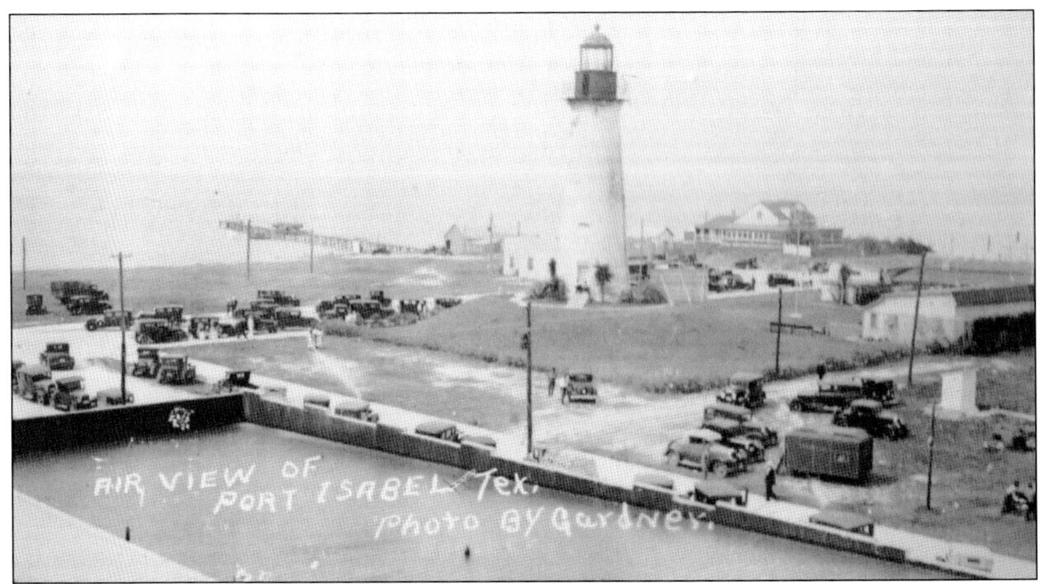

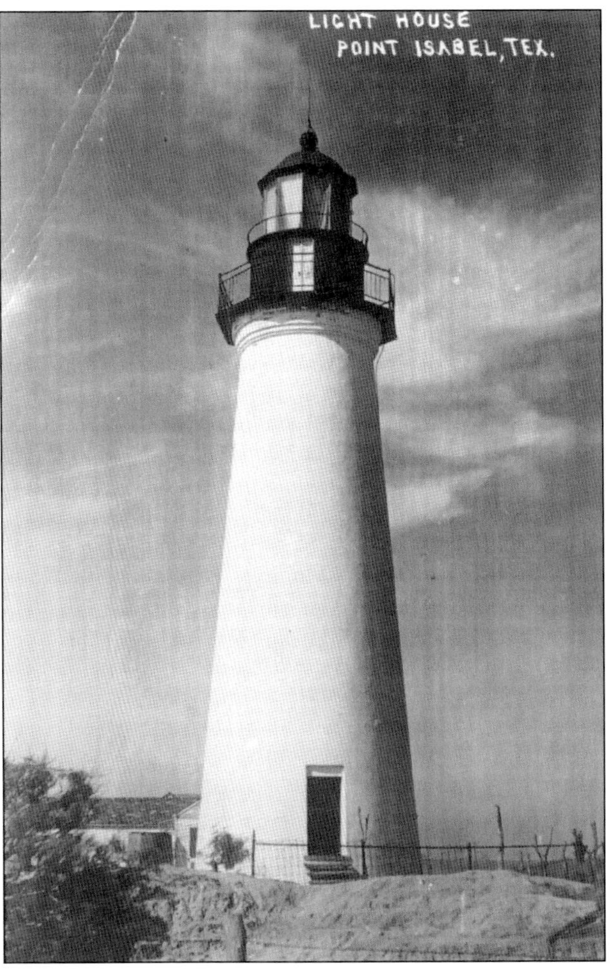

In the early 1920s, the roads around the lighthouse had just been graded to create the hill that the lighthouse stood on. Above, Tarnava and Powers Streets are seen on the left and right, respectively, but the future route for State Highway 100 had not been paved at this point. The area was buzzing with activity as the building of the city was commencing. The house that president-elect Harding stayed in during his 1920 visit is visible on the shoreline to the right.

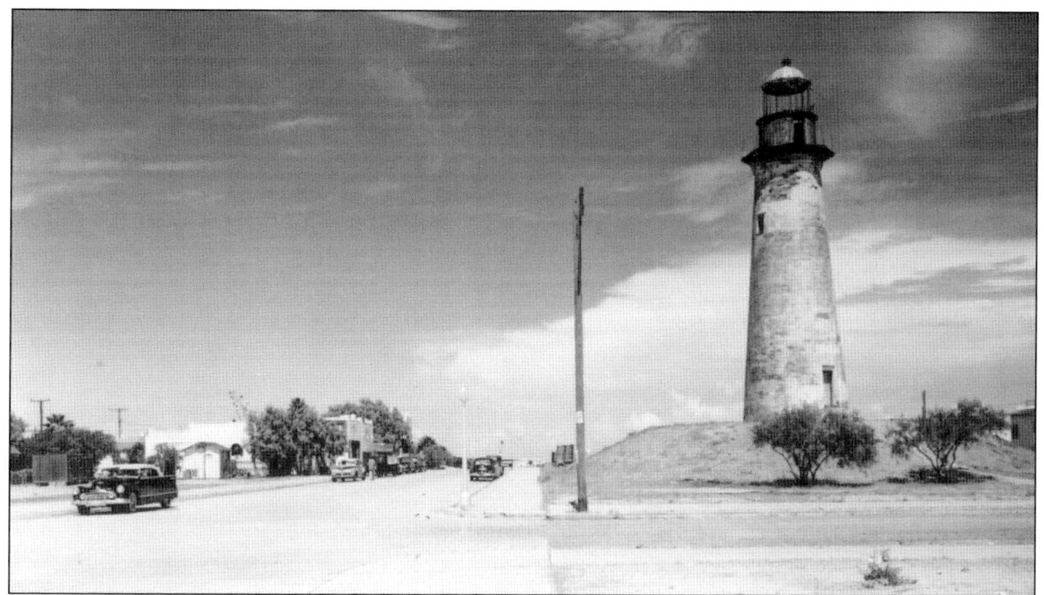

Here is a view down Maxan Street at the intersection of an unpaved Tarnava Street. During the 1940s, the lighthouse deal was picking up steam according to press headlines. Prompted by Dr. J.A. Hockaday, the objective was to have the lighthouse deeded to the state. Lon C. Hill agreed to do so, had the property surveyed, and inquired as to whom to make the deed out to in 1947.

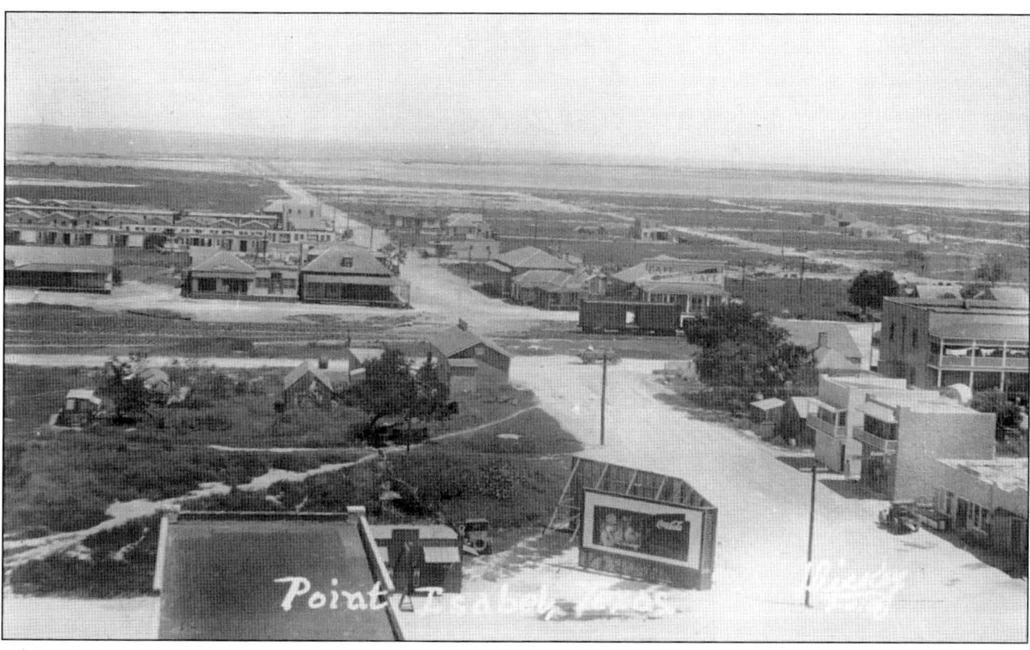

This early-1920s view from the top of the lighthouse toward Powers Street and Railroad Avenue, with an intersecting Tarnava Street, shows an established business district. The large building in the foreground is a new drugstore. Across the railroad from the Champion Brothers Grocery & Market building are a confectionery, an advertisement sign for the Red Arrow Café, Drug Co., Bayview Courts, and several other cafés and restaurants.

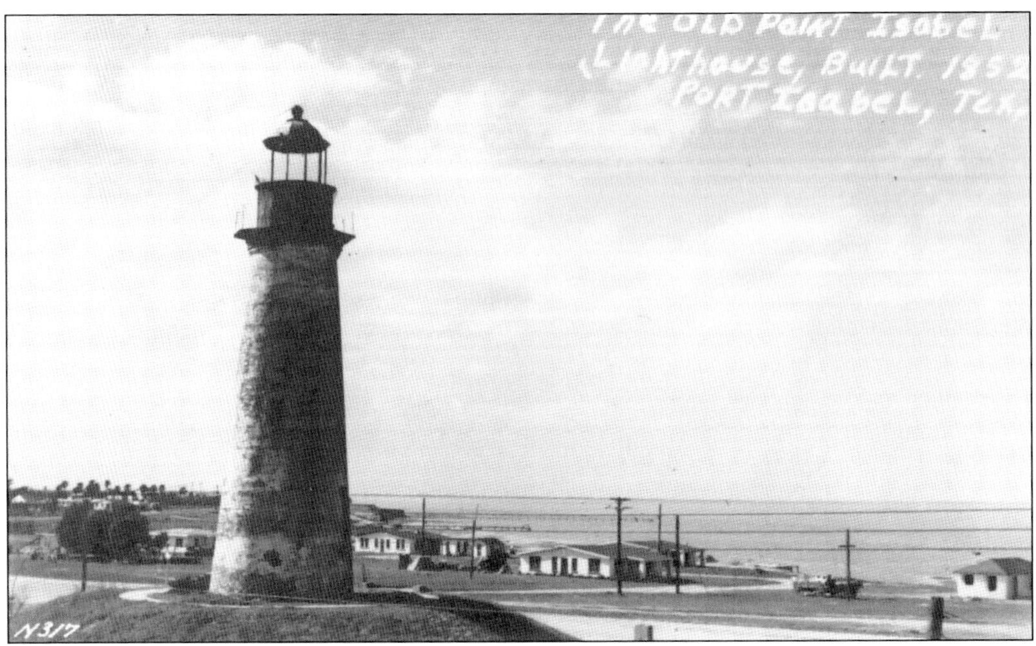

In this 1940s photograph, the lighthouse is missing much of its stucco, all of the eight panes of lantern glass, and at least one cast-iron support that holds the lantern glass. At times, it was feared that the lighthouse would be torn down or fall into hands of promoters who would exploit it. This photograph was taken from the deck of the Ship Café.

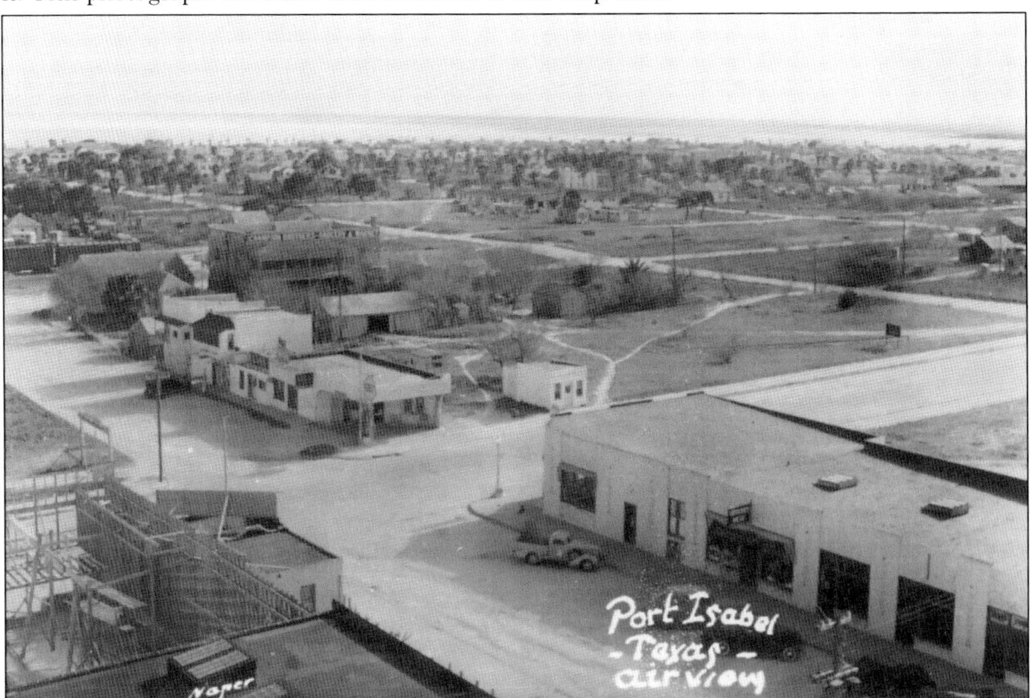

This 1940s view from the top of the lighthouse features the intersection of Powers and Tarnava Streets. Businesses included a Gulf service station, a grocery store, restaurants, and Champion Brothers Grocery & Market. Powers Street was the main street.

Seen here in 1952, the lighthouse stands proudly once again. The cast-iron watch room was removed and taken to Weslaco, where it was sand blasted, and a new, taller lantern was installed. All three tower windows were replaced. A metal band was added to secure the top of the brickwork, and handrails were installed around the lantern. A galvanized wire fence was added around the gallery, and a fixed mercury vapor light was wired to the streetlights.

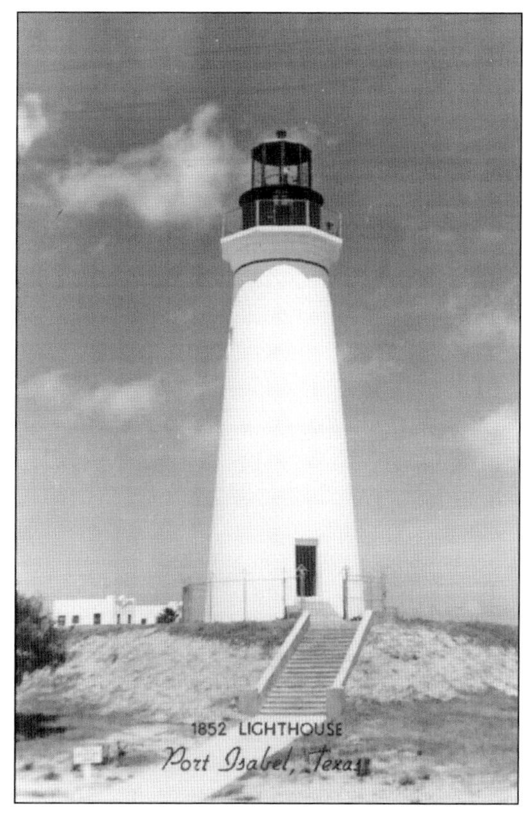

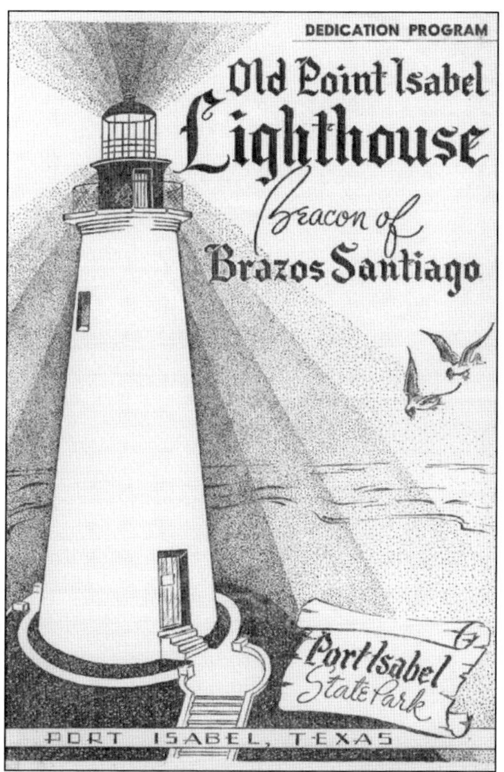

New landscaping was put in place, and the state marker was moved to the northwest corner of the park. New steps were installed on the west side, and so was a parkway. The exterior stucco was removed, and mortar joints were routed to three quarters of an inch and stucco reapplied. A metal plate was welded over the top of the column. The total cost of the refurbishment was $23,500; the contract was awarded on January 23, 1951, to George F. Cail and Son.

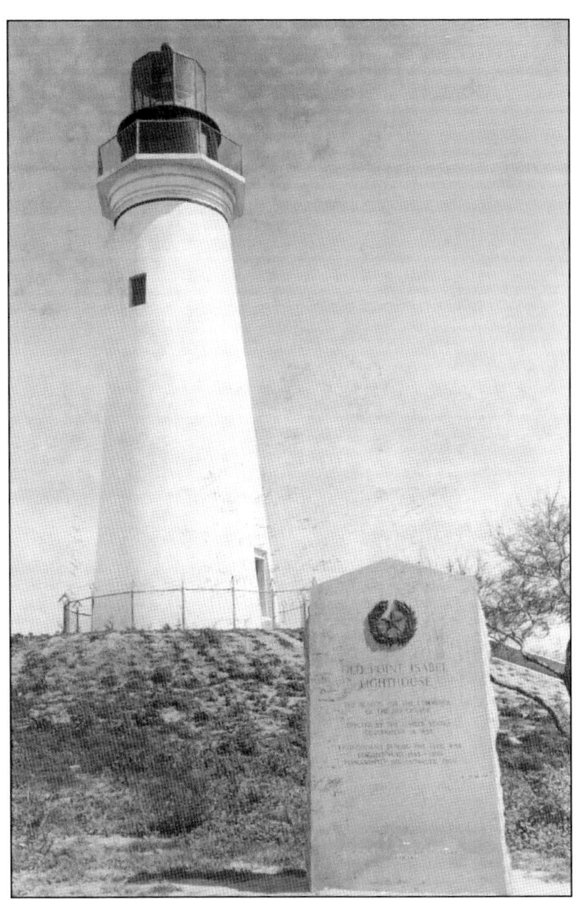

The old Point Isabel Lighthouse, the beacon of commerce of the Rio Grande, was erected by the US government in 1852. It was extinguished during the Civil War, discontinued between 1888 and 1895, and permanently discontinued in 1905. This monument was erected by the State of Texas in 1936. In this 1952 photograph, the lighthouse is standing ready for the dedication of its state park status and centennial. The reverse of this postcard sports a commemorative stamp. Those interested could have their postcards or other covers cancelled and stamped on April 26, 1952, by the Port Isabel Post Office. Ruthie Mras cancelled and sent this card to her husband, F.J. Mras.

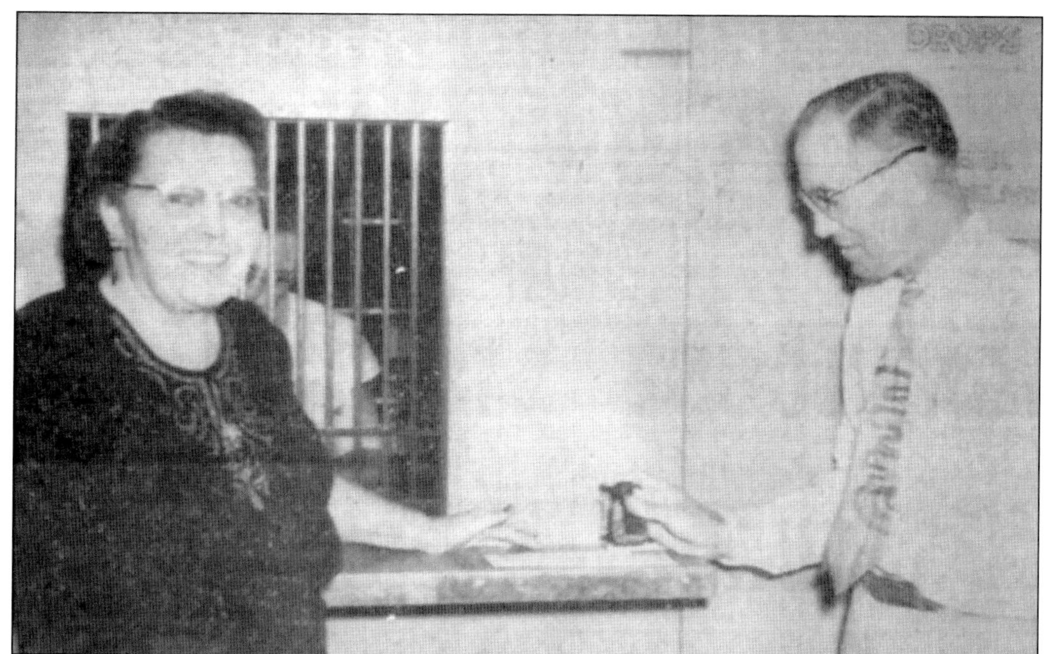

A special mail cachet, shown here, displayed by Port Isabel postmistress Elizabeth Graves and Lighthouse State Park Dedication Committee chairman Ted Hunt, was offered on Saturday, April 26, 1952. A two-day celebration was planned, culminating with a fireworks display on the final evening.

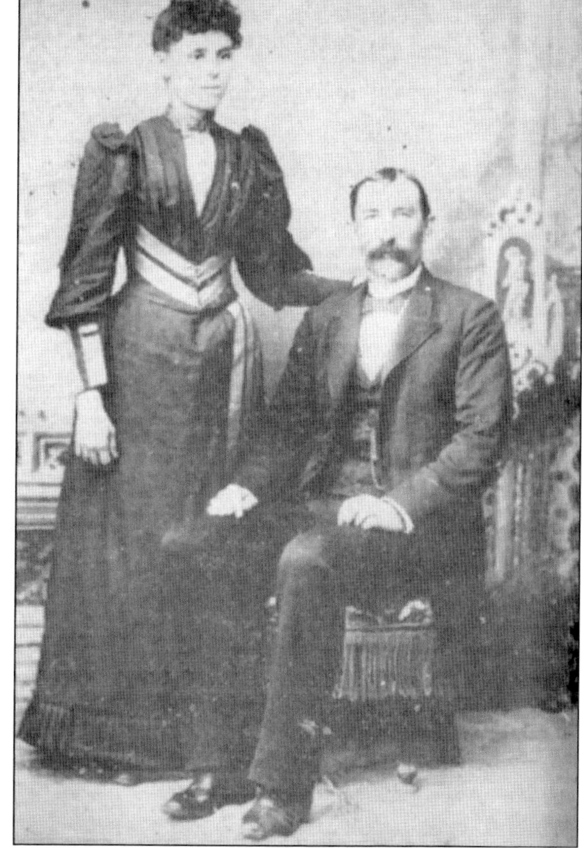

Peter Lambert was assistant lighthouse keeper from January 10, 1896, to January 15, 1899. His wife, former Isabel Gertrude Lightbourne, was born in Port Isabel in 1879. At the time of the dedication of the lighthouse in 1952, Mrs. Lambert was 80 years old and residing in Brownsville. She was known as the only surviving widow of a Point Isabel Lighthouse keeper.

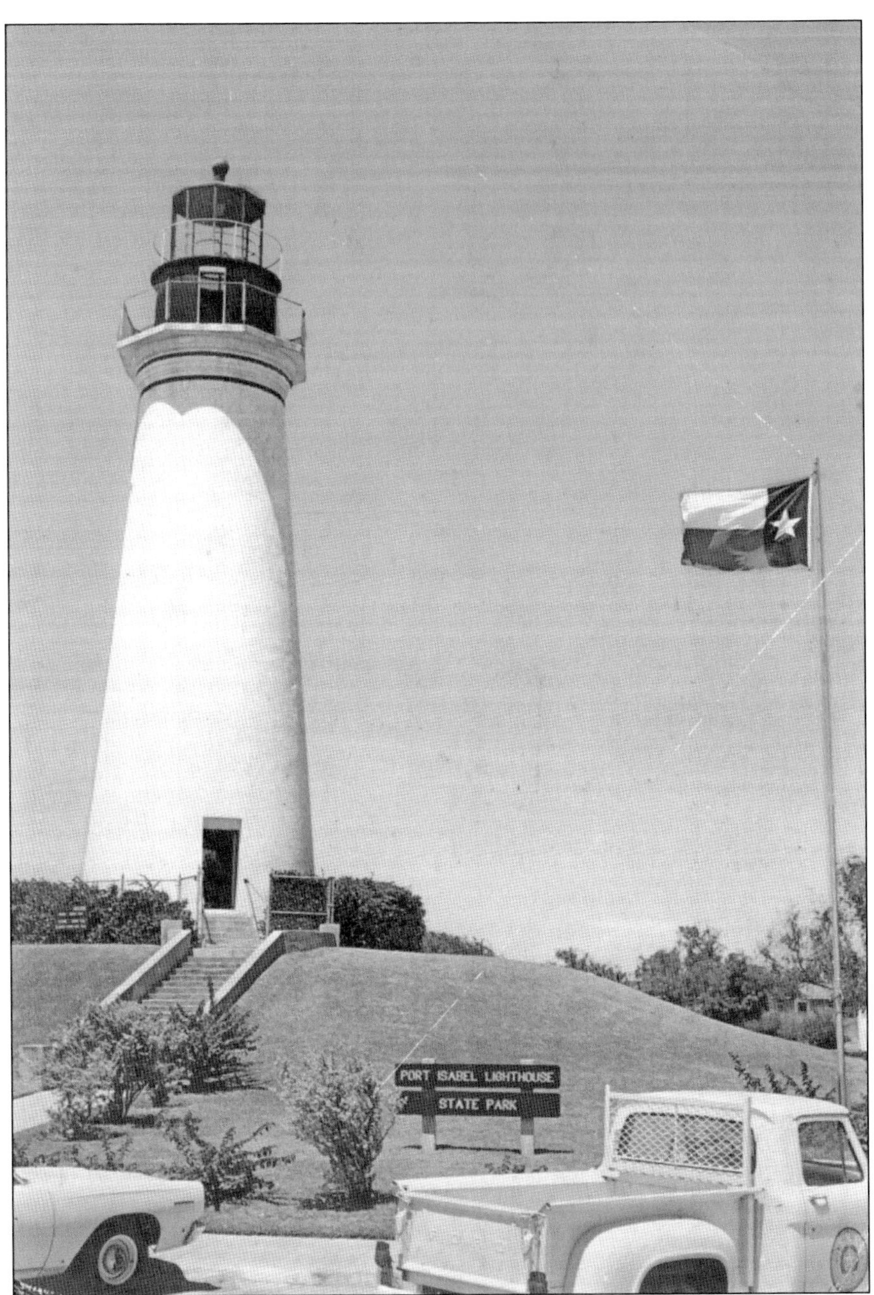

The Port Isabel Lighthouse is open for business as a Texas flag flutters in a stiff south breeze. Port Isabel Lighthouse State Park signage is prominently displayed, and the parking lot sports a Texas Parks and Wildlife Department truck. The lighthouse had regular hours, staff, and maintenance. Today, over 50,000 visitors a year enjoy the lighthouse grounds. The lighthouse is operated by the City of Port Isabel under a Texas Parks and Wildlife Department contract. The keeper's house, rebuilt in 1996 at a cost of $320,000, is a visitors center and home to the Port Isabel Chamber of Commerce. In 2004, the Lighthouse Establishment Cinema was started, with movies projected on the side of the lighthouse during the summer months and other special occasions. This free family-friendly event serves to further endear this old icon to a new generation.

Three

A Railroad, Wireless Station, and Port

In February 1872, Port Isabel's ship came in. Arriving from New Jersey was the Rio Grande Railroad Company's Engine No. 1. The 42-inch narrow gauge began service that would run through 1919.

Freight teams of oxen and mules delivered goods to the interior of Texas and northern Mexico until Simon Celaya of Brownsville established the Rio Grande Railroad Company, which was incorporated on August 13, 1870. Don Chencho referred to Mr. Celaya as his "patron." Chencho helped build the rail line between Brownsville and "The Point." The route of the line was laid out, as the crow flies, for 22.5 miles to Brownsville, Texas. The first train to carry passengers to Brownsville was on July 4, 1872. Overland transportation of freight and passengers to Brownsville served to increase the importance of Port Isabel.

In 1916, Port Isabel became home to one of three wireless stations in the United States designed to increase naval communications. During the seven years of its operations, this state-of-the-art radio facility provided communication between naval vessels in the Gulf of Mexico as well as coast to coast. The Point Isabel location also served as a relay to the Panama Canal until it was disestablished in 1923.

On June 20, 1930, the heavy black headline of the *San Benito Light* read, "PASS PORT BILL. Valley Goes Wild—Bands Head Parade!" The Rivers and Harbors Bill passed the US Senate with an appropriation over $2 million and little trouble was expected in the House of Representatives. A spontaneous parade started in Port Isabel and Brownsville with the Fort Brown Band leading. The parade continued its way through the valley to Mission. Work began on the dredging of the port and a jetties system at the opening of Brazos Santiago, a result of the SOS (Save Our Seaport) program. A valley-wide endeavor, SOS was funded by many neighboring towns and communities. The Rio Grande Valley was now connected with the "four corners of the world."

After nearly seven decades of effort and $80 million, the Gulf Intracoastal Waterway was completed in 1949. The last leg reaching Port Isabel lengthened the project to 1,100 miles. Ships leaving the East Coast could now travel protected from the open ocean via the waterway all the way to the deepwater port of Port Isabel—Port Isabel had purpose.

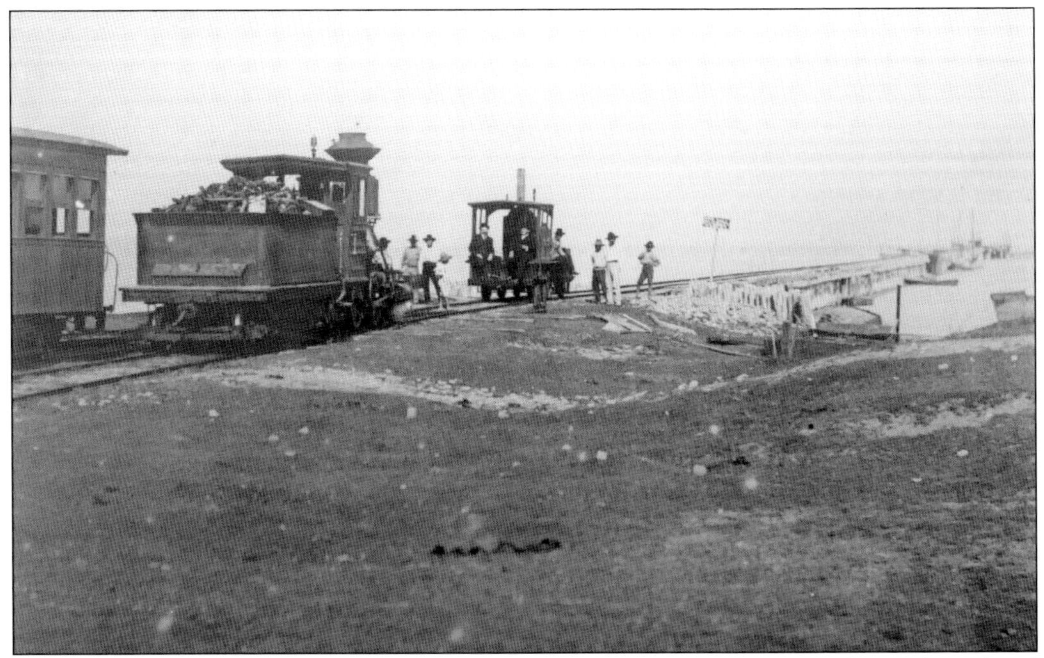

A wood-burning engine on the track approaches what is truly the end of the line. The railroad dock jutted out into the bay 1,500 feet. Lighters and barges would receive cargo to be taken to Brazos Santiago Pass, where it would be loaded on larger gulf-worthy vessels. The car on the track behind the engine is a passenger Pullman car.

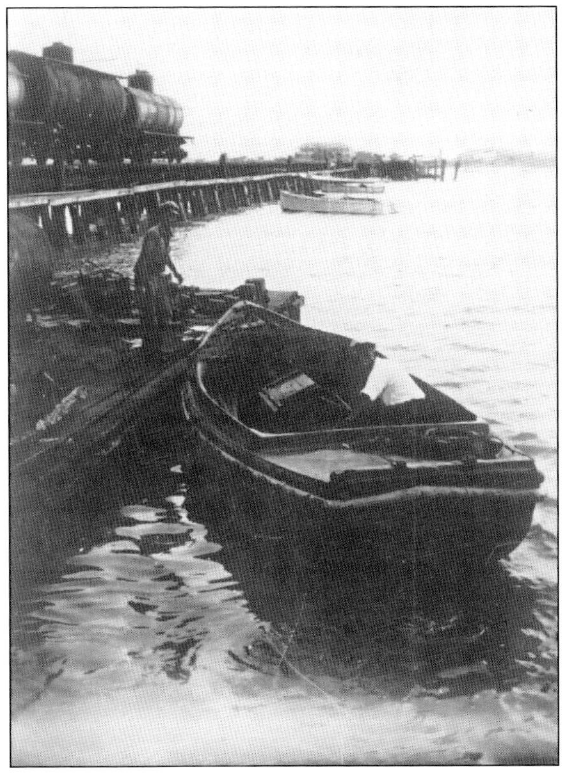

Engine No. 1, designed to run in either direction without being turned, is shown here on the railroad dock. Port Isabel's skyline, including the Queen Isabel Inn, is in the background. While this set-up was thought not as ideal, there was not another sheltered anchorage from Brazos south to Tampico. High water on the route to Brownsville would sometimes extinguish the engine fire.

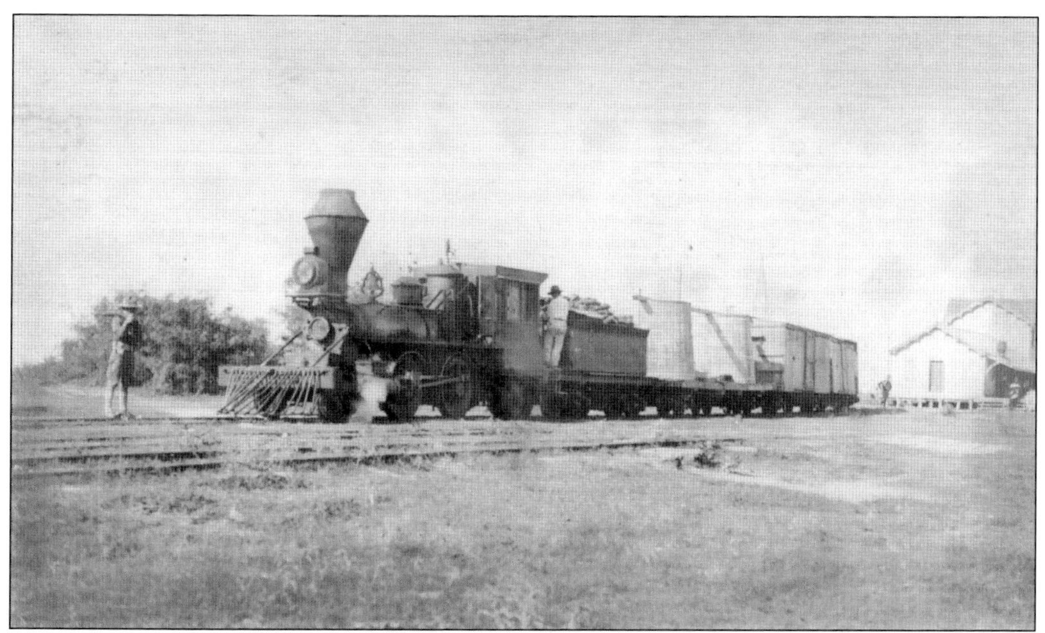

"Fast Mail Limited Brownsville to Point Isabel" was inscribed by a soldier on this photograph. Engine No. 1 is leaving Port Isabel with the depot in the background. The saddle tanks could hold 450 gallons of water, which would not always be adequate for the 22.5-mile trip to Brownsville.

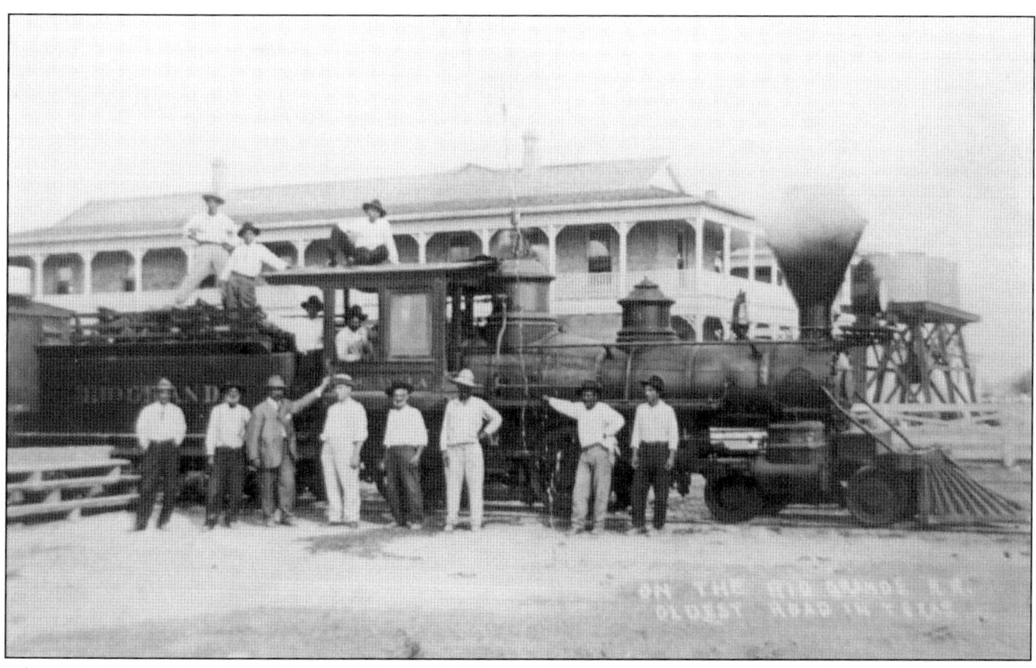

The Rio Grande Railroad served both freight and passengers. The plan to lay track across the Palo Alto prairie, an area just feet above sea level, would prove to be challenging, and the tracks suffered severe damage during the 1873, 1874, and 1880 hurricanes.

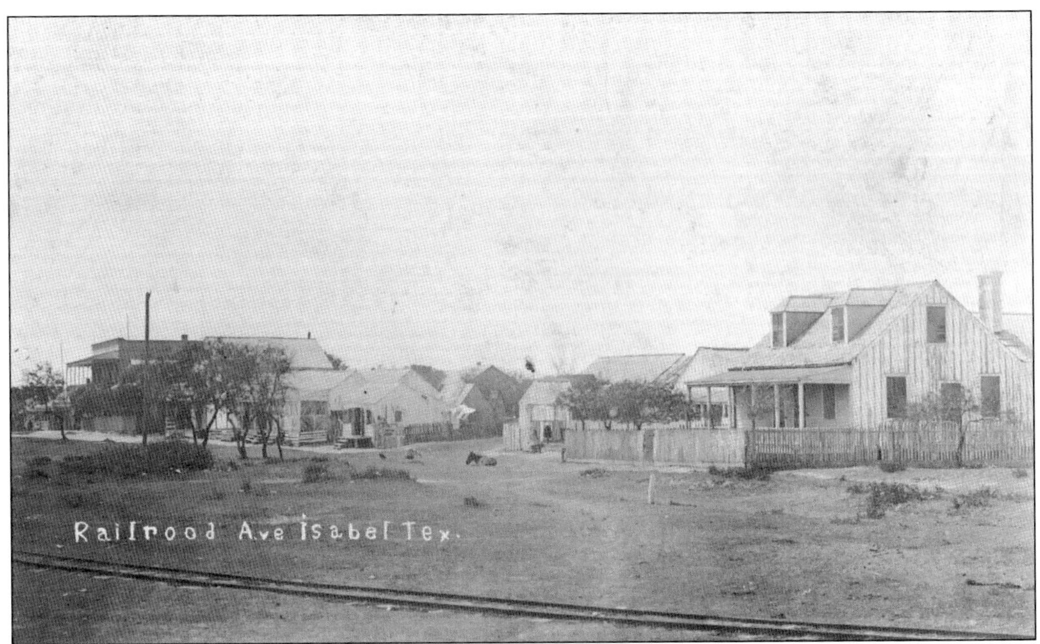

Railroad Avenue ran in front of the Champion Brothers Grocery & Market (left), which was built in 1899; it served as a general store, post office, and later the railroad depot. The area around the building began to develop commercially as traffic increased. In 1953, the City of Port Isabel requested the lowering or removal of the tracks across Tarnava and Garcia Streets.

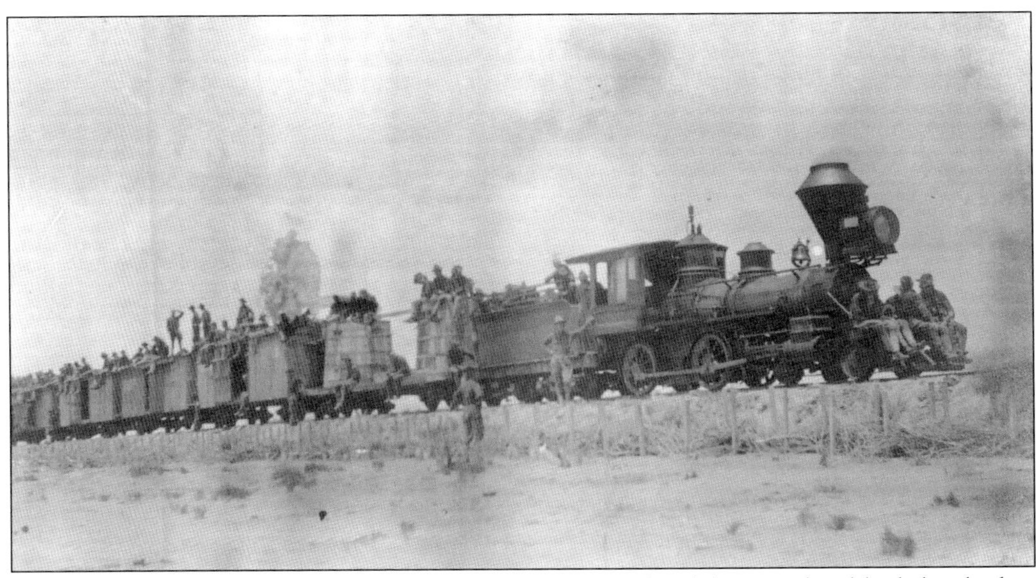

Arriving in Port Isabel from Brownsville, this is an example of the raised rail bed that had to be constructed at various points along the route. Mesquite used for both ties and pilings was cut in Mexico and shipped to Port Isabel aboard the *S.J. Lee*, which the Rio Grande Railroad had purchased from King.

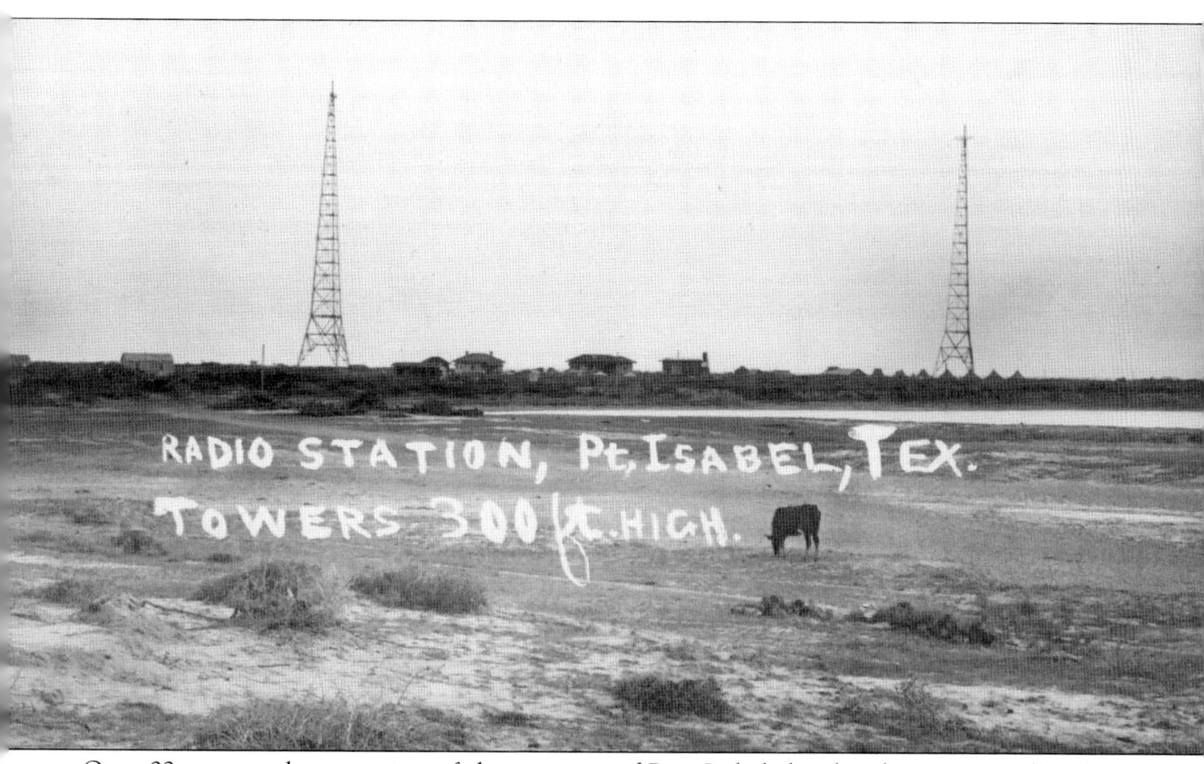

On a 22-acre southern section of the townsite of Port Isabel that locals came to call "The Reservation," two 330-foot wireless towers were built. During construction, the Rio Grande Railroad Company was pressed into service to rush the necessary heavy equipment from Brownsville to the work site, and crews consisting of the 1st New York Cavalry set to work. Between 1916 and 1923, this radio station played an important role in military communications as one of three site selections in the United States. War was declared against Germany and her allies on April 6, 1917, and closer-to-home problems on the border were the cause of much concern. The radio station was vital for strategic communication. By August 24, 1923, the Point Isabel Wireless Station was disestablished, and one of the towers was moved to Fort Brown in Brownsville, Texas, some 20 miles to the south.

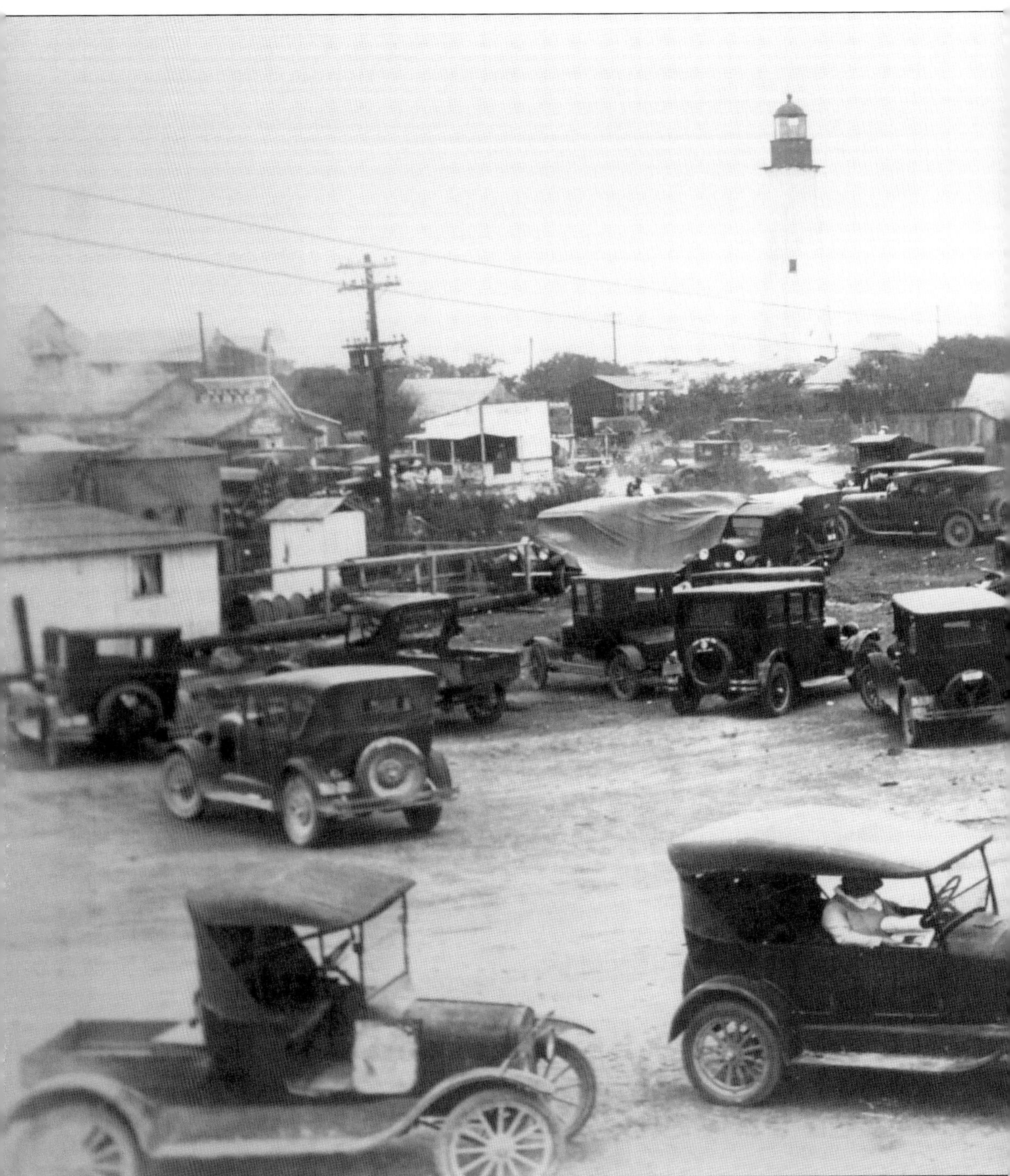

With the building of the railroad and the wireless station, as well as the call for a deepwater port in the Rio Grande Valley, Port Isabel began to experience a boom. Here, in the early 1920s, Port Isabel has a Ford garage and is wired for electricity while attracting motorists from all over south Texas and northern Mexico. One newspaper article started off thusly, "Point Isabel, historic little city of oleanders, fishing nets, and aguadores has undergone a metamorphosis . . . stock roamed

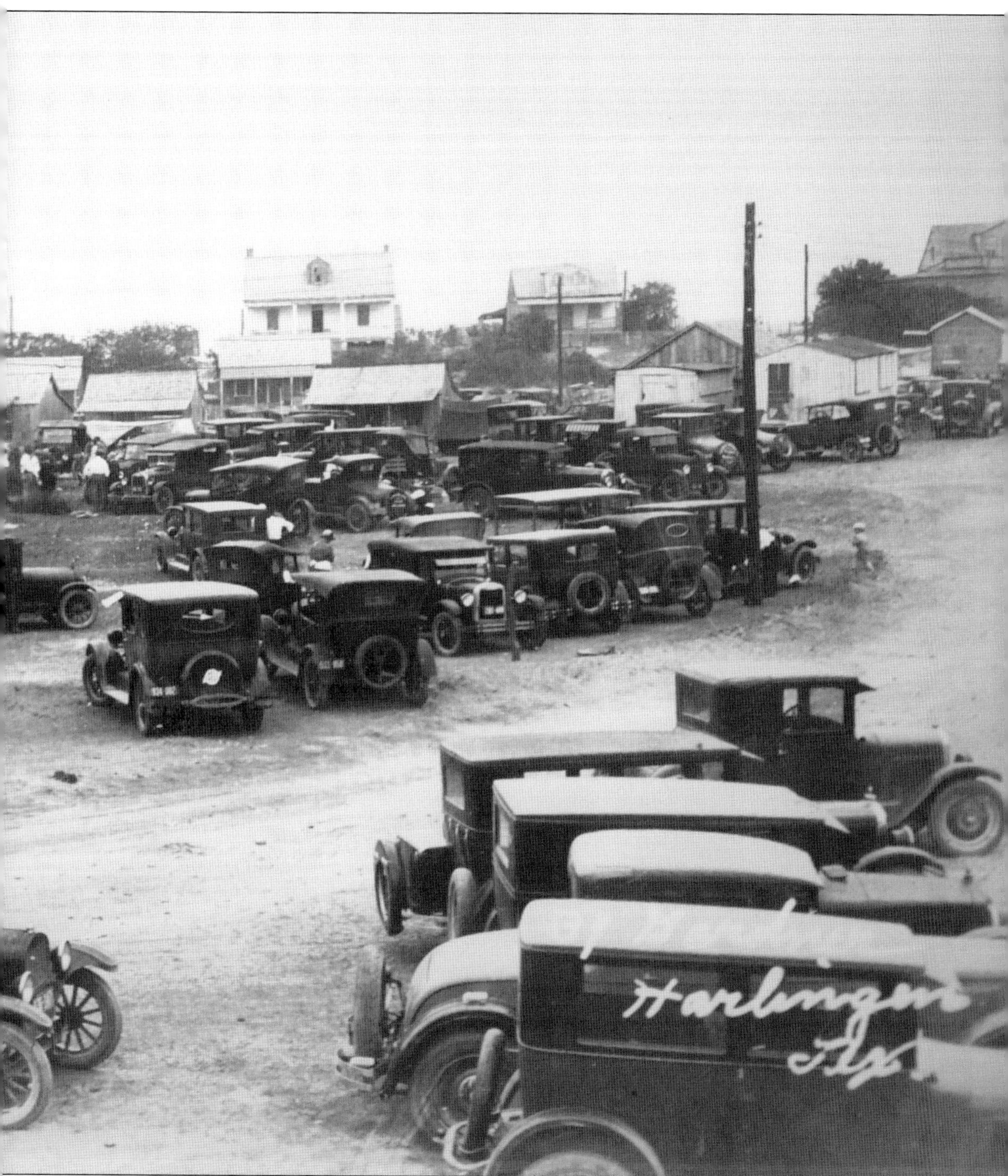

more or less unmolested in the quiet streets and many a picnic basket afforded a dainty repast for an inquisitive hog." Citizens had formed an expedition in self-defense against wild burros, which roamed through town "marauding gardens after nightfall." But here, Port Isabel is poised for its future.

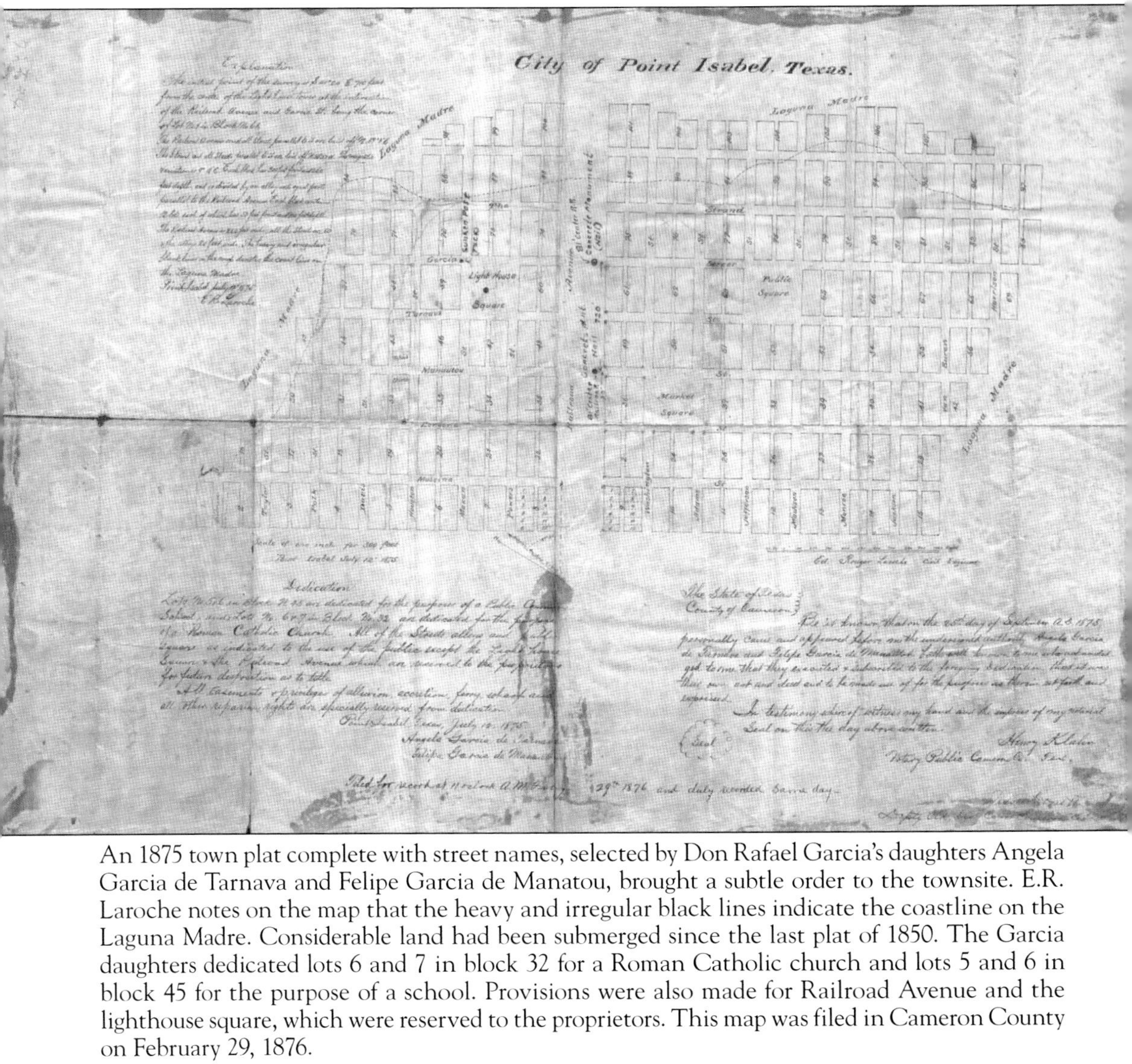

An 1875 town plat complete with street names, selected by Don Rafael Garcia's daughters Angela Garcia de Tarnava and Felipe Garcia de Manatou, brought a subtle order to the townsite. E.R. Laroche notes on the map that the heavy and irregular black lines indicate the coastline on the Laguna Madre. Considerable land had been submerged since the last plat of 1850. The Garcia daughters dedicated lots 6 and 7 in block 32 for a Roman Catholic church and lots 5 and 6 in block 45 for the purpose of a school. Provisions were also made for Railroad Avenue and the lighthouse square, which were reserved to the proprietors. This map was filed in Cameron County on February 29, 1876.

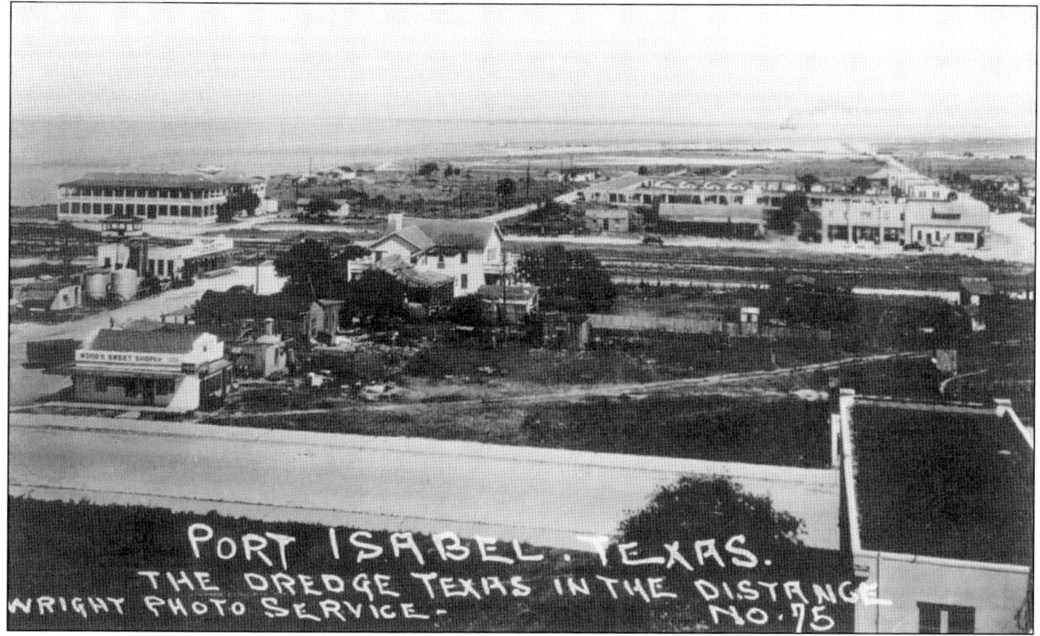

Dredging began on the port project in 1930, as seen by the smoke leaving the engine on the dredge *Texas* on the horizon. A contemporary ad in the newspaper touted, "We dare you to read this and then truthfully say Port Isabel does not have the most glorious future of any city on the American Continent."

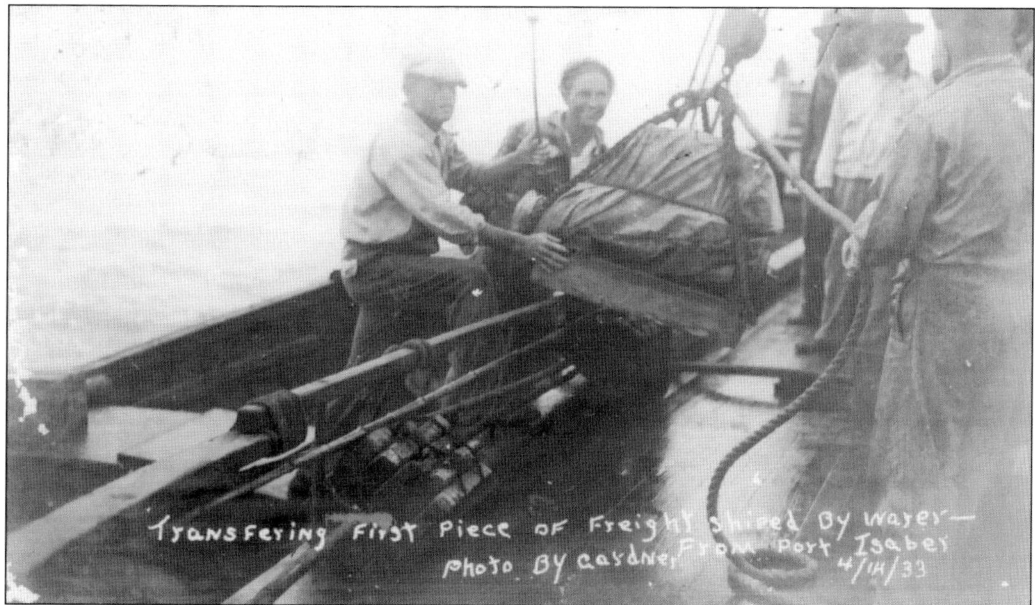

Though several months from the grand-opening festivities, the first piece of freight was transferred to a waiting vessel from the new Port Isabel-San Benito Navigation District. The creation of this deepwater port eliminated the need for the railroad dock. Vessels left the deepwater port and headed directly to the Brownsville Ship Channel before moving on to the Brazos Santiago Pass and then the Gulf of Mexico or Gulf Intracoastal Waterway.

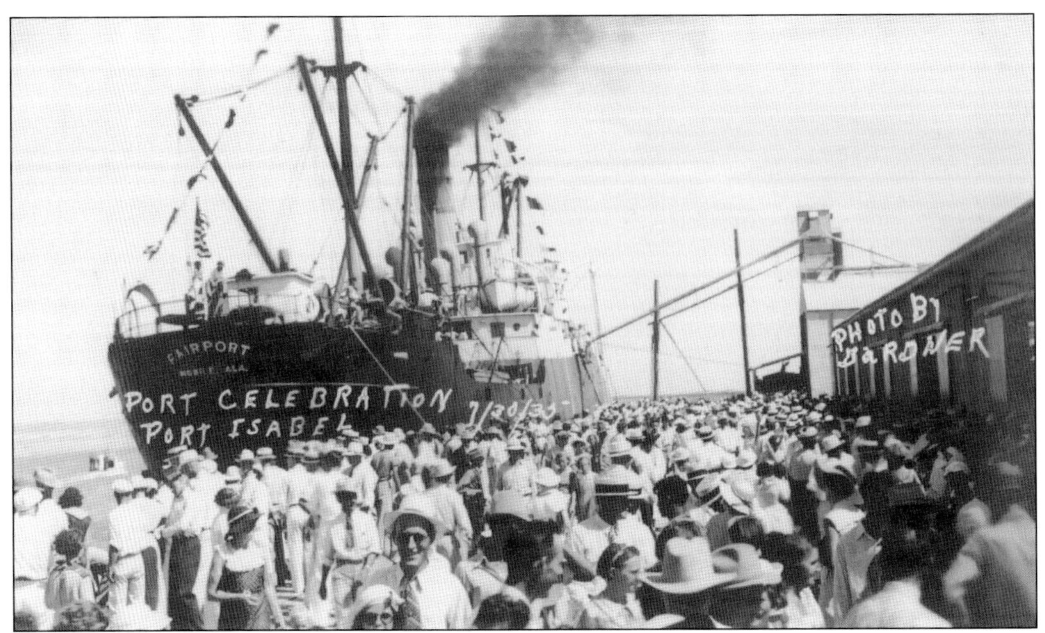

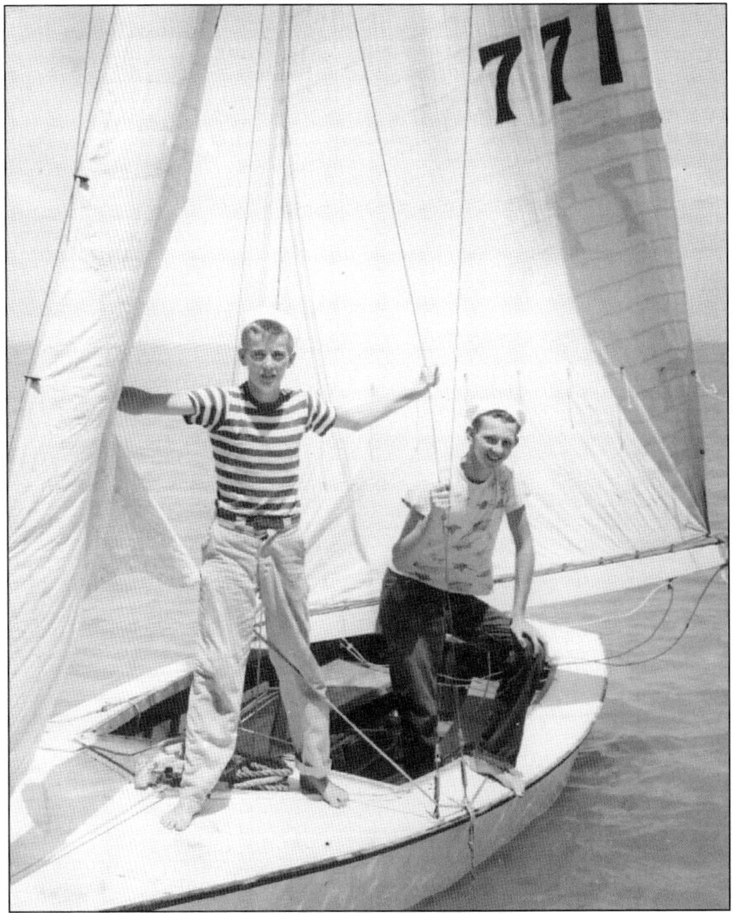

On July 30, 1935, the Port Isabel Celebration started at 3:00 p.m. at the transit shed and was broadcasted by KRGV. Gov. James Allred attended, and hundreds watched the first cargo boat sail. Festivities included boat races, a human fishing contest, and US Coast Guard demonstrations held in the turning basin.

Dick Pitts Jr. (left) and Charles Wilson Jr., both from Brownsville, took their first sailboat cruise down the recently completed intracoastal canal from Corpus Christi to Port Isabel. The 1949 completion of the Gulf Intracoastal Waterway connected the deepwater port at Port Isabel with the East Coast.

Four

Building a City Where a City Belongs

It was a sales pitch to the Rio Grande Valley, to the state, and to the Midwest. "Building a city where a city belongs" was said to be created by public necessity, and the city of Point Isabel was to be the port and playground of the richest, fastest-growing agriculture district in America. The following are some other slogans: "early buyers profit most"; "progress here is No Dream of 'IFs' "; "this city is needed now, where values grow while breezes blow"; "never before, never again, there is nothing like it"; and "demand creates values—there is only one Point Isabel!"

To fill a public necessity is the key to certain success, which is why Point Isabel offered sales brochures. Shipment of winter fruits and vegetables were predicted to triple, and the Rio Grande Valley boasted 140 miles of hard-surface highways with a population between 150,000 and 175,000.

All roads were leading to Point Isabel, to the port for shipment, and to the coast for play despite, as brochures pointed out, the lack of improvements and facilities to enjoy its unequalled natural array of pleasures and sports.

Developers and realtors descended upon, wrote copy on, created maps of, made promises about, and offered excursions around Port Isabel. And since the United States was providing the shipping channel, all the Port Isabel Townsite and Development Company had to do was sell, sell, sell. It was an ambitious program of improvement, which would permit the building of a city and resort destination—almost overnight—by the sheer force of economic demand and public necessity.

A total of $875,000 in bonds was issued. Ten miles of roads were graded over 425 acres of the townsite, and an additional 13 blocks of business district received concrete roads. Over one million yards of fill were used to grade lots and fill in ravines. Two palm trees were planted on each of 2,200 lots, and grass seed was spread. Seven small bridges and one large bridge were built. Nine miles of pipe connected a 10-million-gallon reservoir to the Rio Grande River, and channels were dug. Port Isabel was under construction.

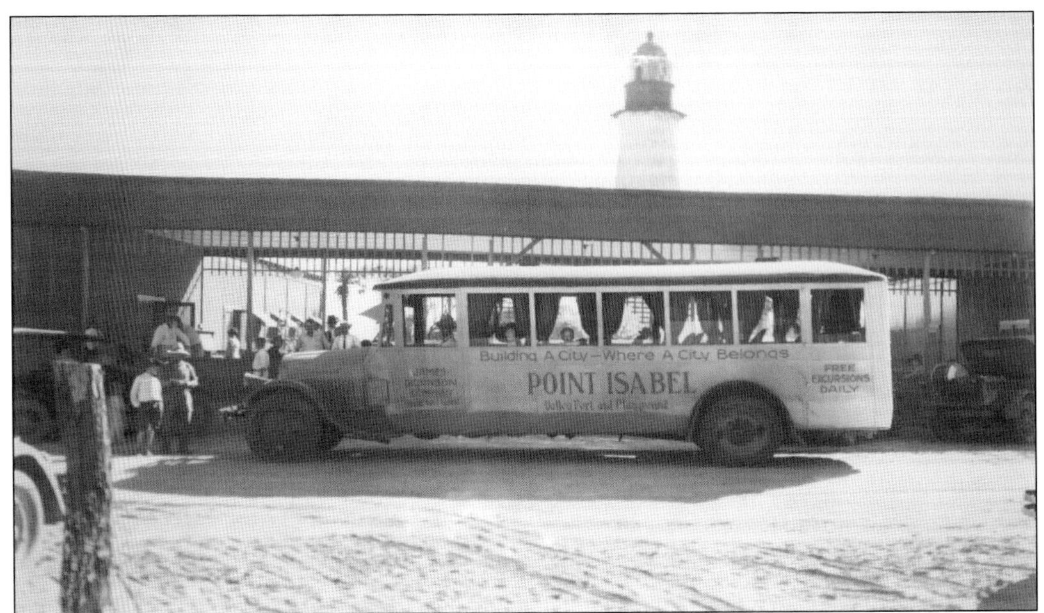

A sales agency's bus ran daily excursions from points in the valley to Point Isabel. The company's Administration Building and government lighthouse in background are shown here. This c. 1925 photograph was taken from the area of what would have been Garcia Street just south of Houston Street.

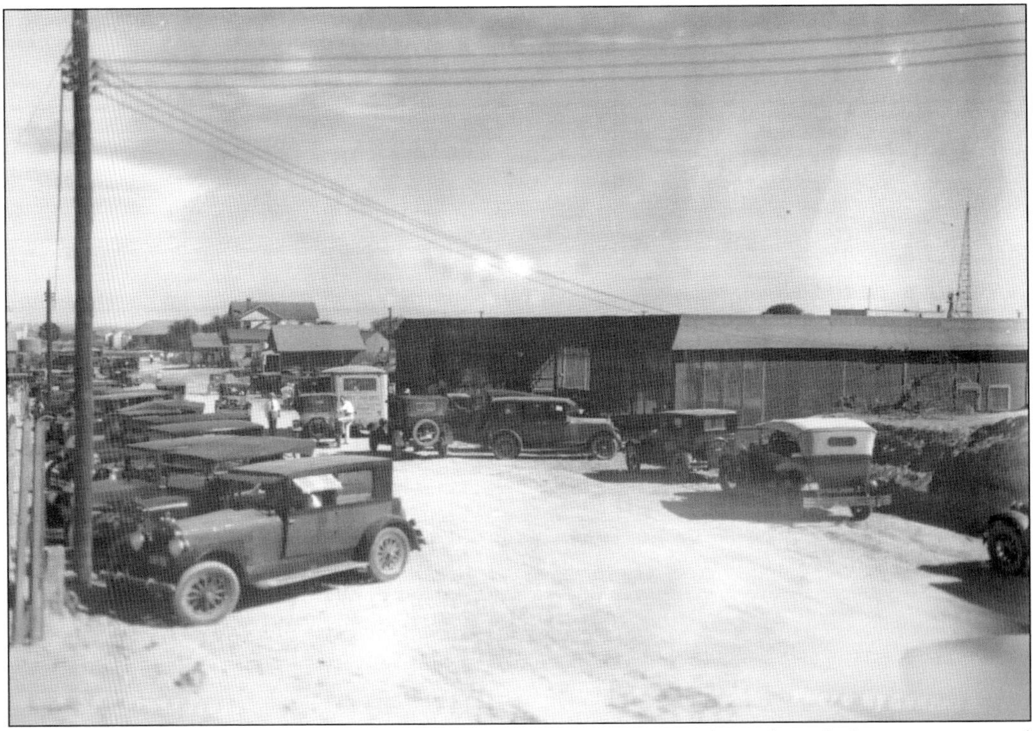

Improvements began as streets were leveled and parking areas cleared, and this was a typical summer weekday in front of the developer's Administration Building (right) on Garcia Street looking south. The excursion bus is visible in the center of the roadway.

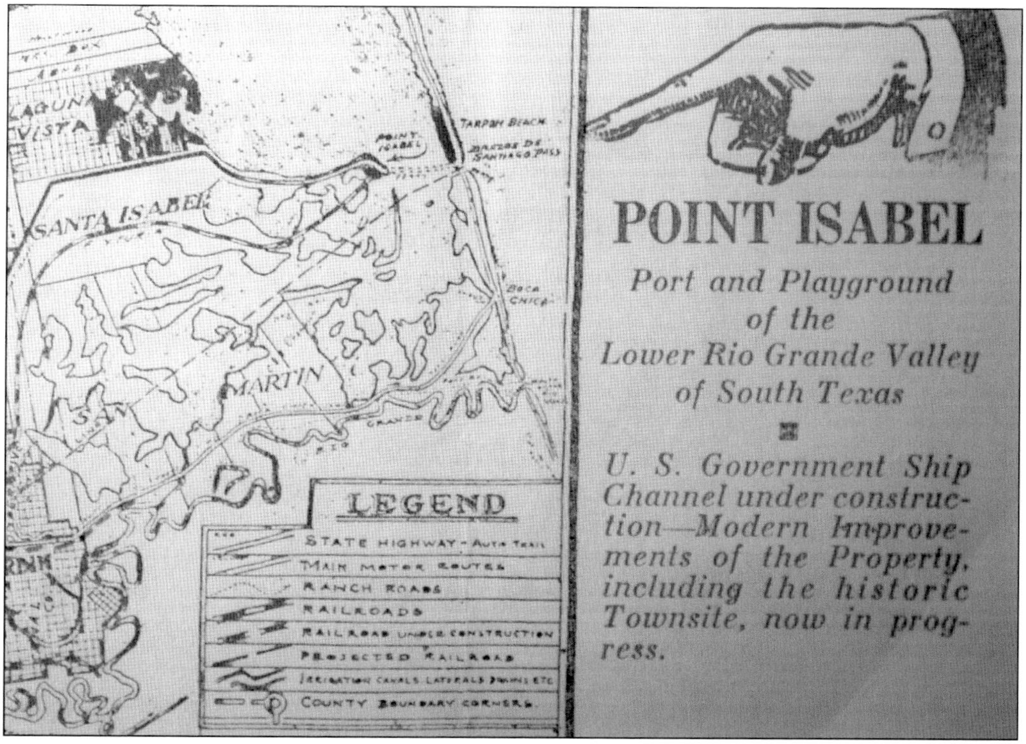

POINT ISABEL

Port and Playground of the Lower Rio Grande Valley of South Texas

U. S. Government Ship Channel under construction—Modern Improvements of the Property, including the historic Townsite, now in progress.

Here, Point Isabel is declared, "Port and Playground of the Lower Rio Grande Valley of South Texas." Port Isabel is located inside the barrier island marked Tarpon Beach (South Padre Island), and the pass is marked Brazos de Santiago Pass. Land parties to the area were furnished with cars and drivers, who were advertised to be residents of the valley acting as hosts.

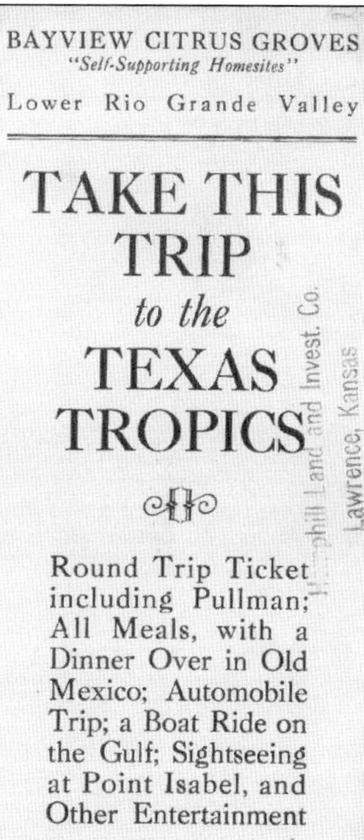

This all-inclusive trip to the Texas Tropics and Port Isabel was marketed to the winter-bound Kansas resident. Leaving weekly from Kansas City on Tuesday evening, travelers were sent by rail to Edinburg, arriving by Thursday morning. This brochure states, "During the tour of inspection, we visit our new town, Port Isabel, on the [G]ulf Coast, where this company is engaged in building a city by the sea." The cost for the entire trip from Kansas City was $40, but "if your wife accompanies you (and we insist that she does) the cost is $60 for the two. This is only a fraction of what the trip costs the company, but it is our method of advertising."

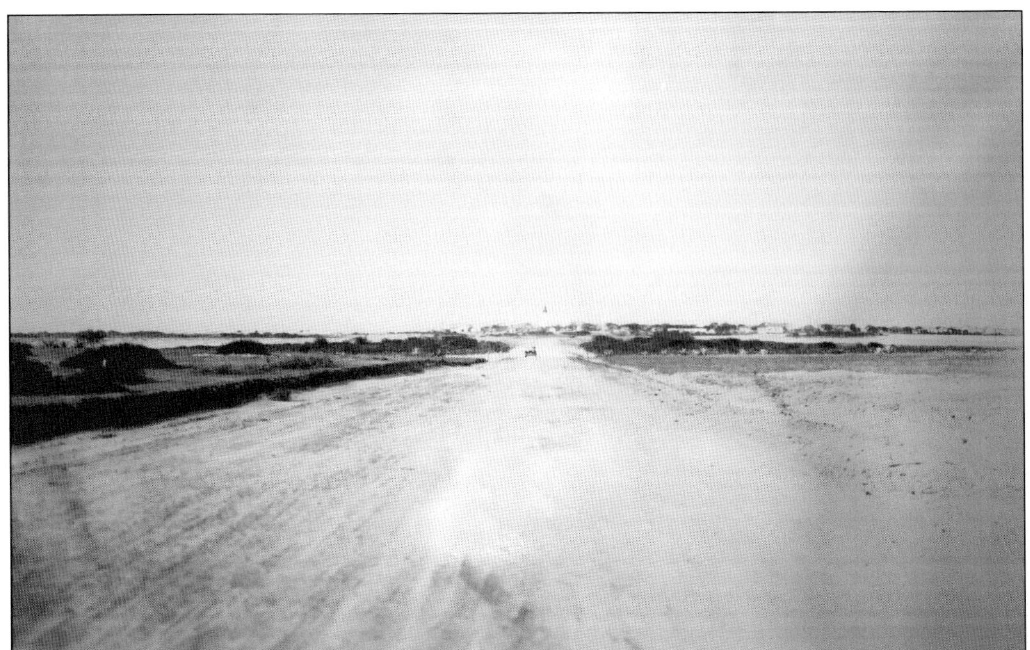

State Highway 100, shown here freshly graded, was meant to be part of the "Main Street" of the Rio Grande Valley, 90 miles long ending at the coast. Concrete paving of the highway was underway to make the drive to the port and year-round resort of the valley one of convenience and comfort.

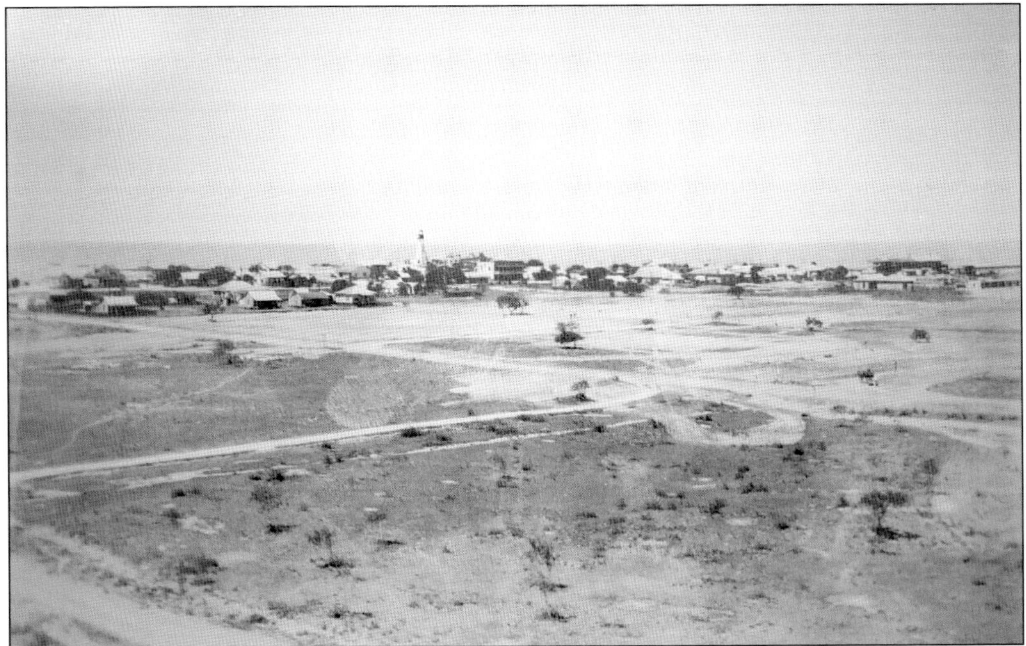

This northeasterly view of the townsite was taken from the government's wireless tower. The buildings on the lots represented those reserved or sold by former owners before the property was acquired by the development company. The elevation of the lighthouse and the keeper's house rise above that of the southern part of the townsite.

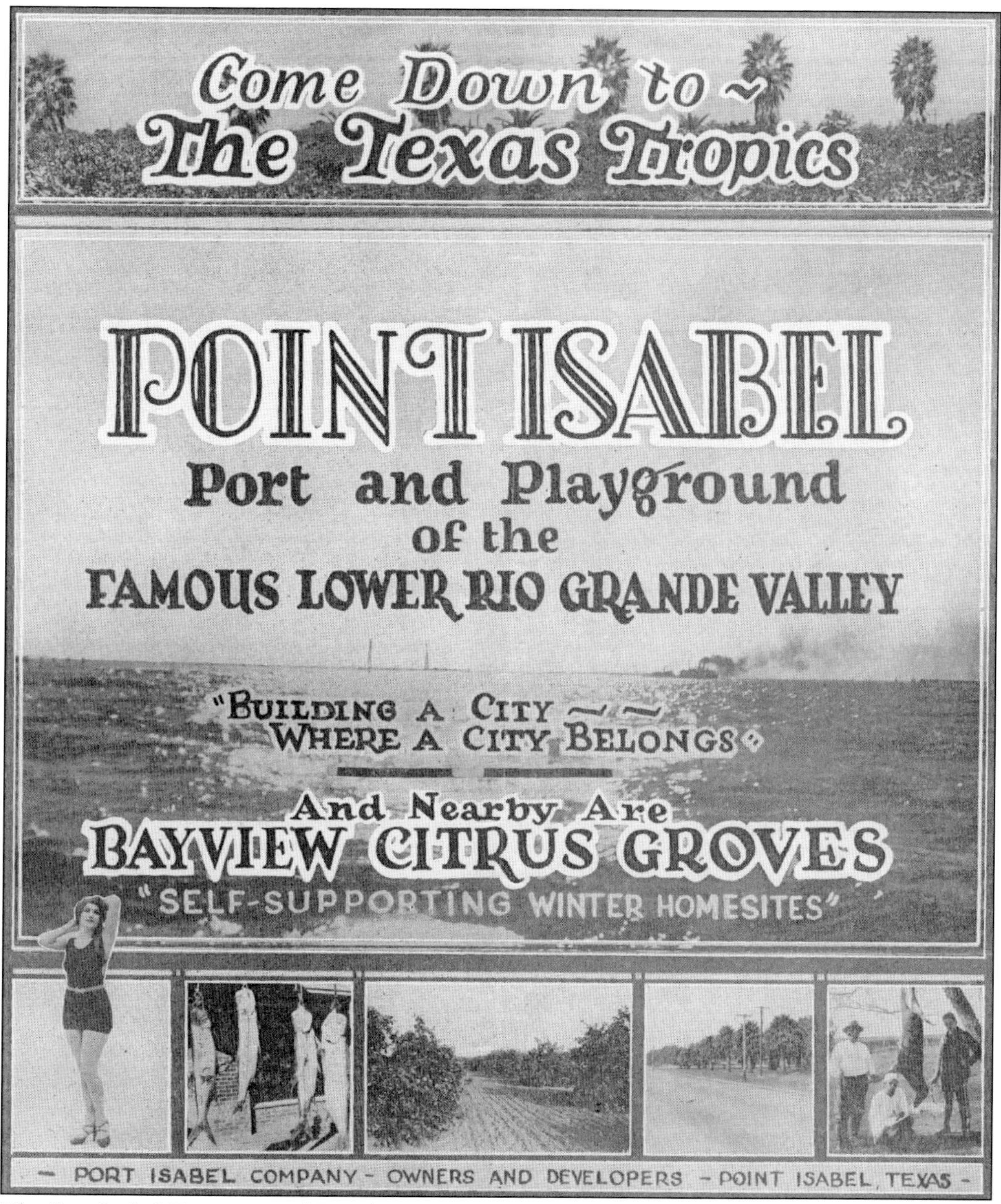

The Port Isabel Townsite and Development Company purchased 800 acres of the original Port Isabel townsite and set about "building a city where a city belongs." With offices in Port Isabel, Brownsville's El Jardin Hotel, and San Antonio, the Port Isabel Company facilitated travel to the area for potential buyers. Nearby Bayview Citrus Groves was also offered as "self-supporting winter home sites." Sportfishing, specifically tarpon fishing, also served as a lure to the area. The close proximity of the Brazos Santiago Pass was a favorite haunt of the tarpon known as the "silver king."

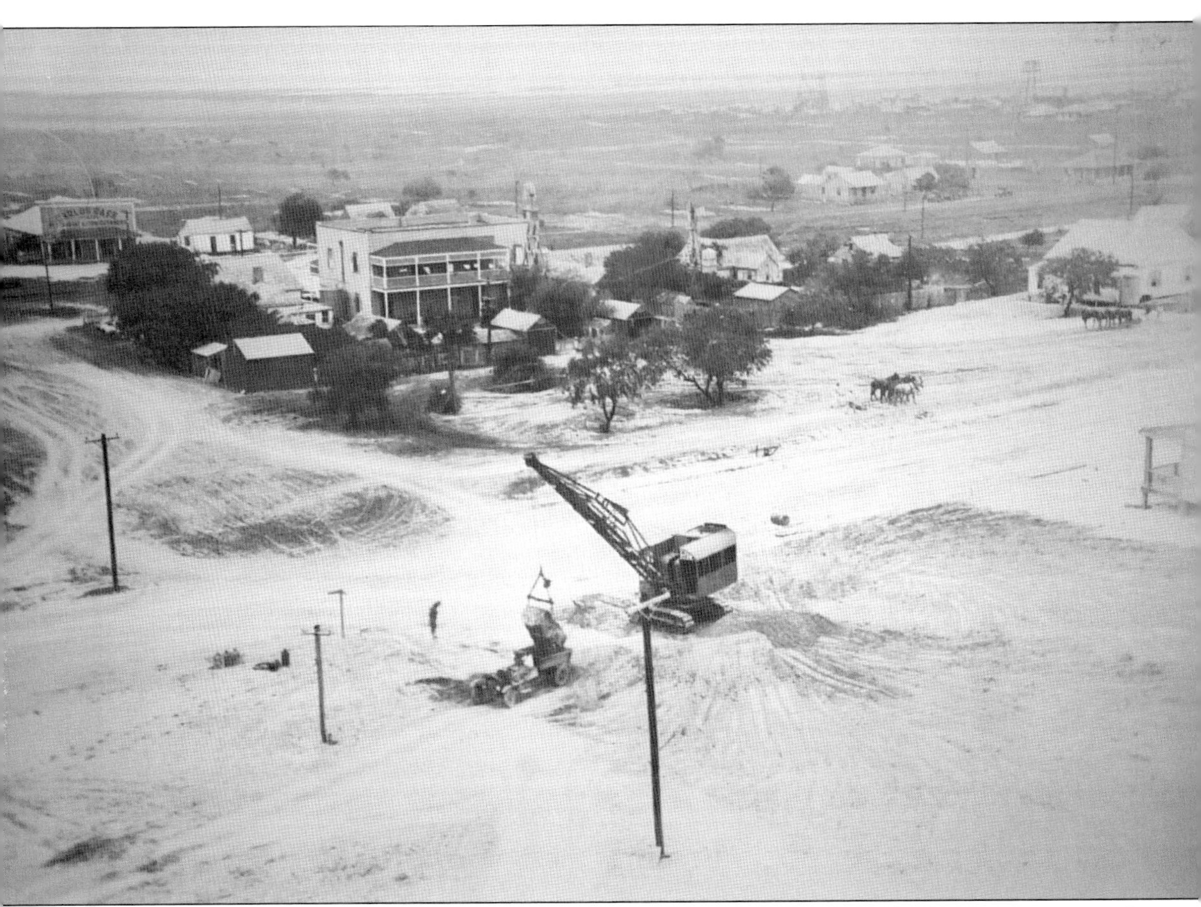

This bird's-eye view, taken from the top of the lighthouse, looks toward the business section of the townsite after tenants' and squatters' shacks were removed. Overlooking Powers Street (State Highway 100) in a southwesterly direction, the image shows the rear of the Charles Champion Building, complete with gallery and fresh laundry fluttering in the breeze. The Champion family lived on the second floor of their business. A cistern on the west side of the building caught rainwater from the center sloping roof. The lot between the Champion Building and Powers Street is being worked by two teams of horses and men using a roller to smooth out the terrain. In the foreground at about the intersection of Powers Street and Tarnava Street, a crane is moving loads of dirt and sand to a waiting truck. Carlos Café (upper left) is just catty-corner to the Champion Building.

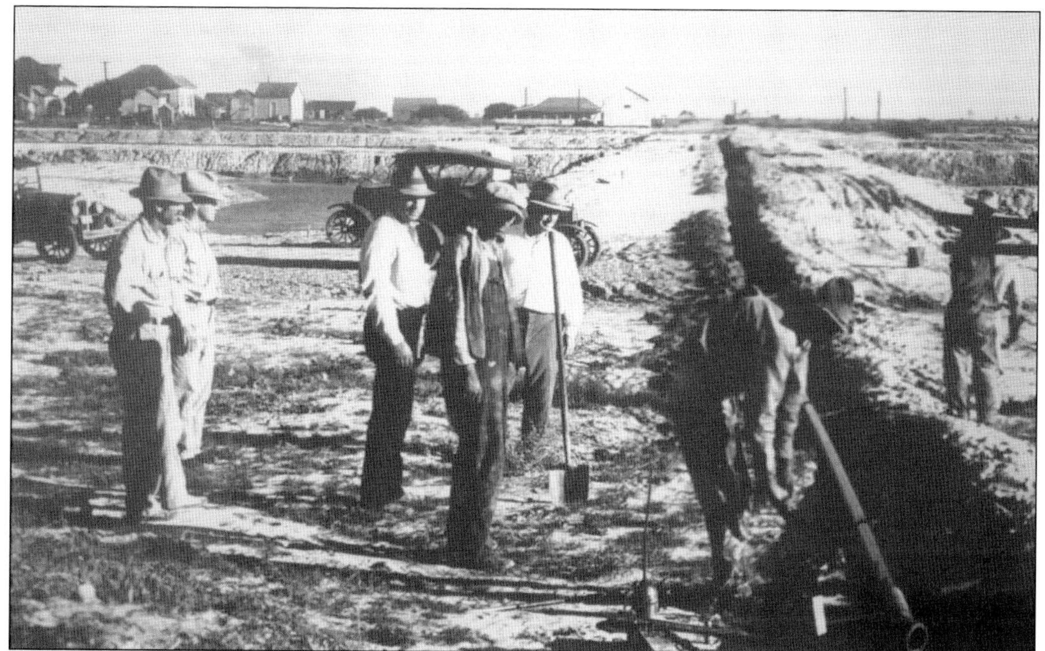

Pipe is being laid in hand-dug trenches as part of the city's water-supply development. Need for such improvements can be evidenced over the workers' shoulders, as the number of new residential structures was increasing rapidly. Six miles of pipe was laid within the townsite.

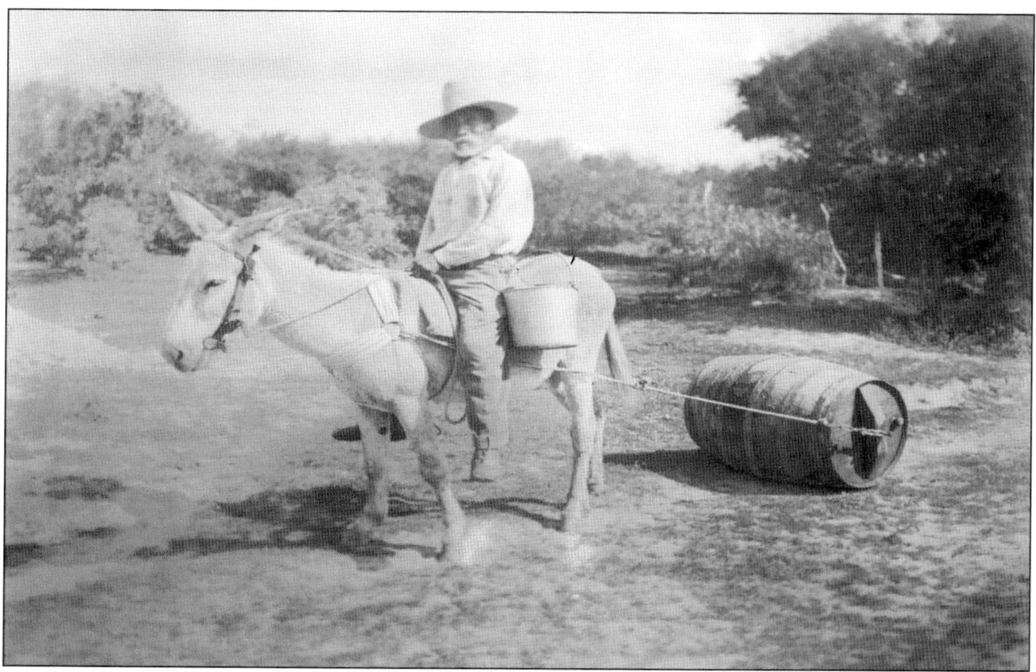

Known as the Point Isabel Individual Waterworks System, water haulers were in use from 1850 until October 1, 1927, when a eight-inch, cast-iron pipeline from Port Isabel to the Rio Grande River was completed at a cost of $90,000. *Aguadores*, or water haulers, would gather at the well each morning and fill their barrels for home delivery.

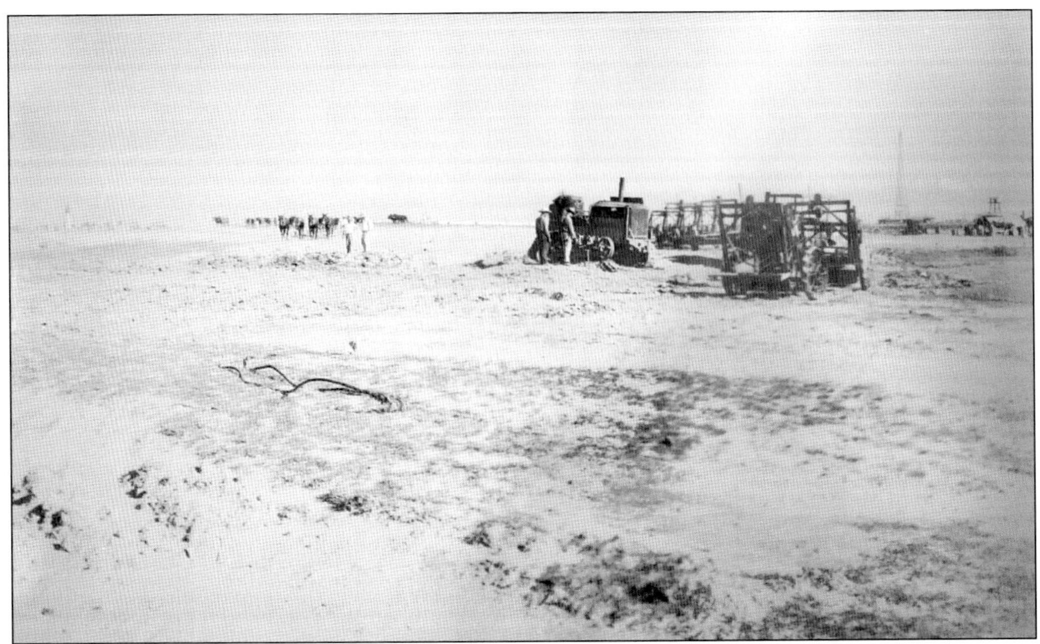

Taken from the west section of the townsite, this photograph shows man and machine working on the development of the city. It appears that a team of horses is dragging a type of grader to smooth out the terrain. In the distance are the lighthouse (left) and one of the wireless towers (right).

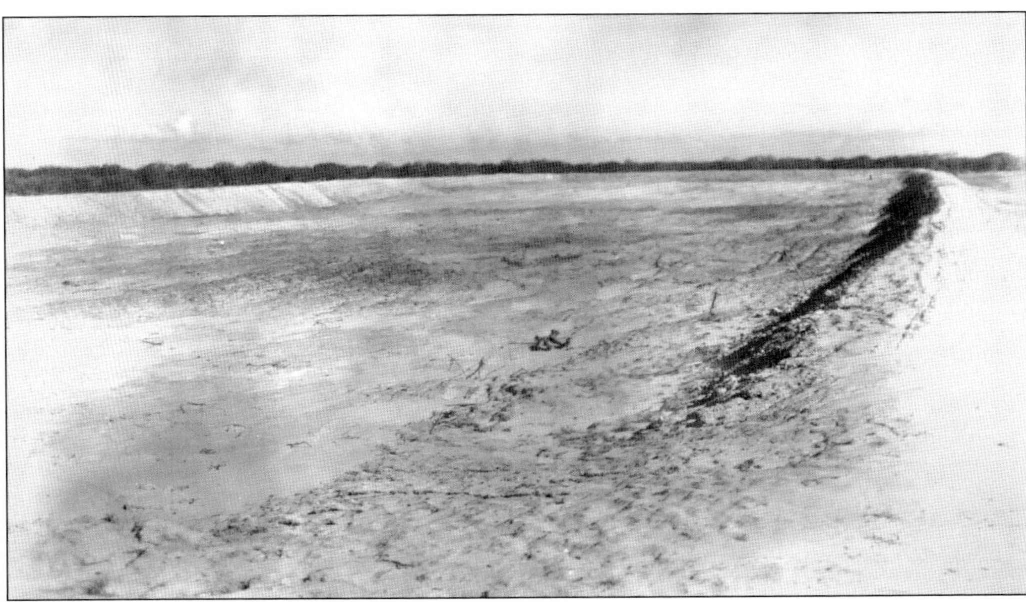

A 10-million-gallon reservoir for the city water supply was dug in the Palangana area. A settling basin of the same size was created nine miles away at the Rio Grande River. The two basins were connected by an eight-inch, cast-iron pipe.

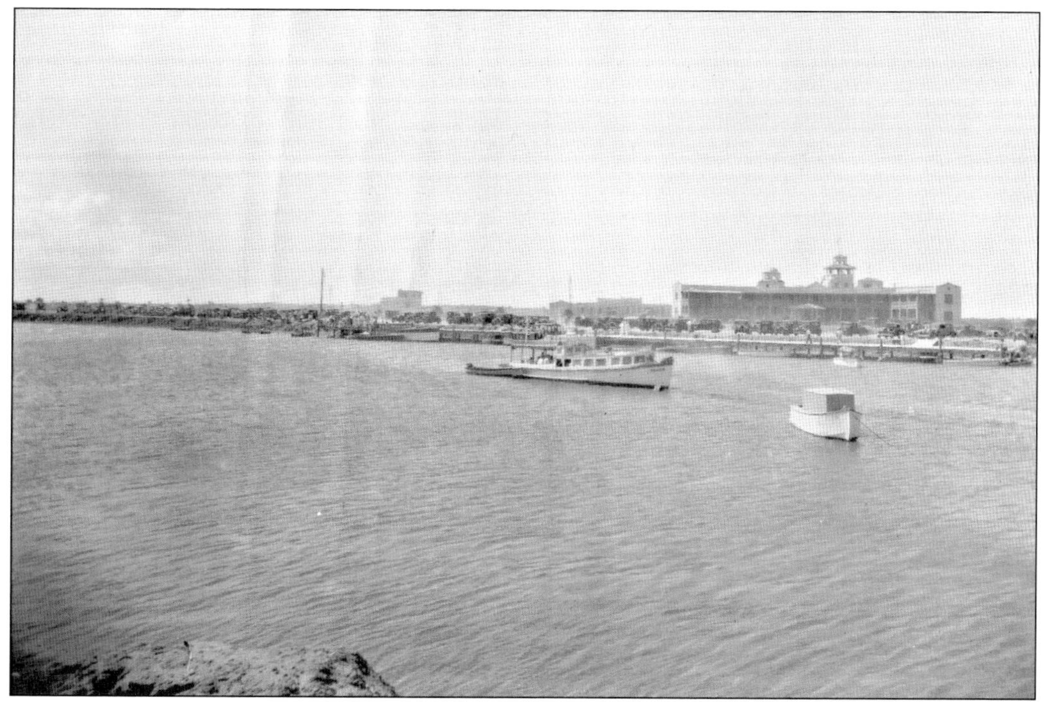

The turning basin in front of the newly constructed yacht club is buzzing with activity. Dozens of cars line Yturria Street along the bank. Visible in the distance on North Shore and Polk Streets are the Alta Vista Apartments and a private residence.

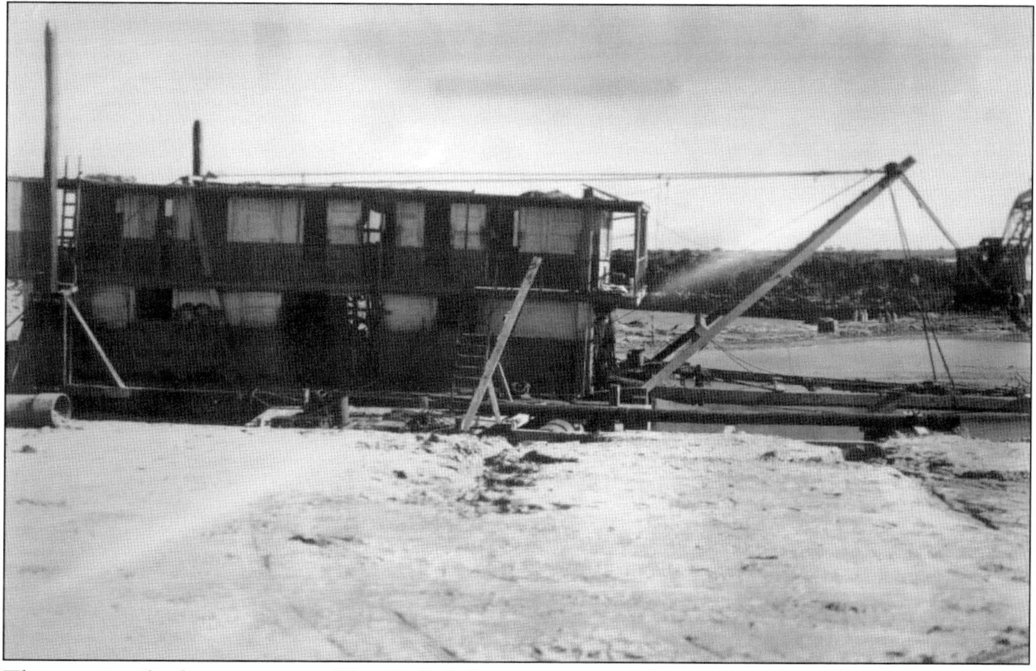

This suction dredge, property of Port Isabel Company, created waterways throughout the townsite, including the Port Isabel Side Channel that ran between the Brownsville Ship Channel and the Laguna Madre Bay to the north. This effectively made Port Isabel an island.

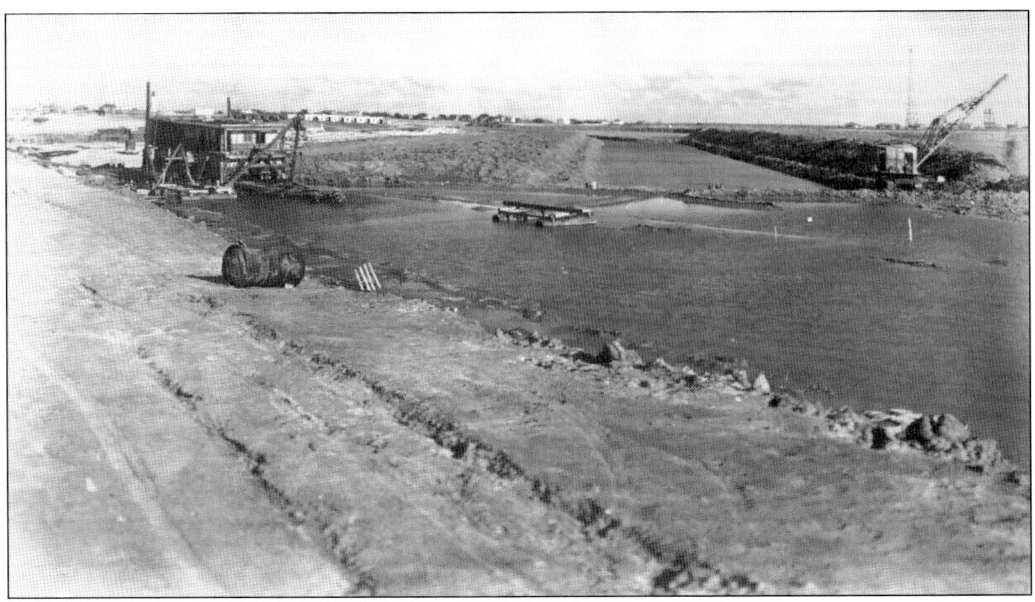

The suction dredge, owned by the development company, works with a crane as they near completion on one of the channels in what was then called the Venetian section of Point Isabel. The photograph was taken from the west side of the still land-locked yacht basin. The Venetian section was also known as "Modern Venice" or "The Fingers."

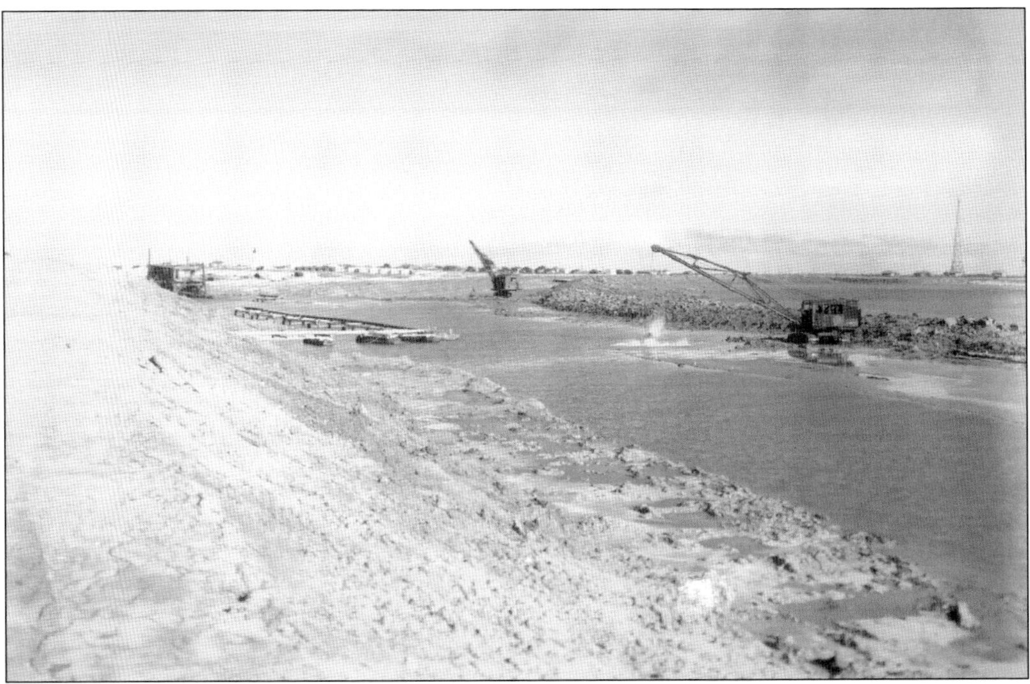

On left in this development scene is the suction dredge, and to its right, two cranes are working a dragline. Channels and blocks are being created in the Venetian section of the townsite. Spoils were used to create additional elevation on The Fingers.

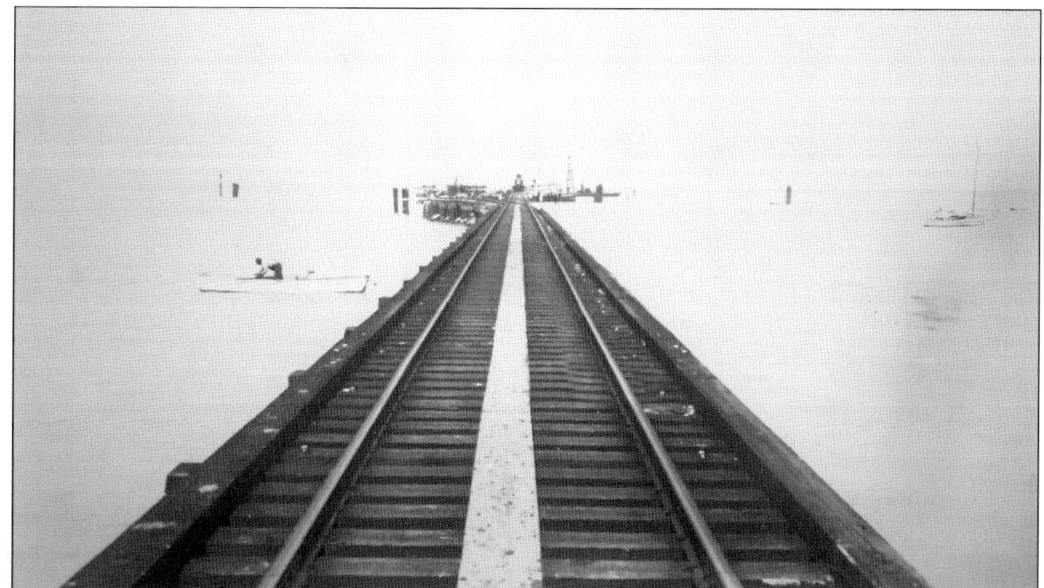

The tracks and trestle of the Rio Grande Railroad extended from the mainland into the Laguna Madre Bay some 1,500 feet to the turning basin at the end of the pier. A train is shown here backed onto the pier and is transferring a load to a waiting barge to go to Brazos Santiago Pass. A fisherman busies himself (left) in a boat lashed to the pier.

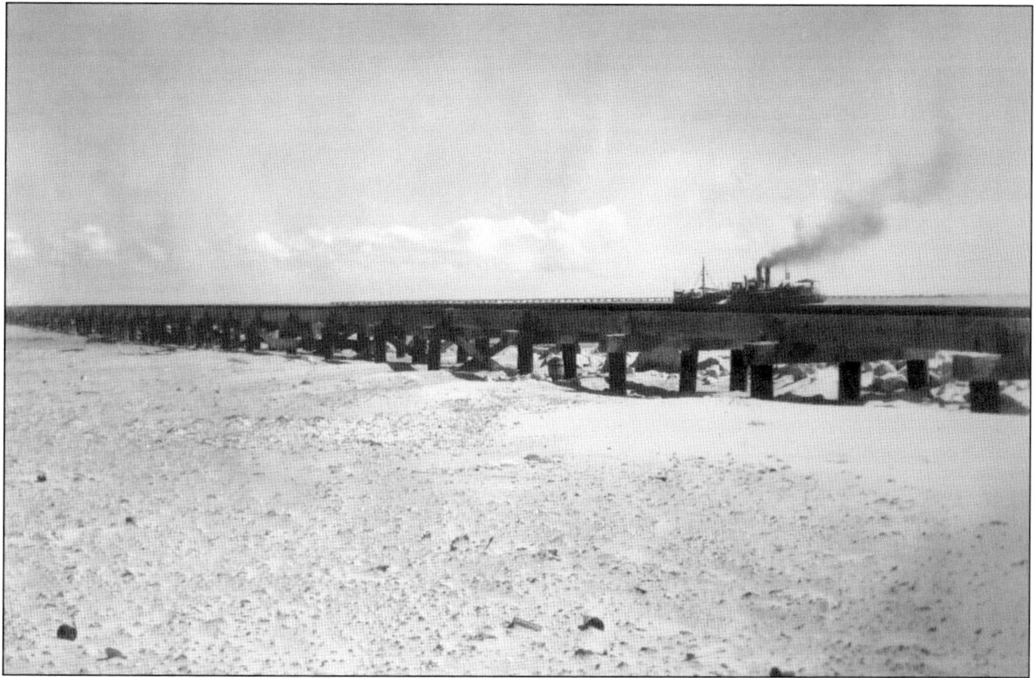

Part of the transition of Point Isabel to Port Isabel included ensuring the stability of the opening at Brazos Santiago Pass between South Padre Island and Brazos Island or Boca Chica Beach. This view of the north jetty, before ballasting was completed, shows the government hopper dredge *Absecon* at work cutting the outer channel to a depth of 18 feet. Dredging was completed early 1928.

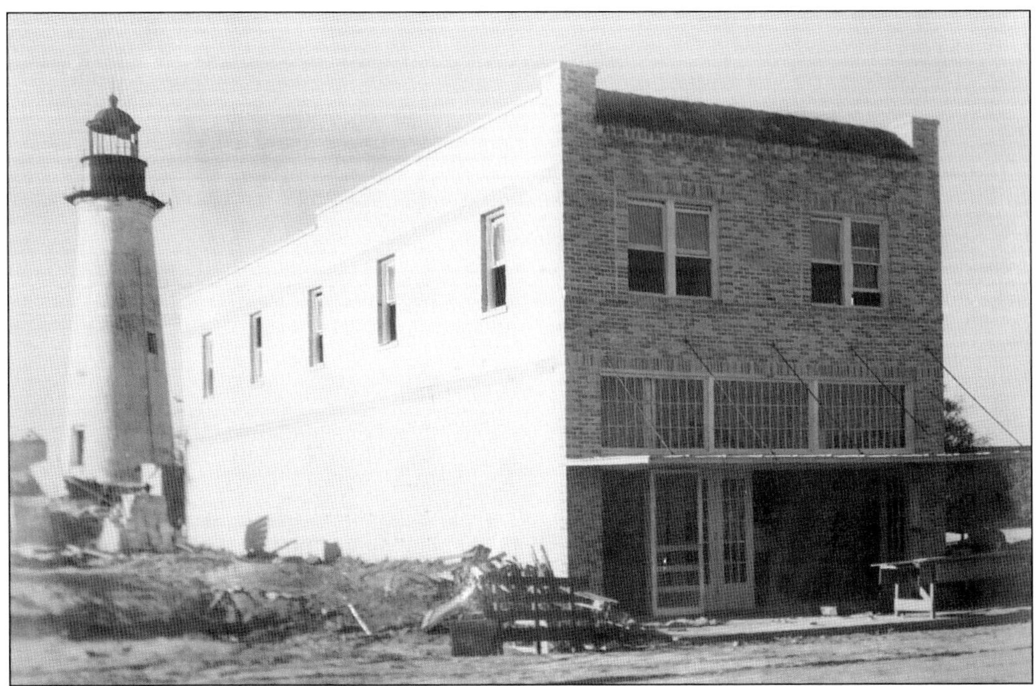

This two-story brick office and drugstore building was just in the process of completion on the south side of the lighthouse on Powers Street. Powers Street was later removed, and buildings were razed to make way for State Highway 100 as the right-of-way for the second Queen Isabella Causeway.

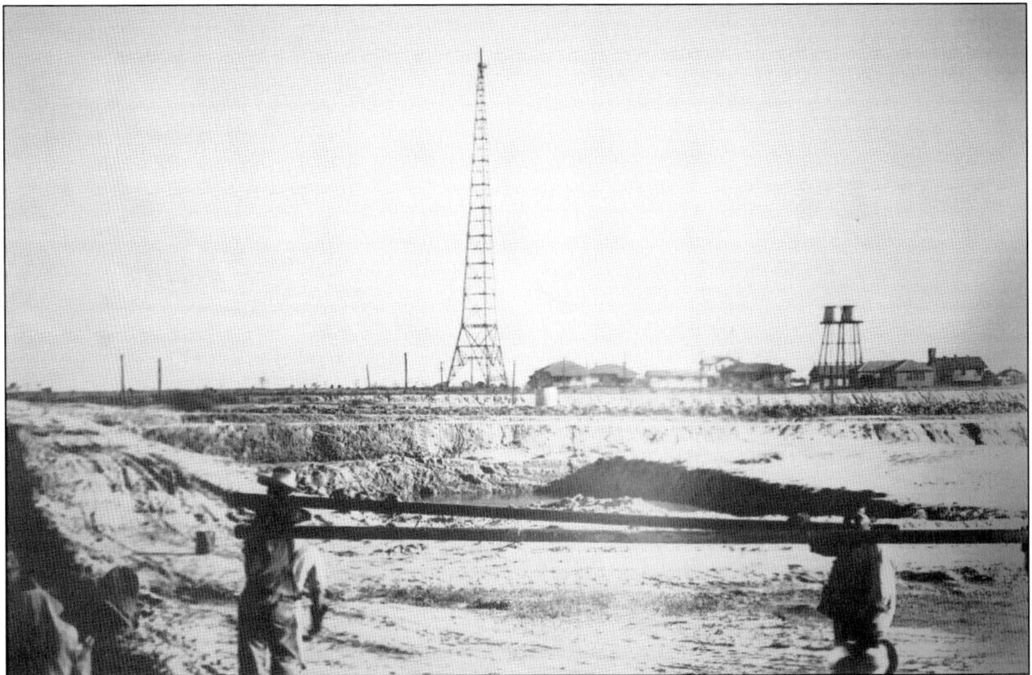

This 1927 photograph, taken during improvements to the city's water supply system, shows two men moving six-inch pipe. The wireless reservation and outlying buildings are visible in the background. The tallest object to the right of the wireless tower elevates four cisterns.

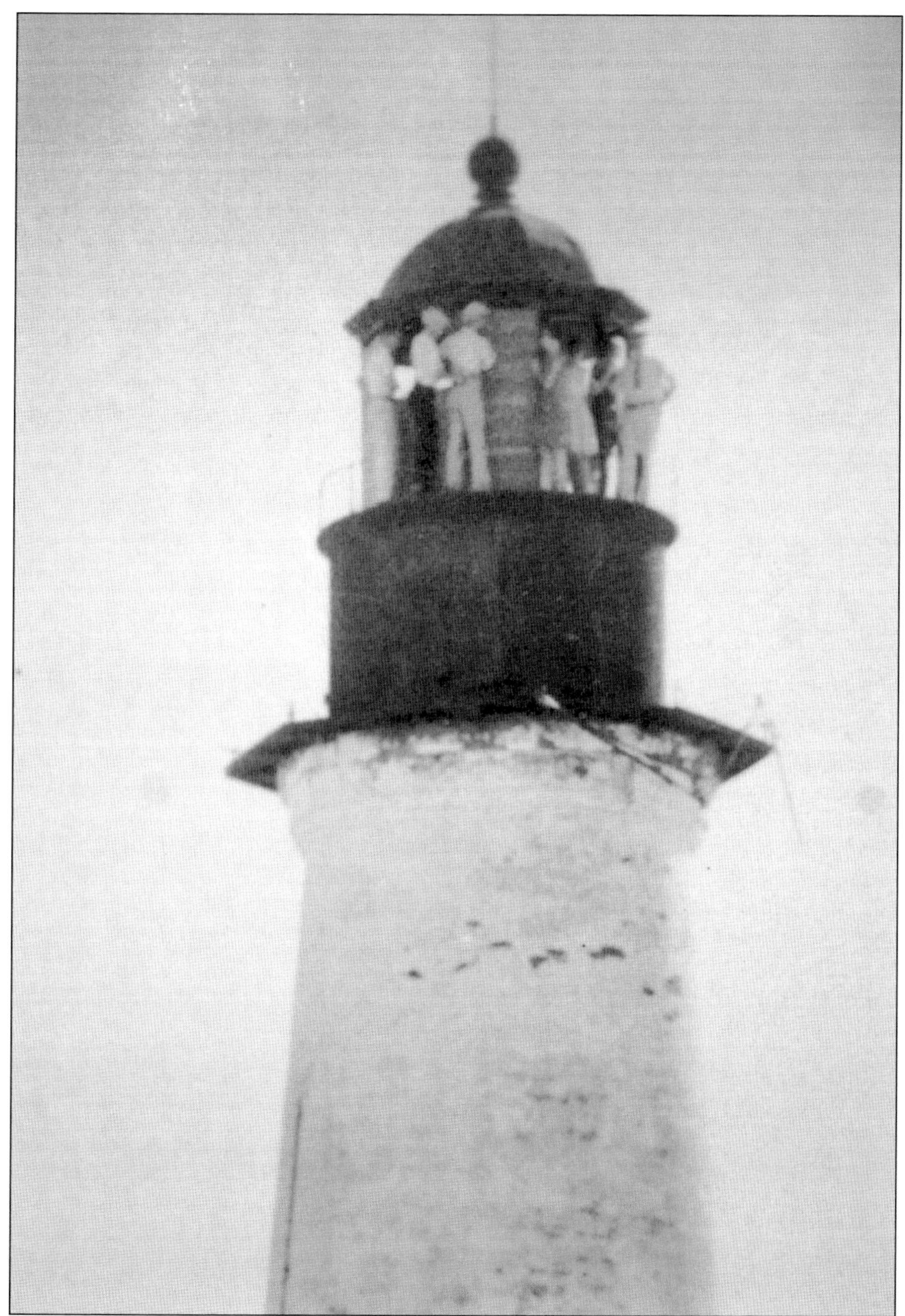

Developers proposed repairs to the Point Isabel Lighthouse, but clearly this photograph was taken prior to those repairs. At least seven people are visible at the top of the lighthouse lantern, clinging to each other and to the cast-iron window openings. The glass is missing from the lantern room, and the railing around it appears to be about knee height, offering little protection against a fall; the catwalk on the level below has no railing at all. Some who considered the lighthouse an iconic emblem also thought that it should be torn down.

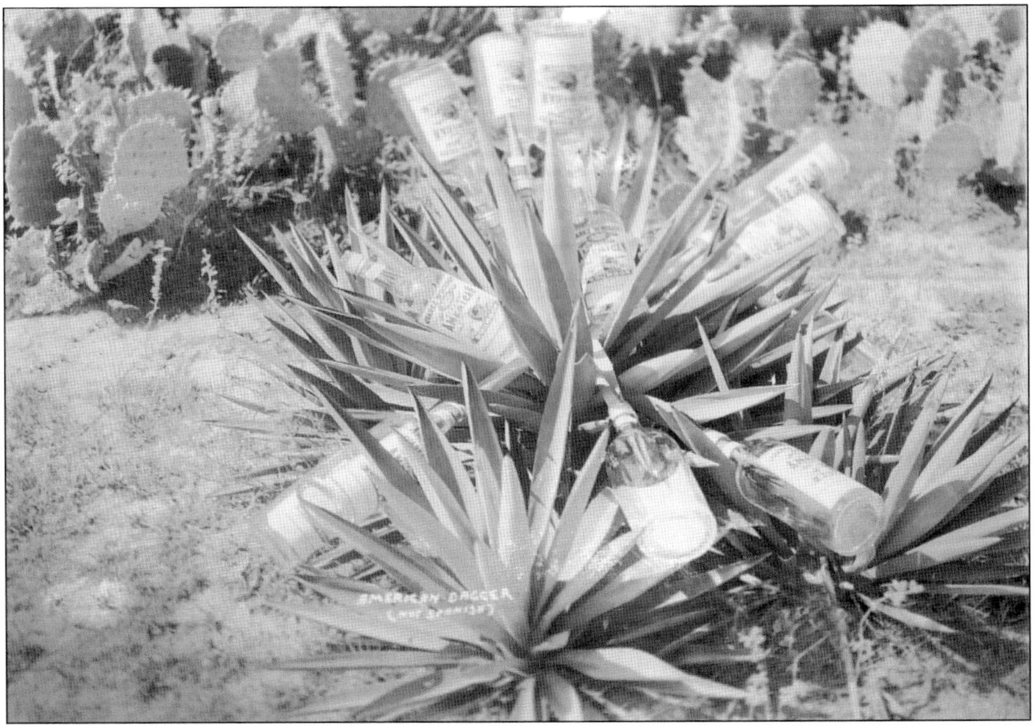

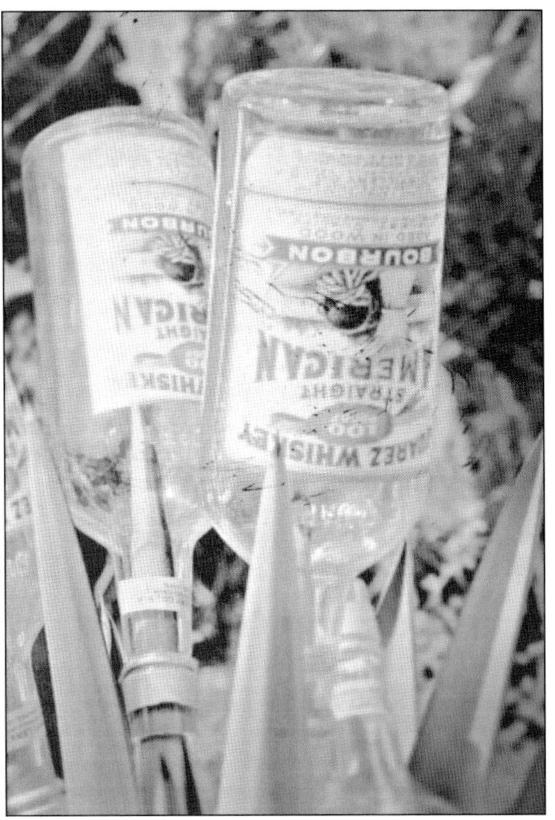

Tucked in a 1927 presentation report of the $875,000 bond issue for the improvement of the Point Isabel townsite was this photograph of an "American dagger." Buds (bottles) shown here were said to have been evidently added to the plant under the cover of darkness from gunnysacks that crossed the Mexican border nine miles away. For the purposes of the report, statistics were not available as to the value of this crop in the Rio Grande Valley. The empty bottles displayed on the leaves of this Spanish dagger plant held 100-proof Juarez Whiskey, straight American bourbon. During Prohibition, the observation of the proximity of the Mexican border was not lost on developers and investors alike.

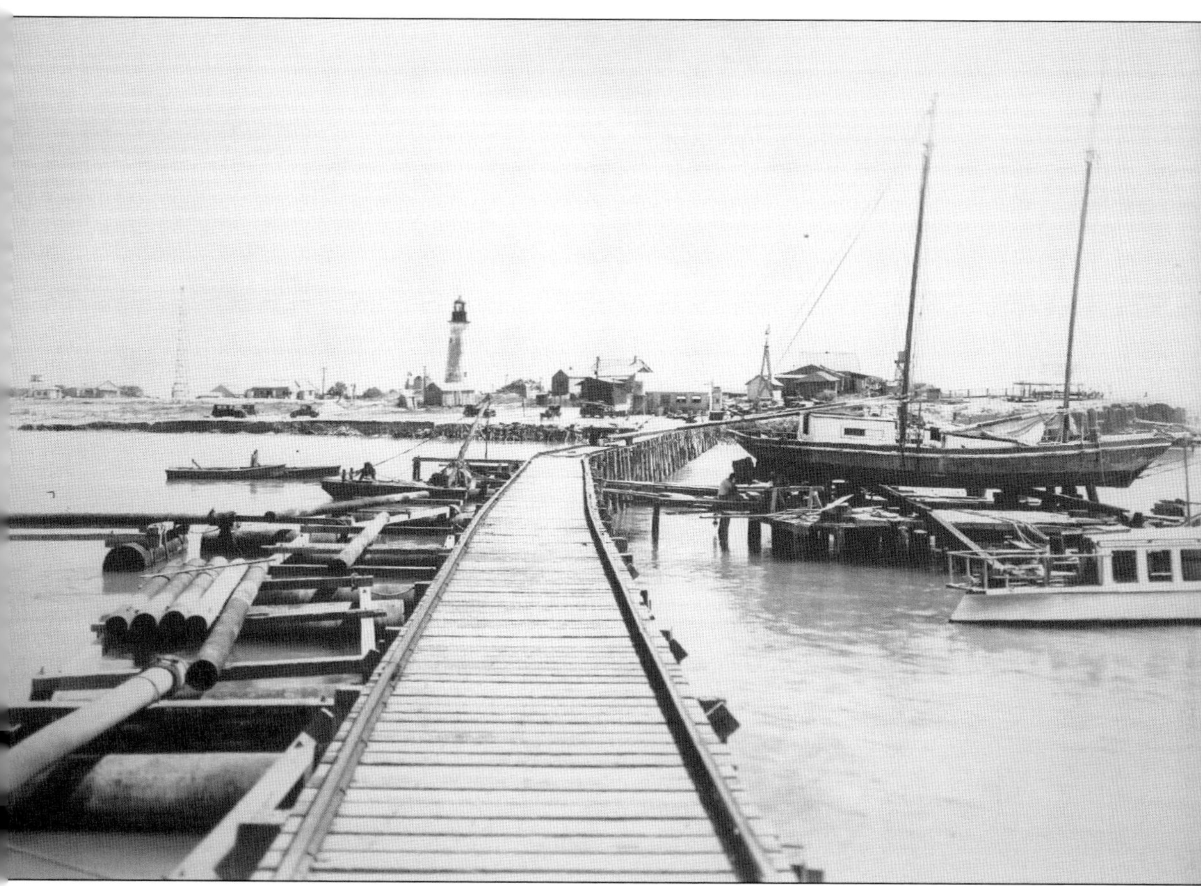

One of the fishing docks in Point Isabel, which appears to be newly constructed, is pictured here. A sailing vessel is dry-docked (right), and workers are performing below-waterline maintenance or repairs. Wooden pilings float atop pontoons to the left of the dock, possibly to be used in the construction of the jetty system on South Padre Island. Slightly above the pontoons are two boats, the type used by local commercial fishermen for fishing in the bay or gathering oysters. In the center of the skyline, to the right of the lighthouse, is the keeper's house. To the left of the lighthouse, one of the wireless towers is visible. Several cars are parked along the waterfront, presumably belonging to those working along the shoreline or out on the bay fishing. A number of structures had cisterns, windmills, or both. Along some stretches of the shoreline, riprap is visible, which was used as a measure against erosion.

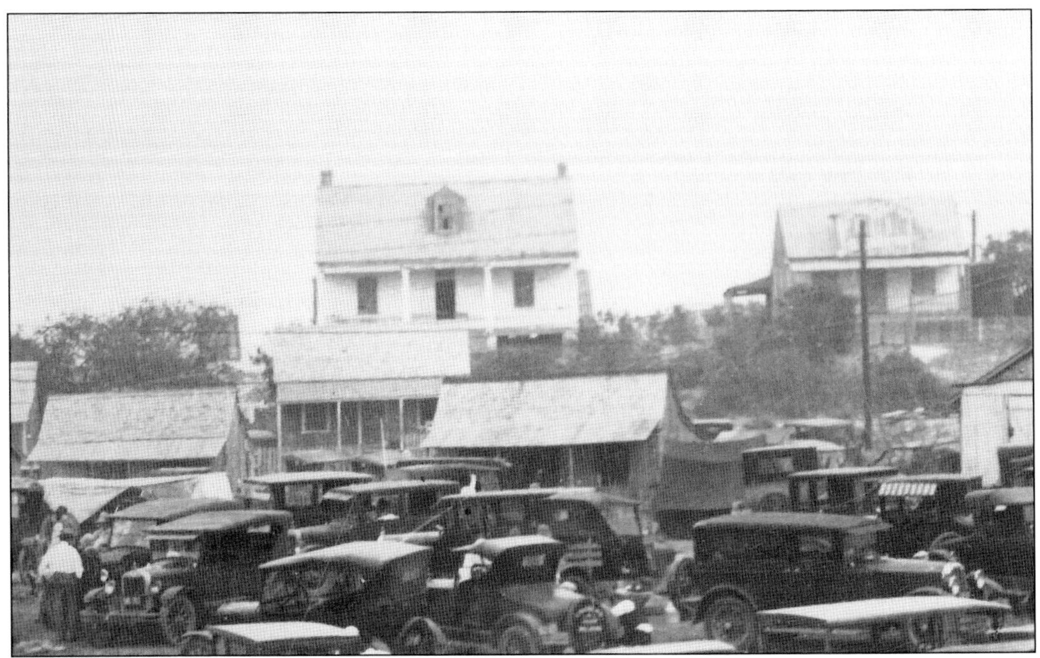

Perched atop the bluff to the northeast side of the lighthouse, the keeper's house, built in 1855, was razed in 1928, and the soil on which it stood was removed to be used for street building and as fill. The structure stayed otherwise empty after the 1905 lighthouse decommission except for five months when, on July 2, 1912, it was rented to John I. Kleiber.

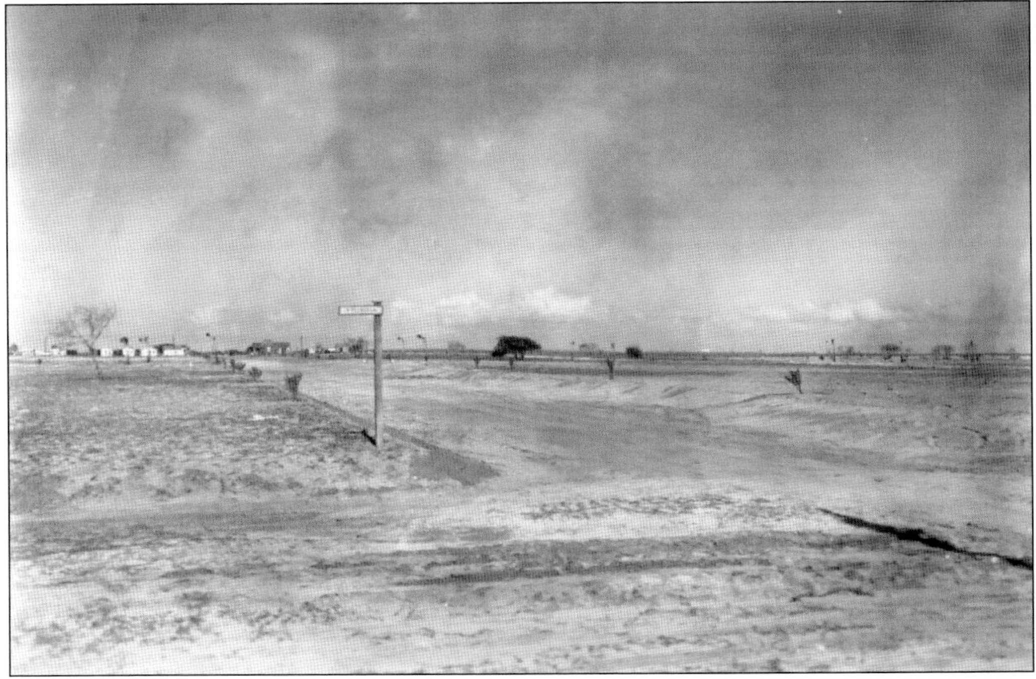

As part of the revitalization of the townsite, residential streets were graded. The street sign in this photograph is of Yturria Street where it intersects with State Highway 100 and heads north. Note the palm trees planted along State Highway 100: two per lot at a cost of $1 each.

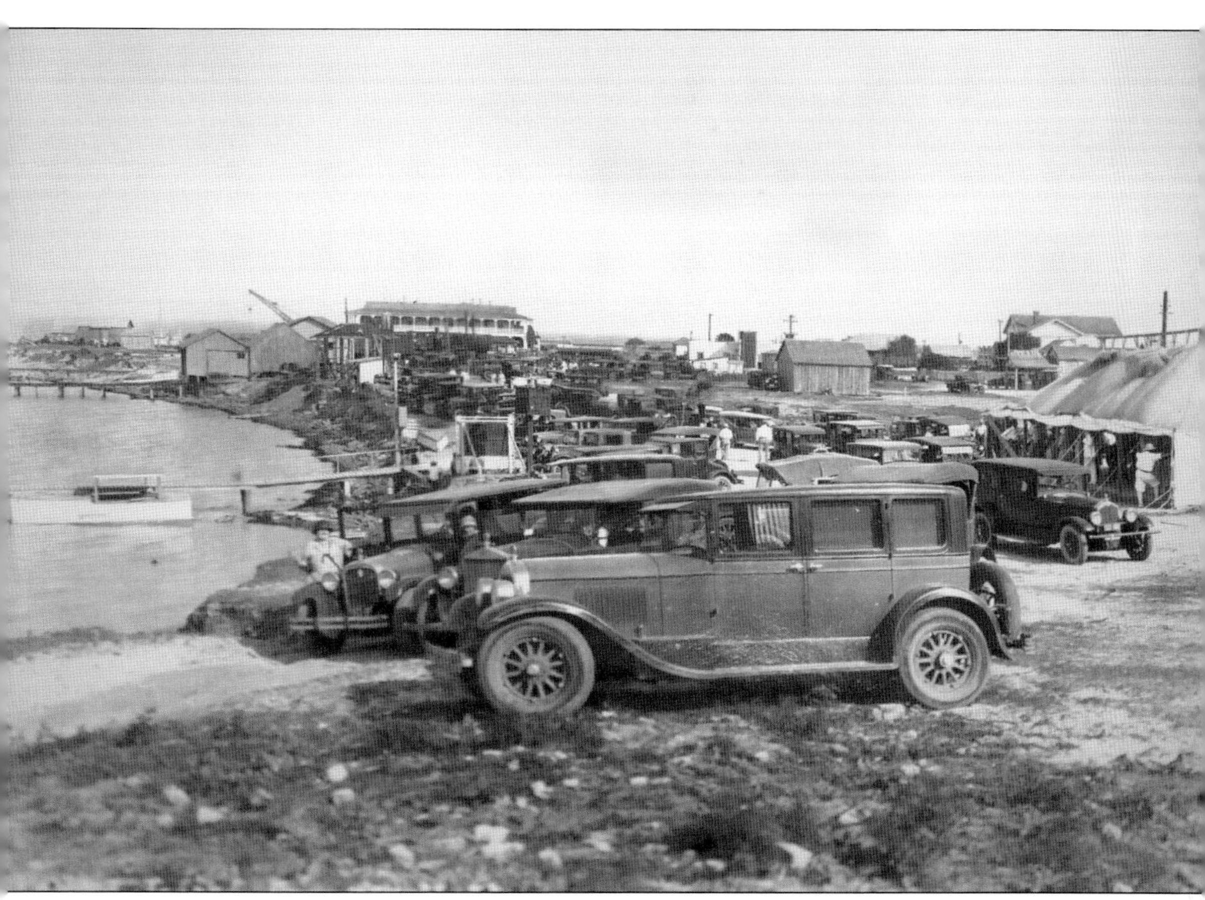

Called a typical Sunday morning scene at Point Isabel, automobiles were parked overnight on the bay front, as accommodations were limited. Visible in the background is the Red Arrow Inn, later called the Queen Isabel Inn. A canteen under the tent (right) offered some provisions.

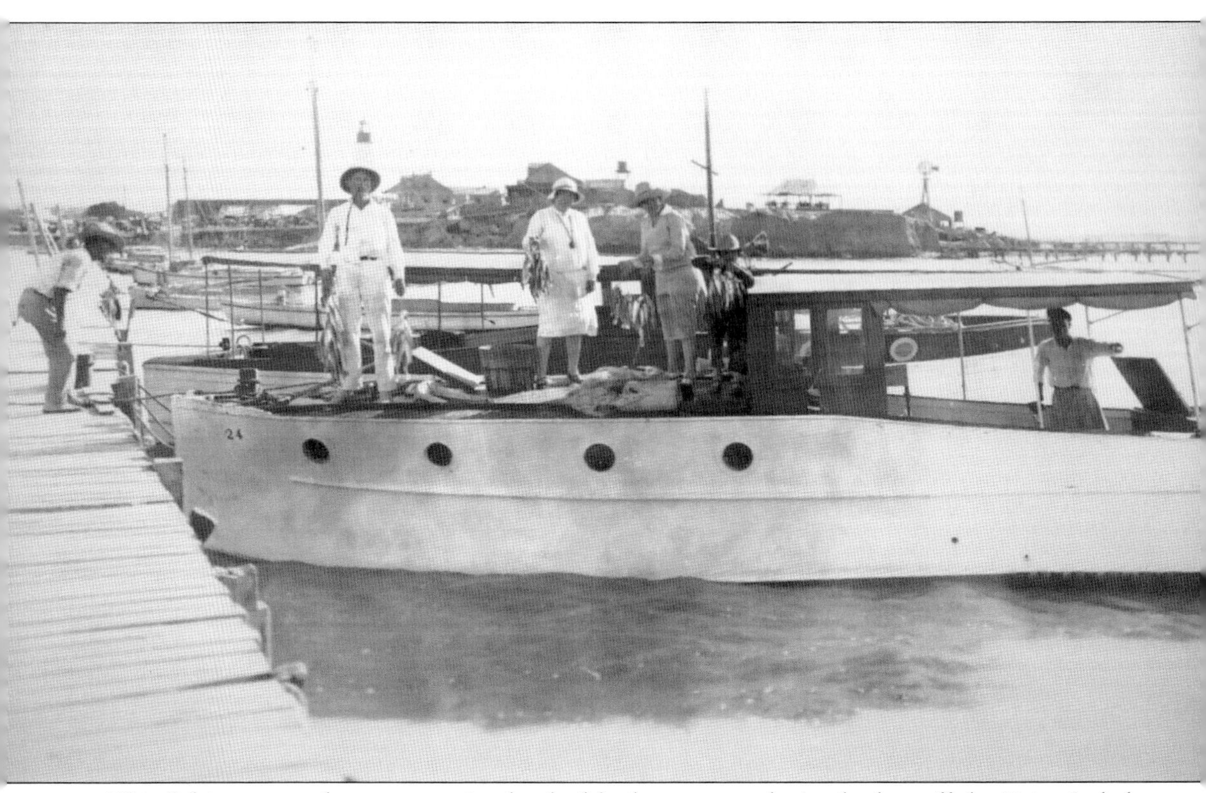

This fishing scene shows a morning haul of fresh trout caught in the bay off the Point Isabel townsite. The fishing party is aboard land developer Al Parker's yacht. Parker's yacht is docked at one of the many piers that jutted out into the Laguna Madre. Behind this proud fishing party is a view of the bluff that Port Isabel was known for. Early accounts put the height of this natural bluff at 30 feet. Eventually erosion and heavy storms claimed upwards of three quarters of a mile of shoreline of the point. Taken from the approximate location of the Colley pier at the end of Maxan Street, or just south of present-day Pirates Landing Fishing Pier, this view shows the keeper's cottage (off the shoulder of the man on the far left in the boat) just slightly north of the lighthouse in its original location. Reconstruction of the keeper's cottage in the 1990s was several hundred feet south of its original location.

This duotone, 24-inch-by-9.5-inch brochure presented an ambitious plan to develop and improve "The Port at Point Isabel Texas." James Dickinson Company, realtors from Brownsville, produced this brochure to encourage investment in the Port Isabel townsite. Early buyers will profit most, it promised. Artwork shared a vision that Port Isabel could one day look like an Atlantic City complete with boardwalks, high rises, and sandy beaches.

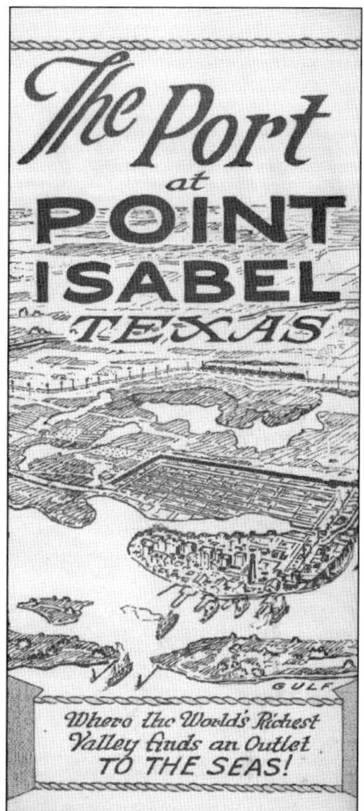

The James Dickinson Company bus, seen here about 30 miles from Port Isabel in Harlingen, is loaded with a band on its way to greet incoming guests with fanfare. Other staff members are suitably attired to attract upper-valley residents and the visiting Midwesterner to a south Texas quality of life.

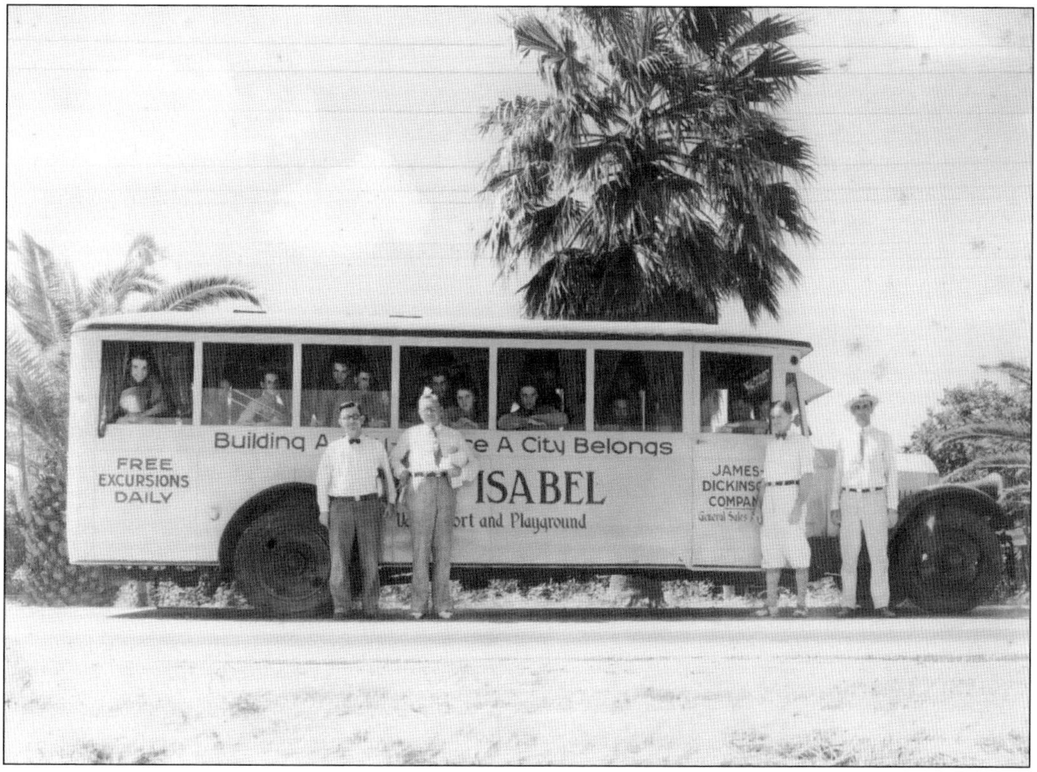

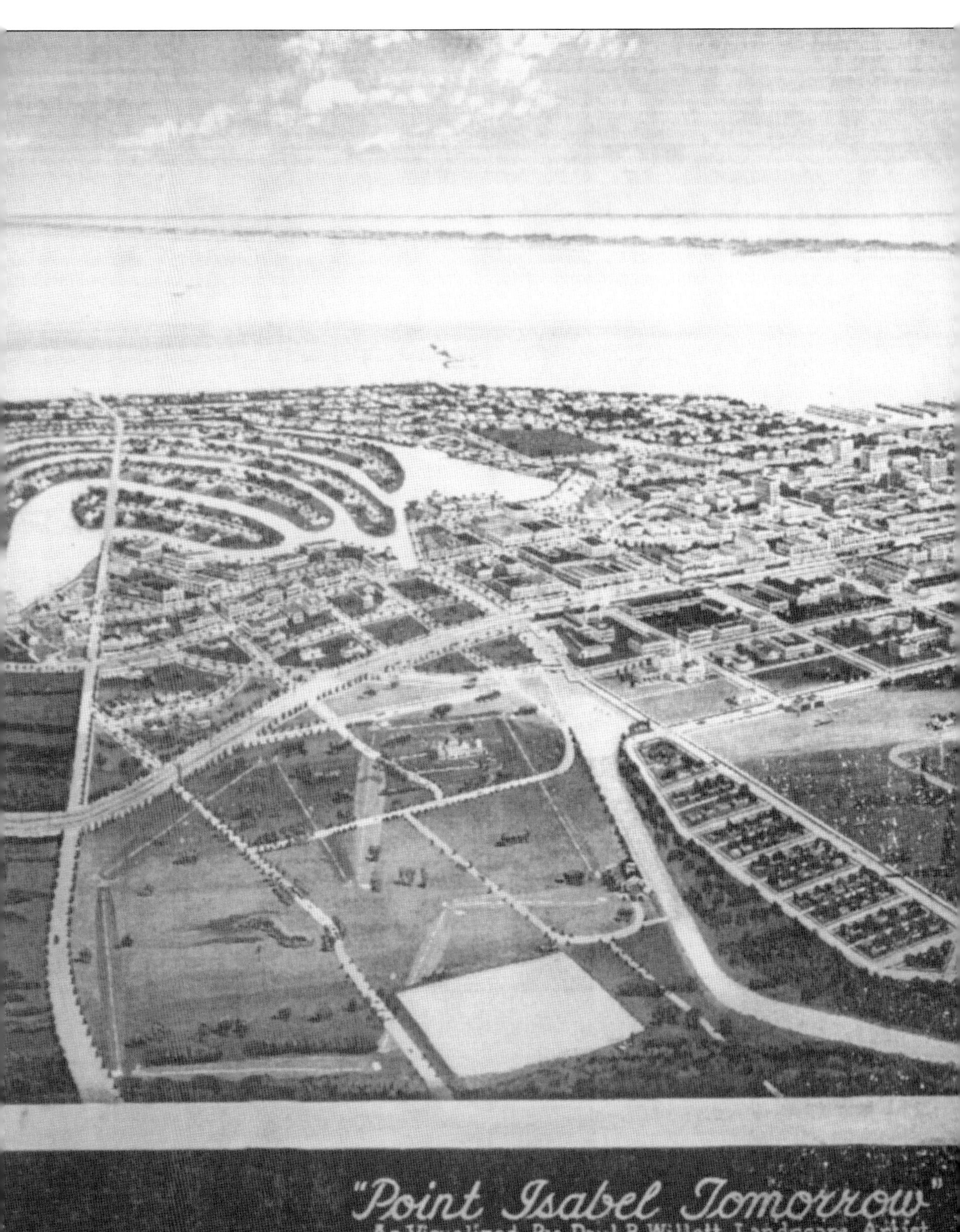
"Point Isabel Tomorrow"
As Visualized By Paul B. Willett Landscape Artist

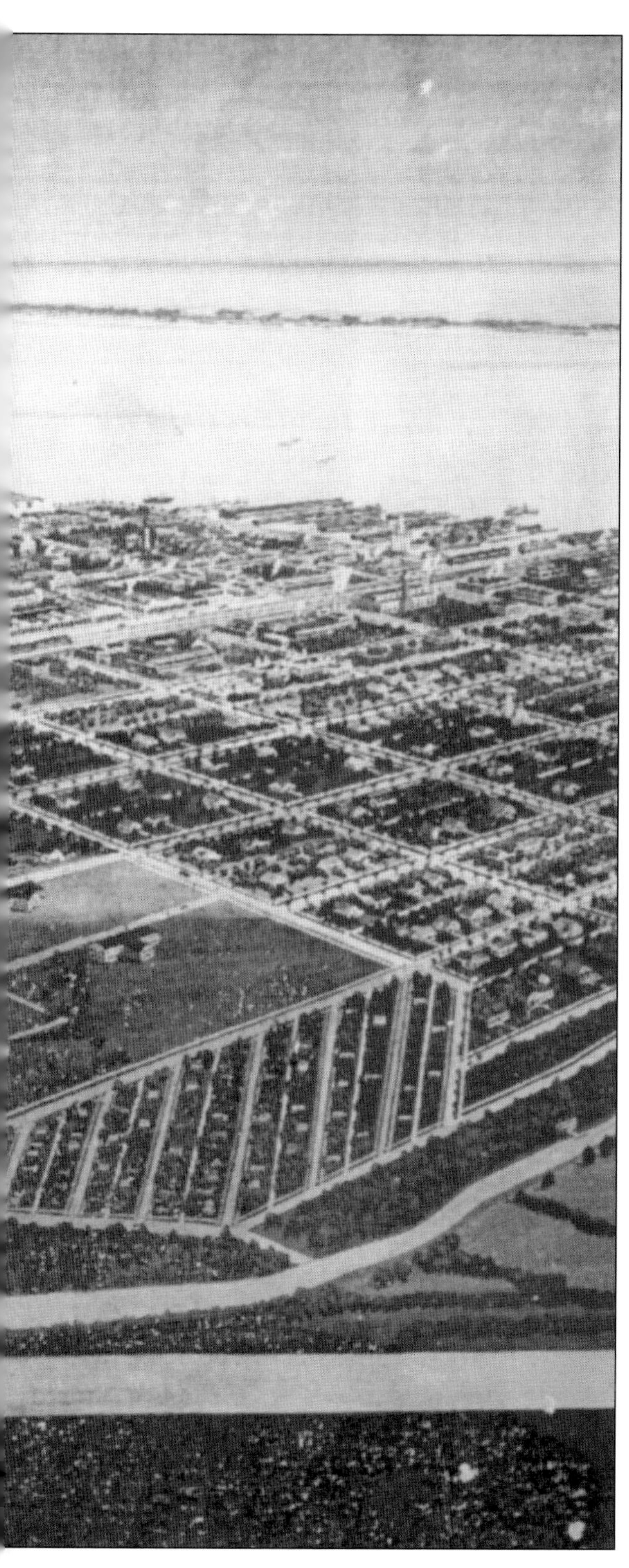

This is an aerial image, titled "Point Isabel Tomorrow," as visualized by landscape artist Paul B. Willett. The Venetian section, also known as Modern Venice or The Fingers (upper left), demonstrates how Port Isabel was carved from the earth and sea. Part of the channel system proposed created the Port Isabel Side Channel. A boater could leave the north side of Port Isabel at The Fingers and motor down the channel to the south side and the Brownsville Ship Channel. A marina has been added to the northern shoreline near the lighthouse area, and South Padre Island is visible in the distant skyline. Public landscaping is emphasized with an abundance of palm trees.

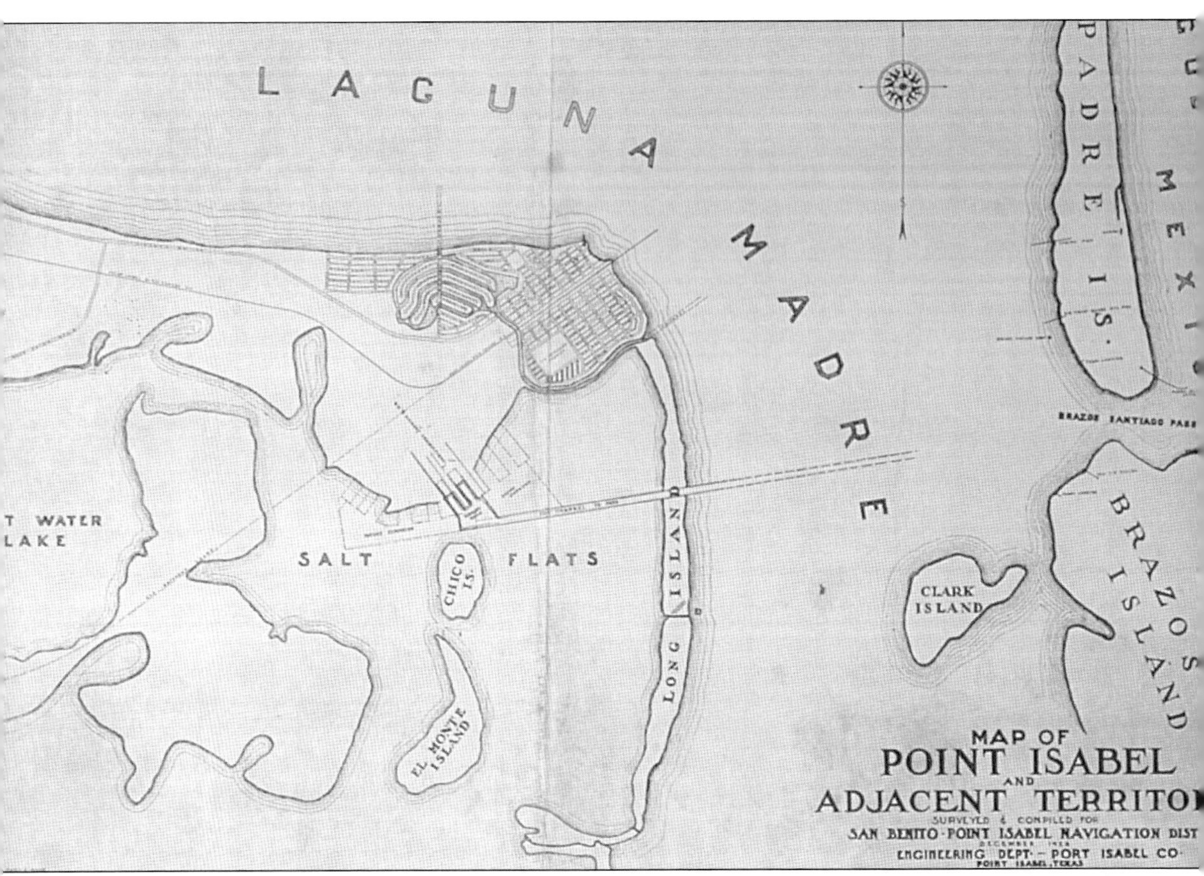

This map shows the location of the ship channel and the turning basin as recommended by the Board of Army Engineers on September 16, 1929. This location was selected for being the most practicable and feasible with the view of future port expansion. Its location is approximately a mile and a half from the business district of Port Isabel. The channel was to be 100 feet wide and 16 feet in depth, with a turning basin 500 feet square. Appropriation for this port was included in the Congressional Rivers and Harbors Bill. Upon passage of this bill by Congress, the port would come to be, which was met with rousing celebration. A parade, with horns honking and flags waving, started in Port Isabel and ended in the upper Rio Grande Valley in Mission. Construction began during the early part of 1930. This was a vital part of "building a city where a city belonged."

Five

Fishing and Catching

Since the earliest times when Port Isabel was visited by the wintering Karanqua Indians, fishing has been an effective lure to the area of the Laguna Madre. A 1930s newspaper article lists the variety of commercially caught fish as redfish, trout, pike, sheepshead, croaker, pompano, and red snapper. Large auxiliary schooners made the 23-mile journey to the red snapper beds. For bay species, a specially designed skow sloop was so effective that is was eventually banned in the interest of conservation.

In 1929, a cannery was constructed for shrimp. When caught in the Gulf by big schooners and their trawl nets, the shrimp were brought to Port Isabel and dumped on the docks of the San Patricio Cannery, where the heads came off before shipment. Also, Port Isabel was the first place in Texas to ship gutted and gilled fish, with the primary market being other parts of Texas.

Oysters were in such demand that they seldom made it beyond San Benito and Brownsville. The Port Isabel oyster was small but delicious and could be eaten year-round.

With an improving economy in the Rio Grande Valley and the introduction of larger gasoline-powered boats with a greater range came an increase in catch sizes and species for fishermen. On the heels of all the success that came with "building a city where a city belongs," Port Isabel faced a challenge. In 1933, the area sustained a great deal of damage when a series of storms and a hurricane devastated the coastline. News reports of the hurricane went nationwide and threatened to derail the tourism train.

City fathers and the Missouri Pacific Railroad set about formulating a plan. In 1934, the first Fishing Rodeo was organized, and a proactive publicity campaign crossed the country. Fishing was great in Port Isabel, and for five days in August, it was open to competitors vying for 26 prizes. When things got tough, the tough went fishing—and they caught fish!

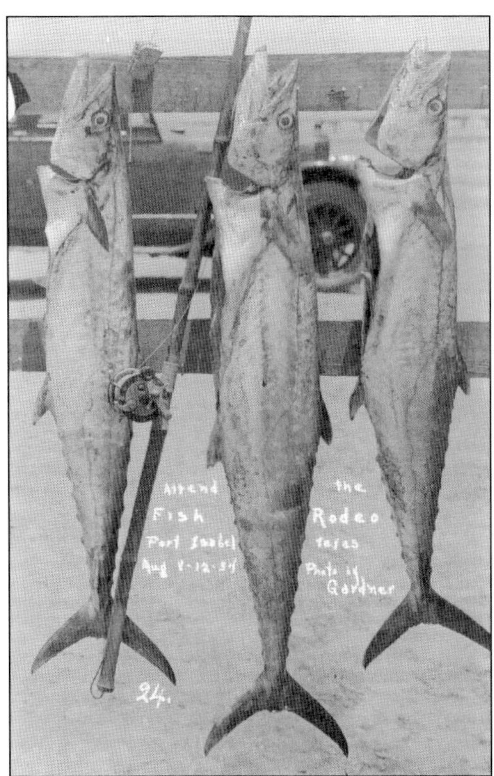

August 1934 brought with it the first Tarpon Rodeo, which was later to become the Texas International Fishing Tournament. Promotional items like this card, which in part reads, "Attend the Fish Rodeo, Port Isabel, Texas, Aug. 8-12-34," were used to bait anglers and their families. Following the devastating hurricane season of 1933, community leaders partnered with Missouri Pacific Railroad and decided the best way to promote Port Isabel and its recovery efforts was to promote sportfishing. And the fishing was good, as demonstrated by this catch of Spanish mackerel.

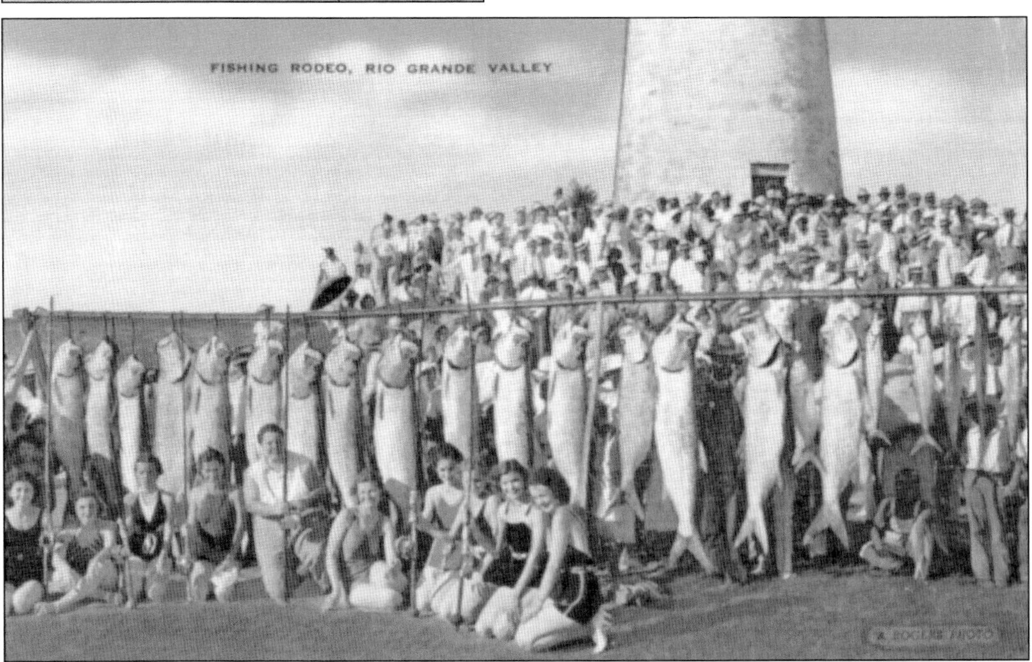

Less than a decade after the Tarpon Rodeo began, silver was still king. Following a day of fishing, anglers and their catch of tarpon made their way to the hill surrounding the lighthouse to pose for this photograph. Dozens of tarpon were displayed, which helped make the point that Port Isabel offered some of the best sportfishing in the United States.

The first annual Rio Grande Valley Fishing Rodeo brochure promises five days of fun and frolic. Wednesday, August 8, 1934, started off as follows: "The Rodeo begins you know, / When Old Sol peeps his head / Out over the Gulf of Mexico, / And sluggards are in bed. / So do not wait, but get the bait / Out in the waters blue. / By eve you may accumulate / A ton of fish or two!"

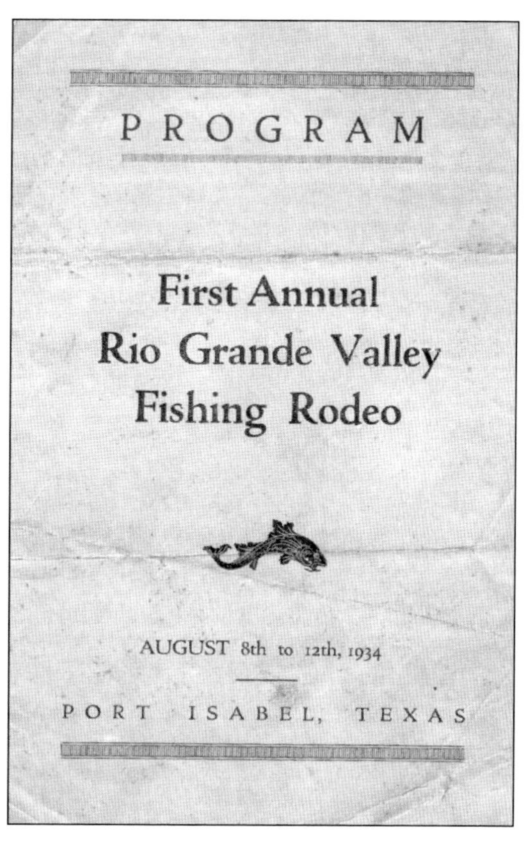

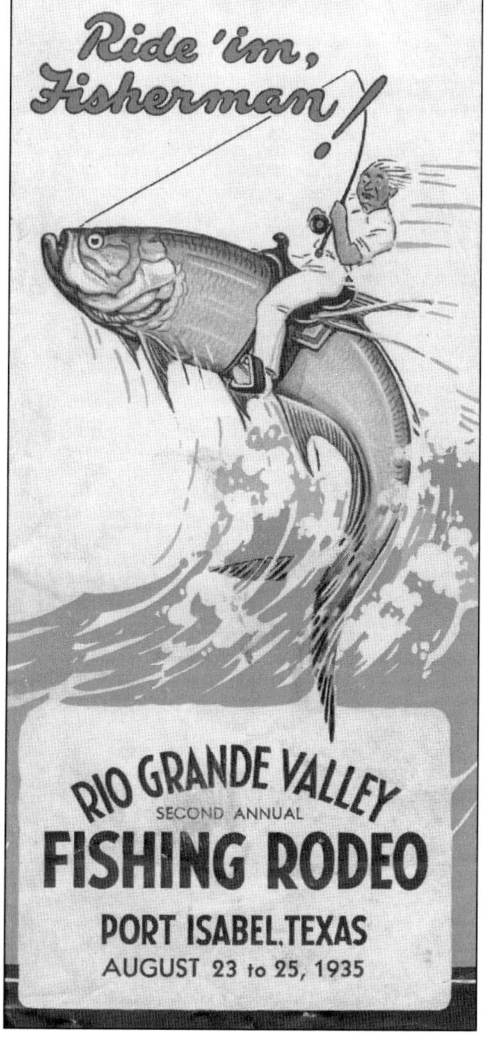

Day two of fishing, Thursday, August 9, 1934, brought this little rhyme: "The early bird, you've often heard / Most oft' the fish procures. / Your luck was poor? Don't be disturbed, / Today you may get yours! / A ball game hot, out on the "lot," / Tonight will entertain you. / You may relax and like as not / The effort will not pain you."

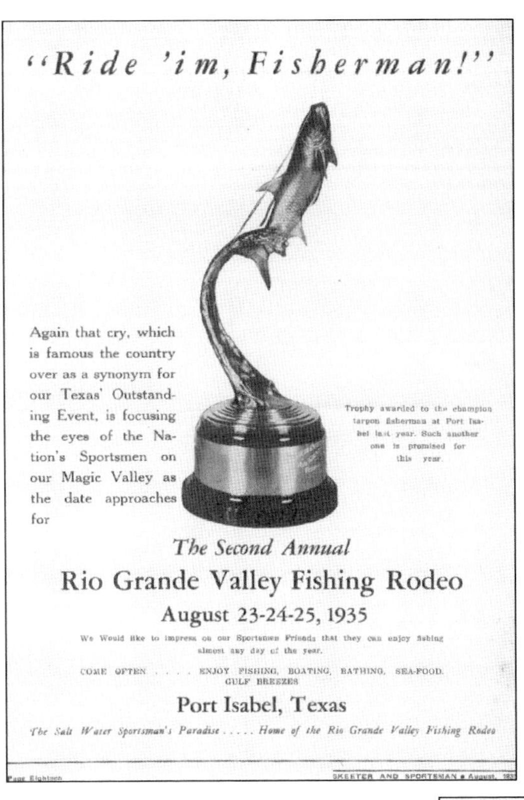

Friday, August 10, 1934, day three of fun and frolic, brings this challenge: "Friday, fish day! How we wish they / Would grab our line. / Maybe angling's not our dish.--Say! / Wasn't that a strike this time? / Now don't forget the big banquet / By Valley Lions sponsored. / If food and fun you fain would get / Your prayers will there be answered!"

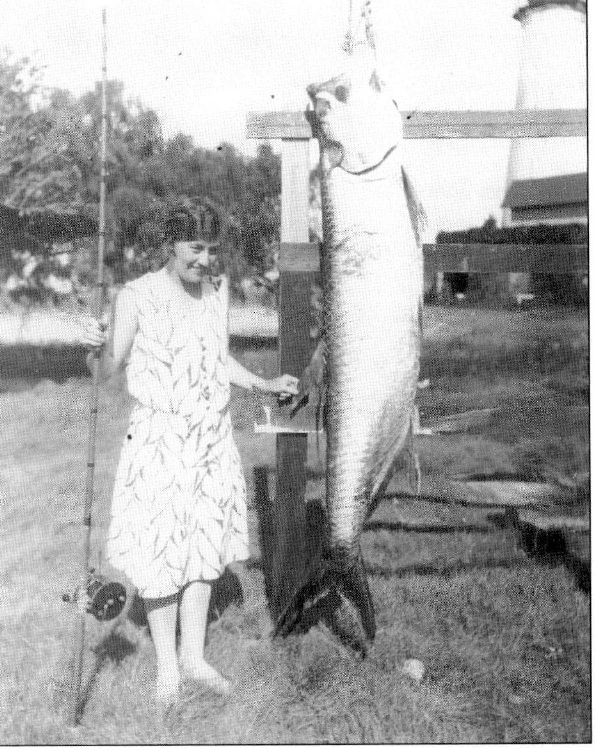

Saturday, August 11, 1934, was paired with this verse: "Another day upon the Bay / Or maybe so 'outside,' / By now you should be 'impasse,' / To things like time and tide. / To Mexico this night we go / To feast on fried 'frijoles' / And maybe hoist un gran' vaso / Con otros Espanoles!" Roxie Burto poses here with her with 1934 Tarpon catch.

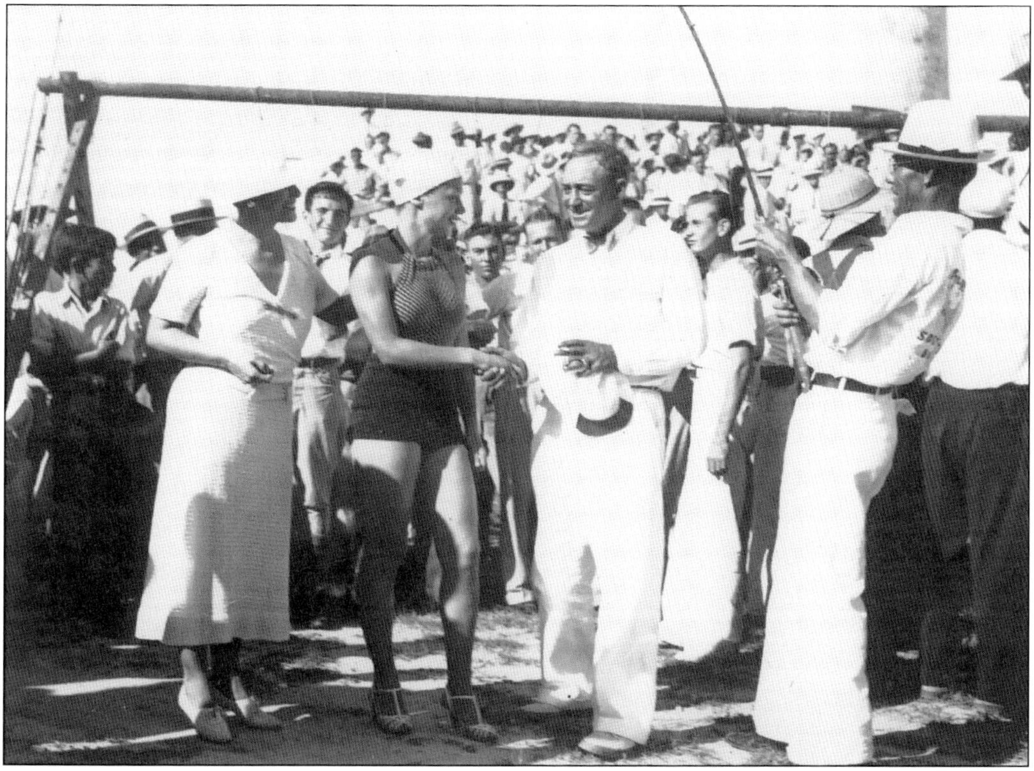

Sunday, August 12, 1934, had the following rhyme: "A final chance for to enhance / Your records in the book; / For prompt at two the fishing's' through, / And win or lose, HERE'S LUCK! / A program rife with thrills and strife / (as hereinafter stated) / Will occupy the time 'till five / When winners are related." What followed was a human fishing contest, porpoise-riding contest, parachute jump, fishing awards at the lighthouse, and a free street dance. Above, the gentleman with the fishing pole to the right has caught the lady in the center. Walking the plank was another popular activity for spectators.

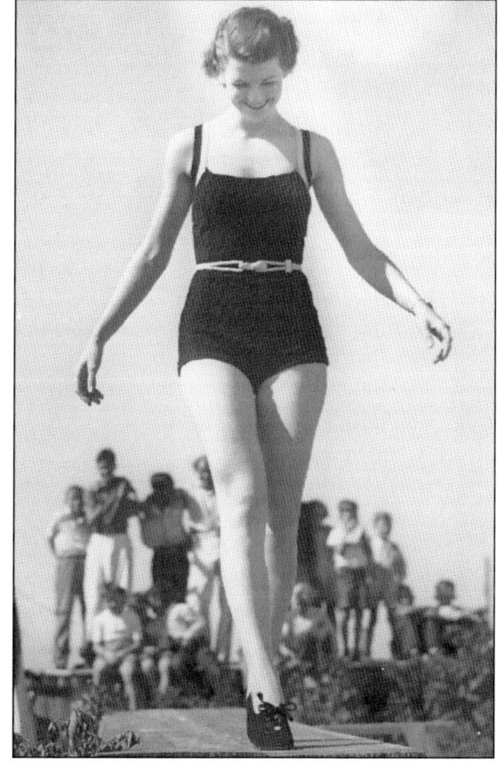

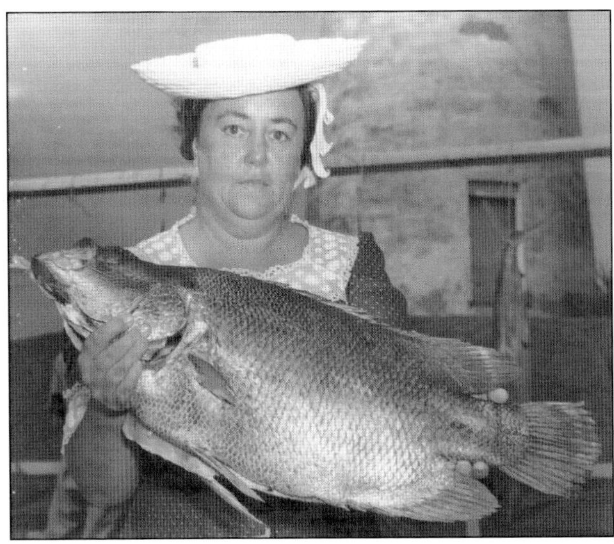

In the 1934 fishing rodeo brochure, fishing "widows" were cordially invited to make the Shary Yacht Club and Brazos Hotel their event headquarters. Bulletins were posted with alternative entertainment. The Mission Flying School had a fleet of planes, advertised as safe ships, available for short or extended trips, taking off from the Port Isabel Landing Field. Many women took part in the fishing contest, such as the angler pictured here posing in front of the lighthouse with her tripletail as darkness falls. The fashion of the day often found anglers of both genders in their Sunday best.

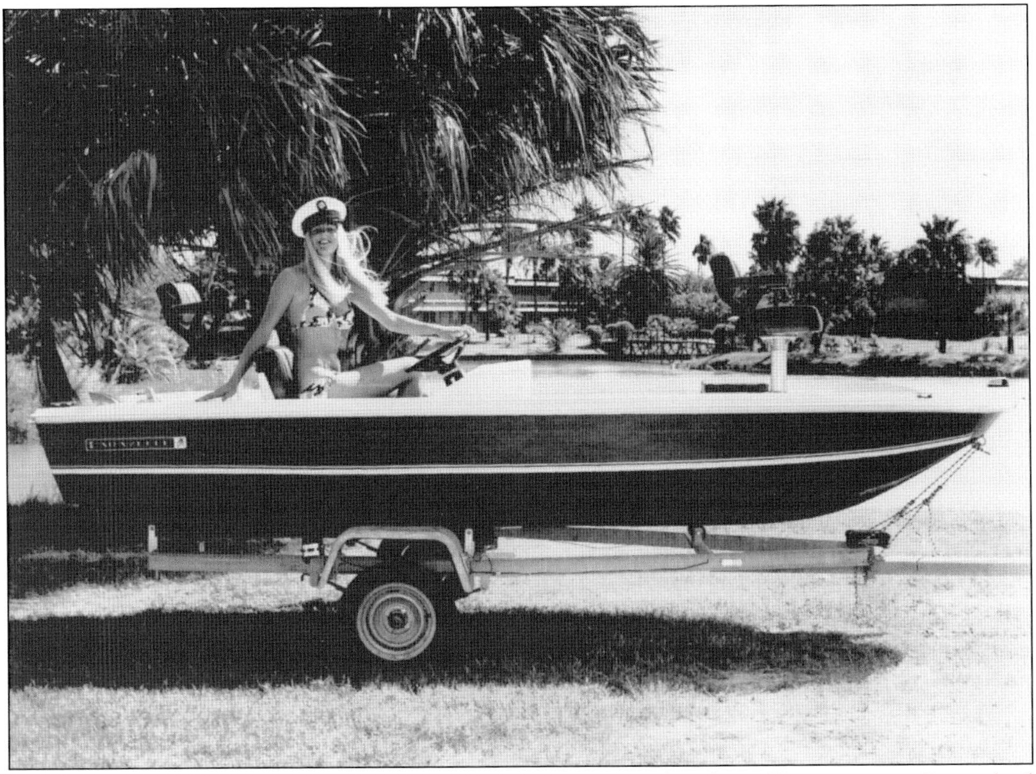

In 1974, June Keys represented the 36th Texas International Fishing Tournament. Prizes had escalated beyond a rod and reel to this bay boat and trailer. Sponsors saw the value in the competitors this event attracted and were anxious to get their message in front of them.

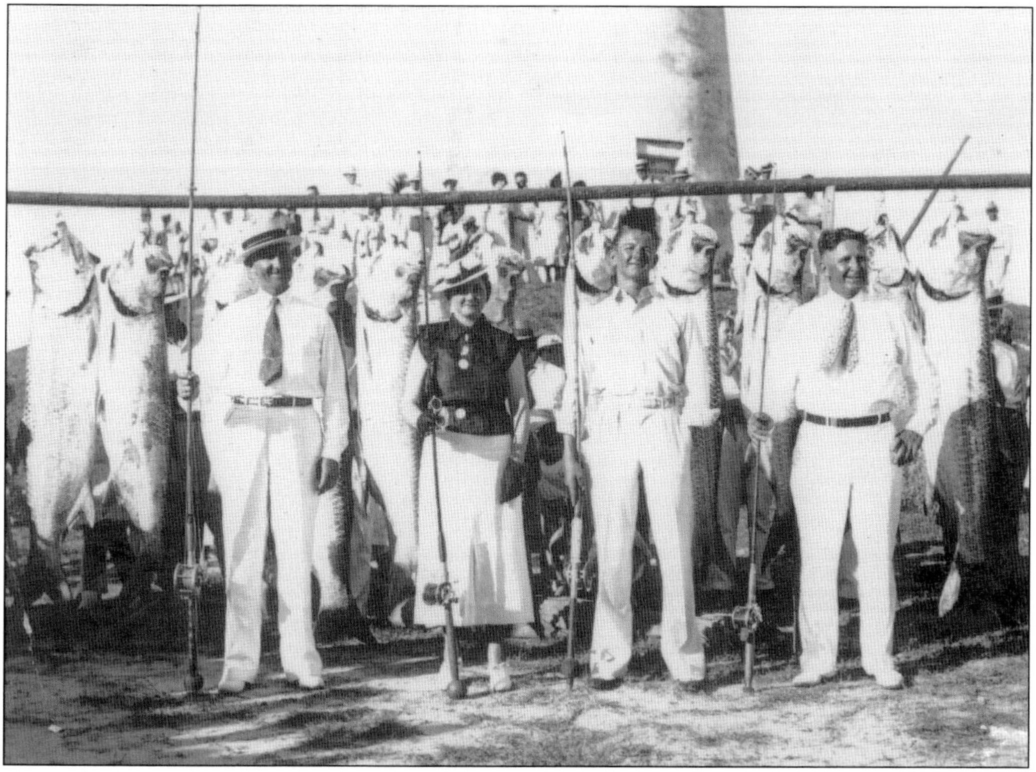

Mr. and Mrs. David M. Lide (left) and son Bobby of Shreveport, Louisiana, pose in front of the lighthouse with some of the tarpon they caught during the first fishing rodeo. The Lide family won 6 of the 26 prizes offered. Bobby won the juvenile division, and Mrs. Lide won the women's division. Mr. Lide was nosed out in the last hour by another Louisiana angler.

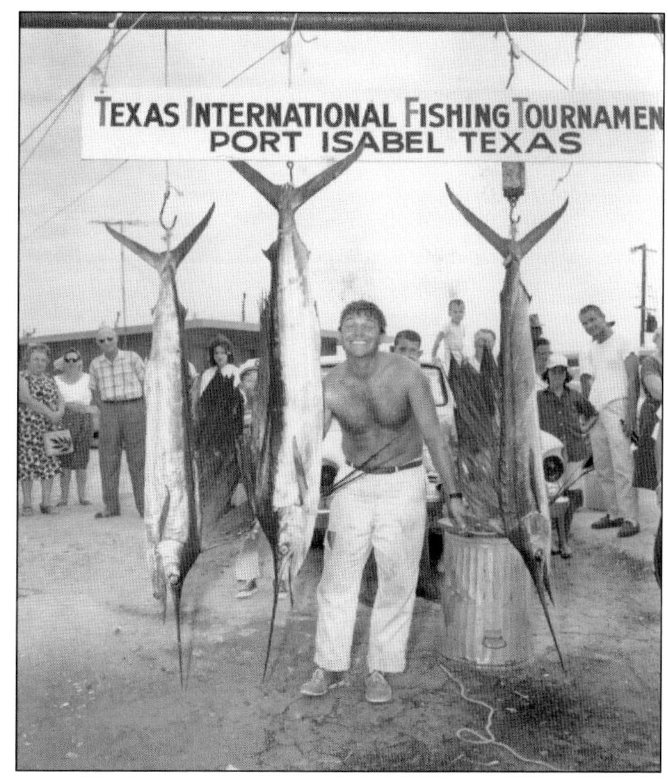

At the 23rd annual fishing rodeo in 1961, Bob Relay won first place in the Men's Sailfish category as the Texas Grand Champion and is pictured here with his prize catch. The local economy was positively impacted, as competitors hired boats and captains, bought supplies, and stayed in hotels.

Port Isabel, Texas.

Nov. 23, 1 9 3 1.

Gentlemen:

I hereby swear that the following statements are the truth.

Kind of Fish Black Sea Bass Weight 547½

Length 7 ft 9½ inch Girth 72 in

When caught Nov. 21st 1931 Where Caught Port Isabel

Rod used 6 ft Horrach Ebbotson Line von Hofe, Celebrated #27

Lure or bait 4 inch live Perch on 11-0 Sobey hook.

Caught by O. C. Gaskill

City Port Isabel State Texas

Sworn to and subcribed before me this the 23 day of

Nov. A. D. 1931.

Mrs. R. Berry

NOTARY PUBLIC CAMERON COUNTY

Fish witnessed and weight and measurements verified by

Jim McWilliams ADDRESS Port Isabel

Sig Were. ADDRESS Port Isabel

Port Isabel is a superlative, and from time to time, the paperwork is available to back it up, as seen here, dated November 23, 1931:

> I hereby swear that the following statements are the truth. Kind of fish, Black Sea Bass. Weight, 547 ½. Length, 7 feet 9 ½ inch. Girth, 72 in. When caught, Nov. 21st, 1931. Where Caught, Port Isabel. Rod used, 6ft. Horrach Ebbotson. Line, Hofe Celebrated #27. Lure or bait, 4 inch live Perch on 11-0 Sobey hook. Caught by, Ole Gashill. City, Port Isabel. State, Texas. Sworn to and subscribed before me this the 23 day of Nov. A.D. 1931. Mrs. R. Berry, Notary Public Cameron County. Fish witnessed and weight and measurements verified by, Jim McWilliams and Sig Were.

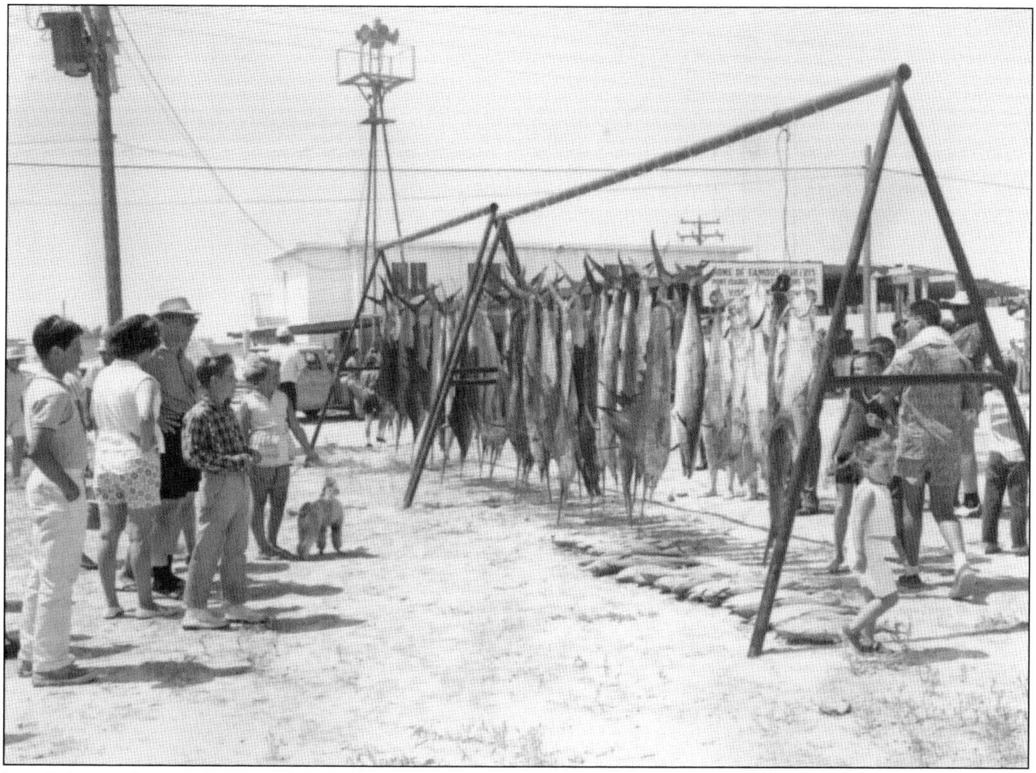

In 1961, at the 23rd annual fishing rodeo, 33 sailfish were brought in. Such sights were not only popular to anglers but also to non-fishing spectators who drove from all over the valley to witness the event. Pictured in the background is the Port Isabel Volunteer Fire Department, "Home of the Famous Fish Fry."

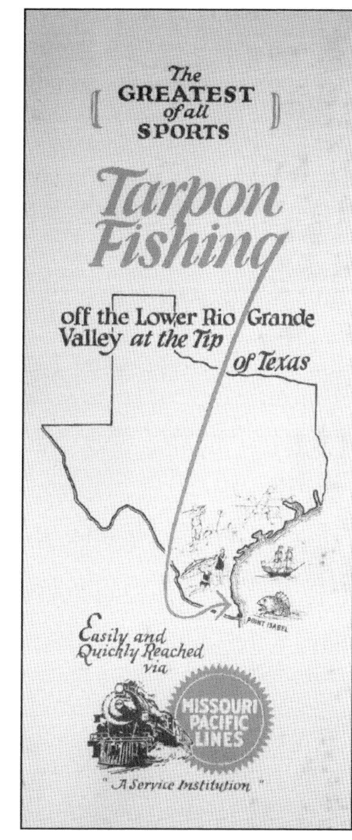

In the late 1920s or early 1930s, Missouri Pacific Lines built a railroad and offered the greatest of all sports at the end of the line: tarpon fishing. Missouri Pacific was an early partner in competitive sportfishing, creating a line that ran from San Benito to Port Isabel. This brochure was circulated to attract passengers with fishing poles.

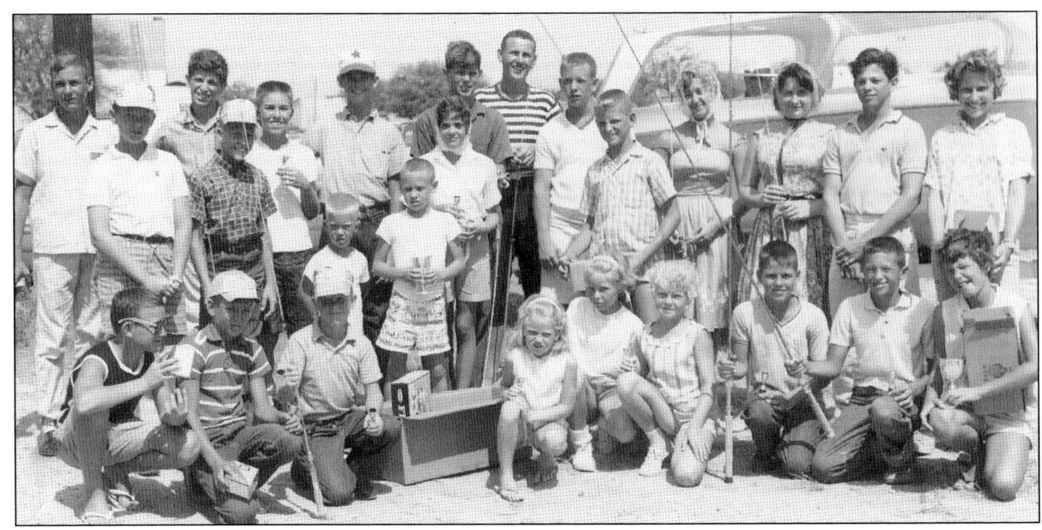

At the 23rd Texas International Fishing Tournament, young prize-winning anglers included Vere Charles Wells; Jay Meade; King and Ben Etz; Dorothea, Margie, and Kathy Meade; Steve Noell; Billy Massey; Sammy Jones; Tom Flory; Paul Fowler; Peter, Steve, and Pope Noell; and Bob Hawkins. Today, the fifth generation of youngsters is partaking in the event.

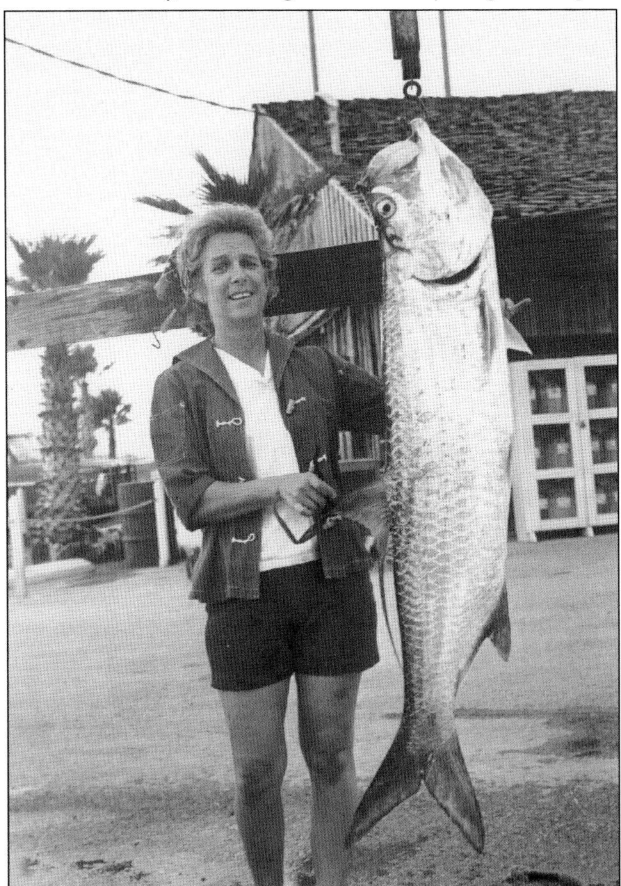

Lifelong resident and angler extraordinaire Bobby Wells won the Tarpon Division Grand Championship in 1974, 1984, and 1989. Wells is shown here with her biggest prize, a 160.5-pound silver king that took over two hours to land on son Capt. Vere Wells's boat. Coming in after dark and just in time for the 10:00 p.m. news, these were the fish stories that became legend.

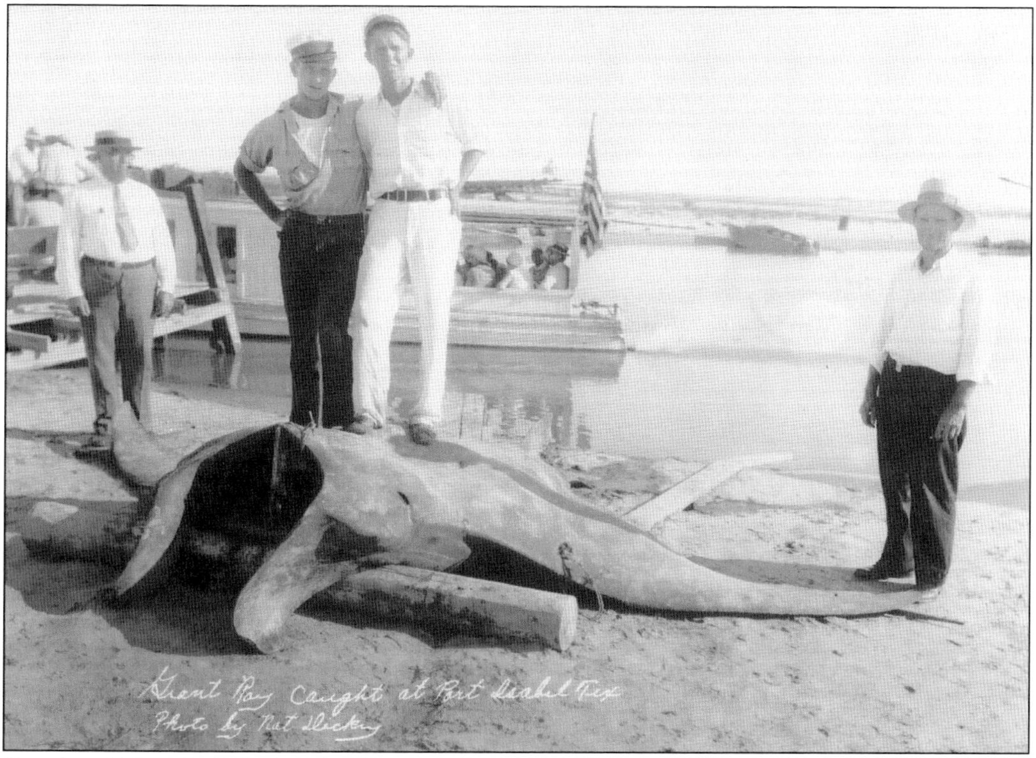

Caught off Port Isabel, this devil ray was one of the species that fed the imagination of the marine adventurer. Sometimes weighing in at upwards of 3,000 pounds, this species would be harpooned and fought for hours while pulling at times multiple boats through the Gulf waters off of Brazos Santiago.

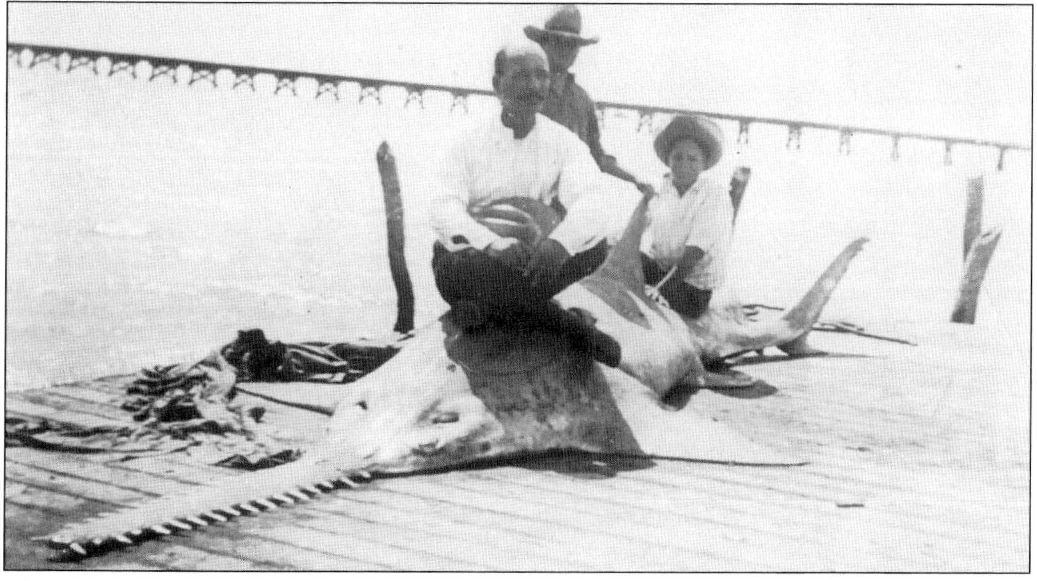

This proud angler sits atop his 17-foot, 2-inch sawfish caught off Port Isabel. Sawfish bills were sometimes used as souvenirs and sold in local shops. The Port Isabel Lighthouse's likeness or other nautical subjects would be painted on them.

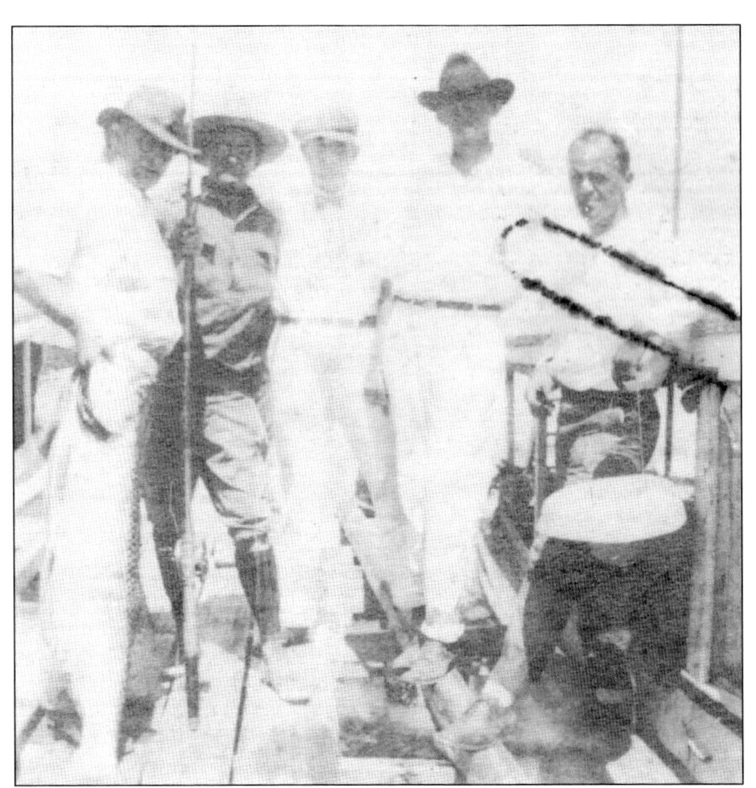

R.C. (left) went on a fishing trip in October 1921, and the catch was memorialized with this photograph. He is holding a tarpon about waist high. Al responded to the photograph with an observation, "You will probably be interested in this picture of your 9 ft. Tarpon. Signed Al." Clearly, it is not a nine-foot tarpon. R.C. made a notation on the letter, "Save this Sis and phone Al that the 9' length is about ok for size." Having a photograph of the catch can sometimes debunk the fishing story.

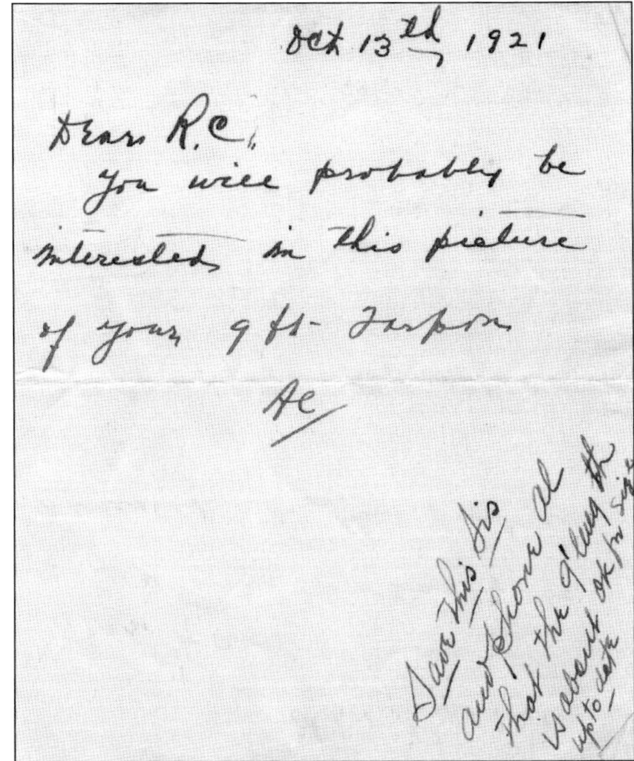

Oct 13th 1921

Dear R.C.,
You will probably be interested in this picture of your 9 ft- Tarpon

Al

Save this Sis and phone Al that the 9' length is about ok for size up to date

As the tournament progressed through the years, an entire court of young ladies from all over the valley would compete for the title of queen. In 1937, Jane Johnson was the fourth-annual queen of the Rio Grande Valley Fishing Rodeo. She is pictured here with her tarpon catch.

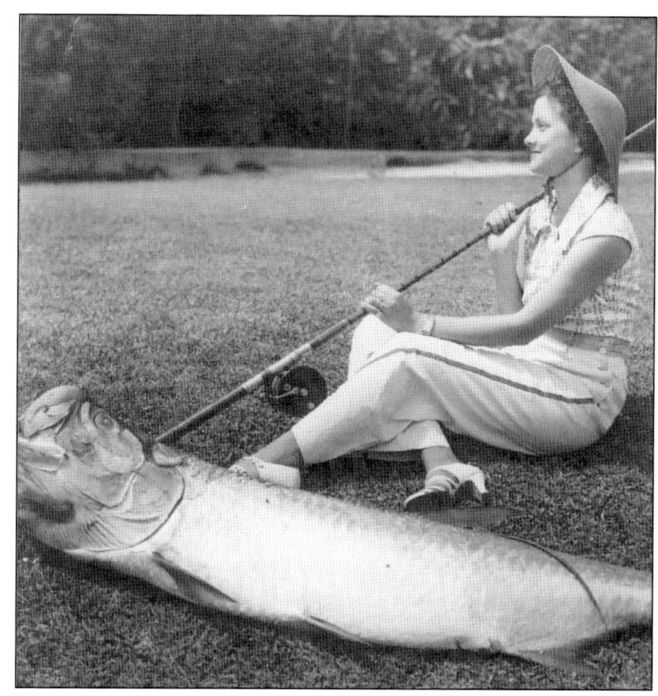

The 24th annual Texas International Fishing Tournament had a new mascot, as someone brought a big cat to a big fishing tournament. This lioness was tied off in front of the yacht club during the fishing tournament's festivities in 1957.

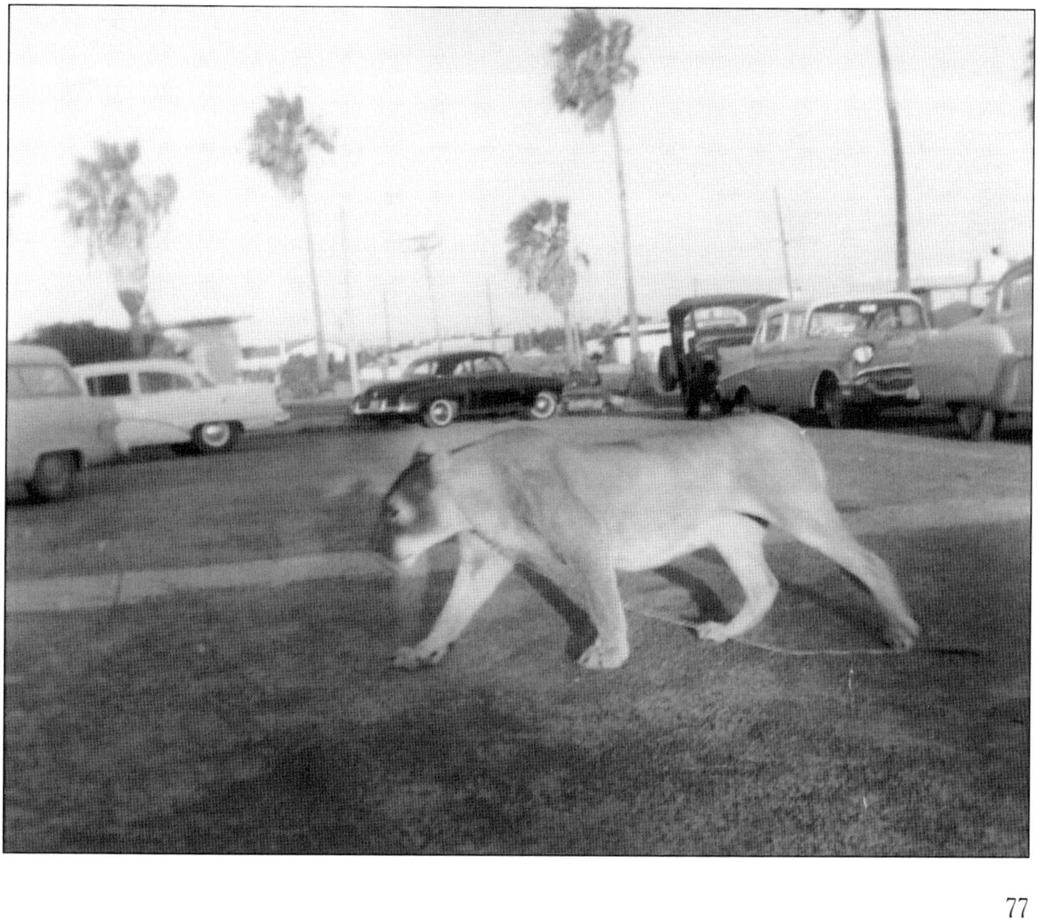

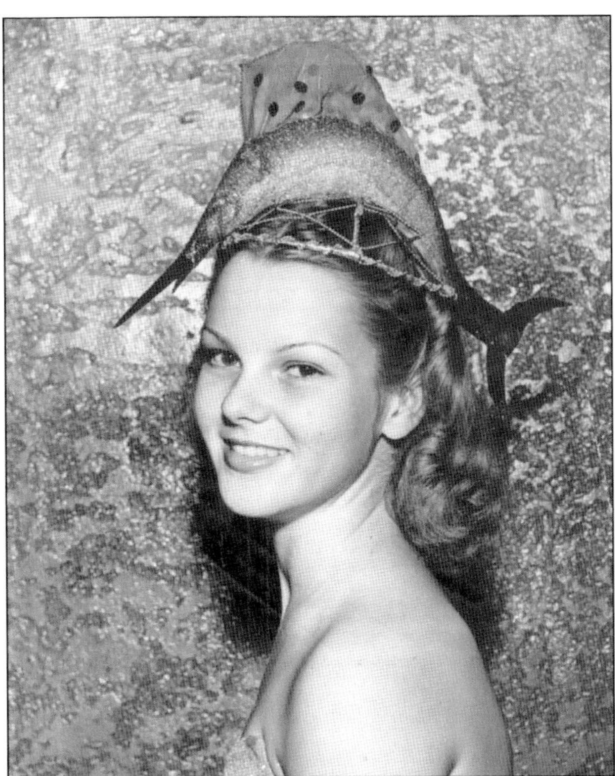

In 1938, at the fifth annual Rio Grande Valley Fishing Rodeo, Beatrice "Skeets" Johnston of Harlingen was crowned queen. Her sailfish crown was designed by Sheila Shields. As the competition for queen drew from towns all over the valley and featured many social events, the Rio Grande Valley Fishing Rodeo was indeed a Rio Grande Valley product.

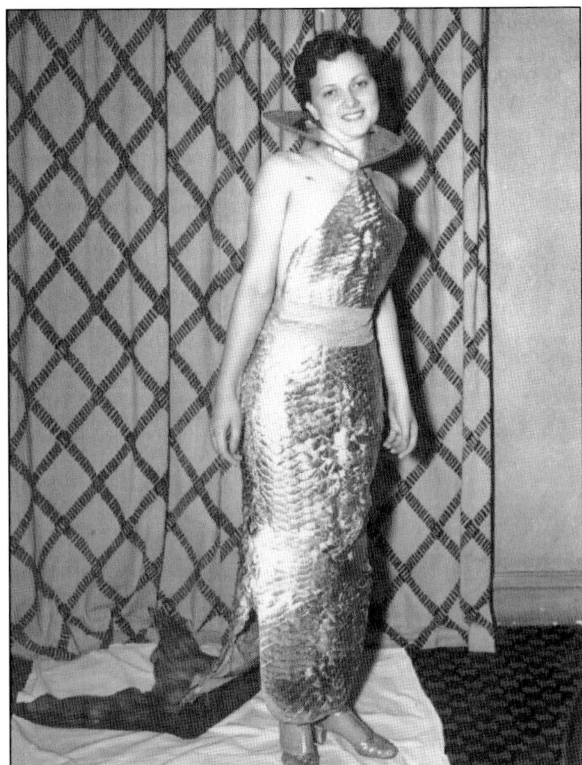

In 1937, at the fourth annual Rio Grande Valley Fishing Rodeo, Jane Johnson of Rio Hondo was the Tarpon Rodeo queen. A series of publicity photographs were taken of her in an evening gown made of tarpon scales.

Six

Visitors Arrive

Even before the 19th century, El Fronton was drawing visitors. Fresh sea breezes wafting off the Laguna Madre Bay and great fishing were just the ingredients needed to create traffic. And traffic created piers, ferryboats, fishing boats, restaurants, souvenir stands, and hotels and motels.

At the turn of the 20th century, border-region skirmishes caused the deployment of a number of troops to Port Isabel. Most of those troops came from the Midwestern portion of the United States. After being pulled out of the area, these men found their way back to the coast as visitors. In the early 1920s, the Port Isabel Land Co. was formed and began a proactive outreach to the Midwest—and it worked. Travelers in fur coats would disembark from a train and be presented with a grapefruit or orange, along with a slice of south Texas hospitality.

In 1927, Point Isabel incorporated and enacted the slogan, "building a city where a city belongs." Road improvements and a growth spurt in the business community gave Port Isabel the reputation of a phoenix rising from the ashes.

For the next several decades, Port Isabel continued to develop into a coastal destination. Postcards featured the lighthouse, souvenir shops, a distinctive coastal landscape, shrimping fleets, the beach, charter boats and ferries, lots of fish of all sizes and varieties, local characters, and hotels and motels. Snapped up, stamped, and sent back home, these messages encouraged more people to travel to deep south Texas. Souvenirs bearing all things Port Isabel were packed back home and served as advertisement and promise for a unique travel experience. As the rest of the Rio Grande Valley developed with paved highways and expanded train routes, trade and travel increased.

Today, Port Isabel still boasts great fishing, piers, boat rides, a lighthouse open to the public, museums, restaurants, all kinds of souvenir shopping, great Tex-Mex and fresh seafood, and relaxed sea breezes.

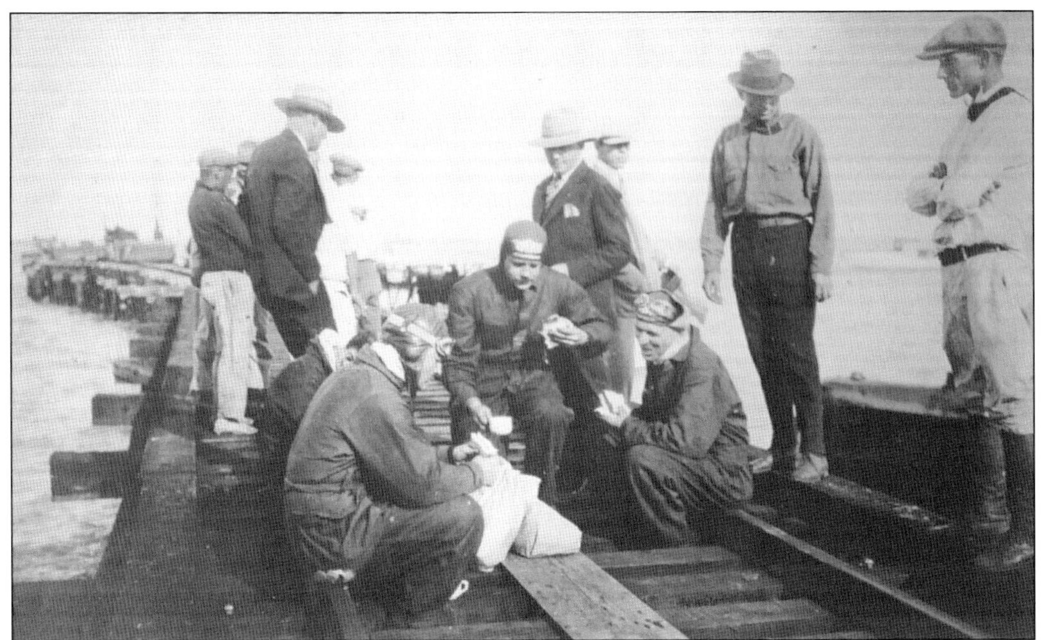

The Pan American Goodwill Flight landed in Port Isabel in late 1926. On a mission to take messages of friendship from the US government and promote commercial aviation, the Pan American flyers stopped in Port Isabel. En route to Central and South America, the flyers are seen enjoying a picnic lunch complete with sandwiches while sitting on the railroad dock.

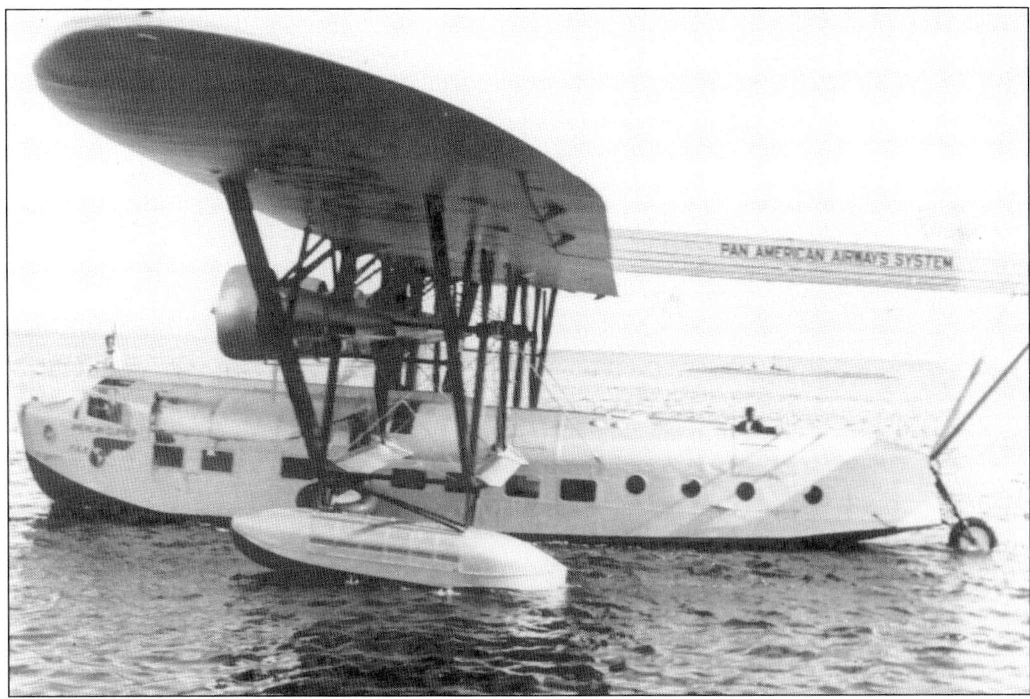

The Pan American Goodwill Flight crews of 1926–1927 chose the motto "no work, no ride." Few facilities and assistance made it necessary for each flyer to be an accomplished pilot and mechanic. Port Isabel was a possible fuel stop on the way to Central and South America.

During the Mexican Revolution and border skirmishes of 1916–1917, Pres. Woodrow Wilson sent soldiers like these Iowans south to Texas. Bugs, Ster, and Clint enlisted on June 16, 1916; five days and four nights in Pullman Sleepers found them arriving in Brownsville, Texas, 11 days later. They have gathered for a photograph near the railroad docks where vessels offered a trip across the Laguna Madre Bay to South Padre Island. Most soldiers made their way to Port Isabel to enjoy some time at the coast.

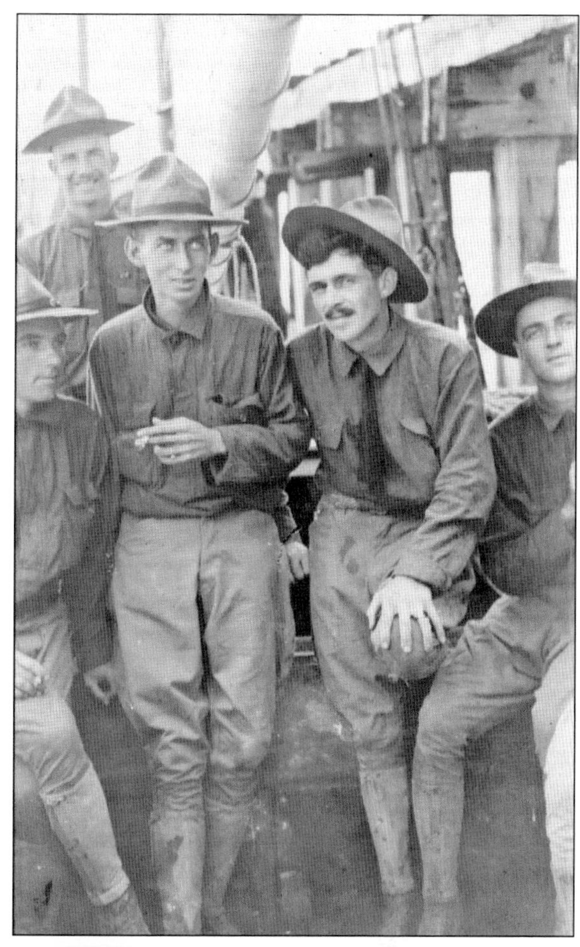

"Bob Burns, Roy Remy, and Earl Fort" reads the handwritten caption from a border-service photograph album with this 1916 image. Pictured in front of the Charles Champion Key to the Gulf General Store, Earl Fort sits on a burro, which is pulling a rolling water barrel. Port Isabel residents relied on this method of water delivery. One of the two boys to the left was the aguador.

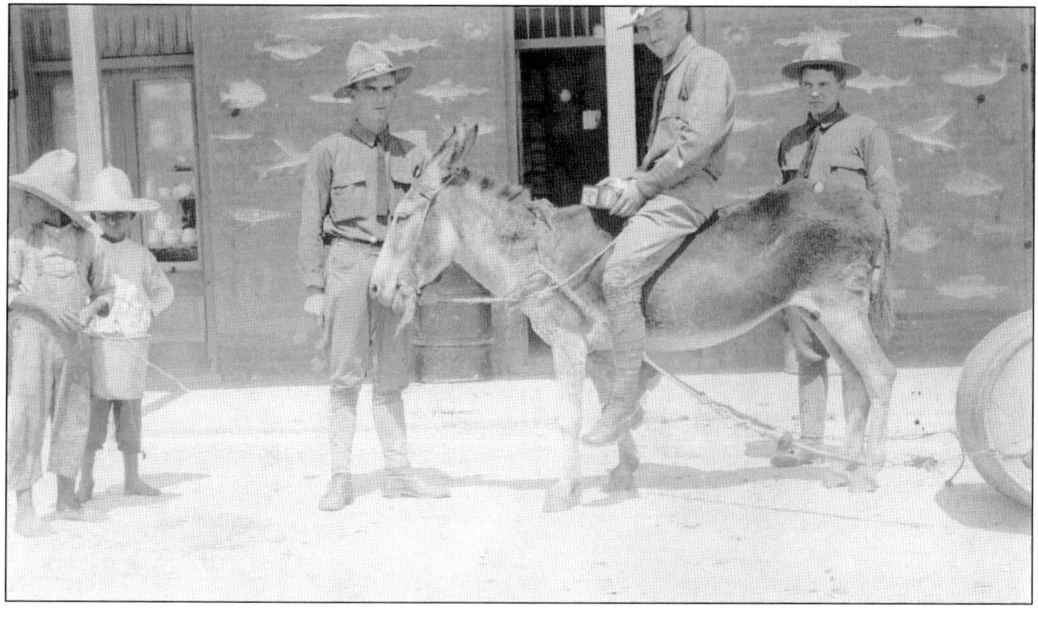

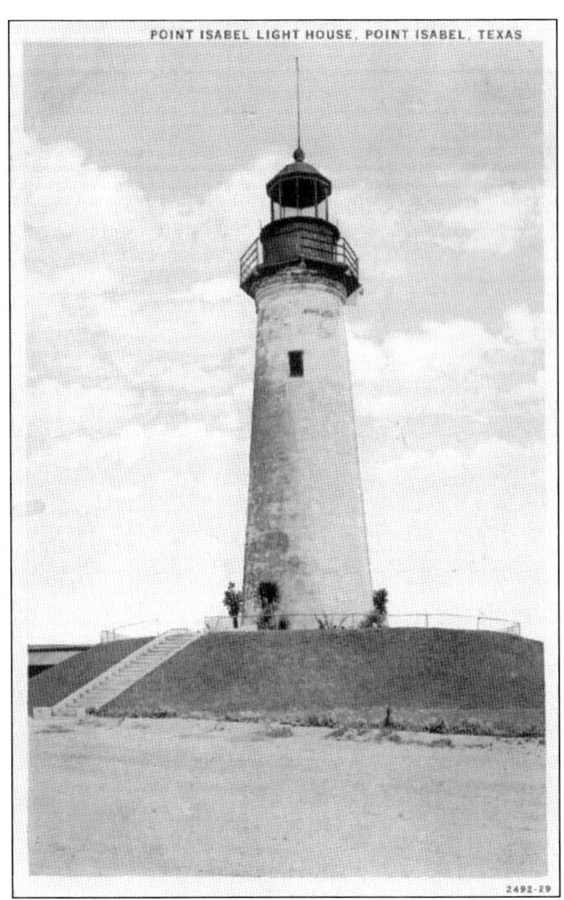

"Hello Ceach, Here we are at the jumping off place. Guess we'll have to turn around and start the other way." This 1929 inscribed postcard sent back to folks in Hooser, Kansas, expresses the highlight of the trip to Port Isabel as its proximity to the end of the world. Located at the southernmost point in Texas, Port Isabel was often marketed as sharing latitude with Miami, Florida. At the time this photograph was taken, the Point Isabel Lighthouse had been decommissioned for nearly 25 years. It became a beacon for tourists. When they were operable, lights positioned beneath the catwalk illuminated the tower at night.

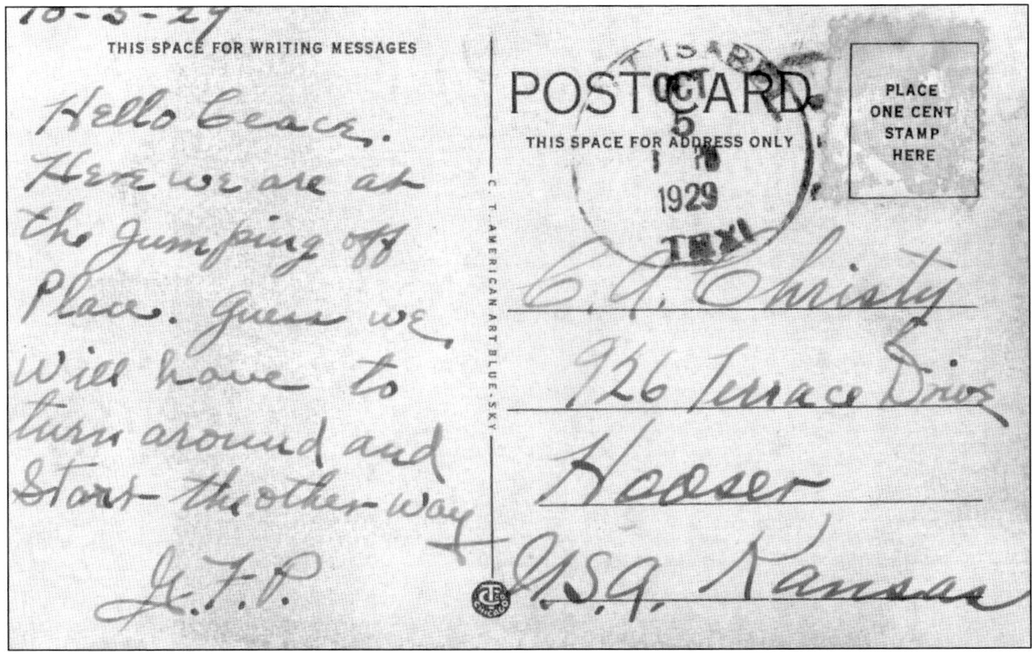

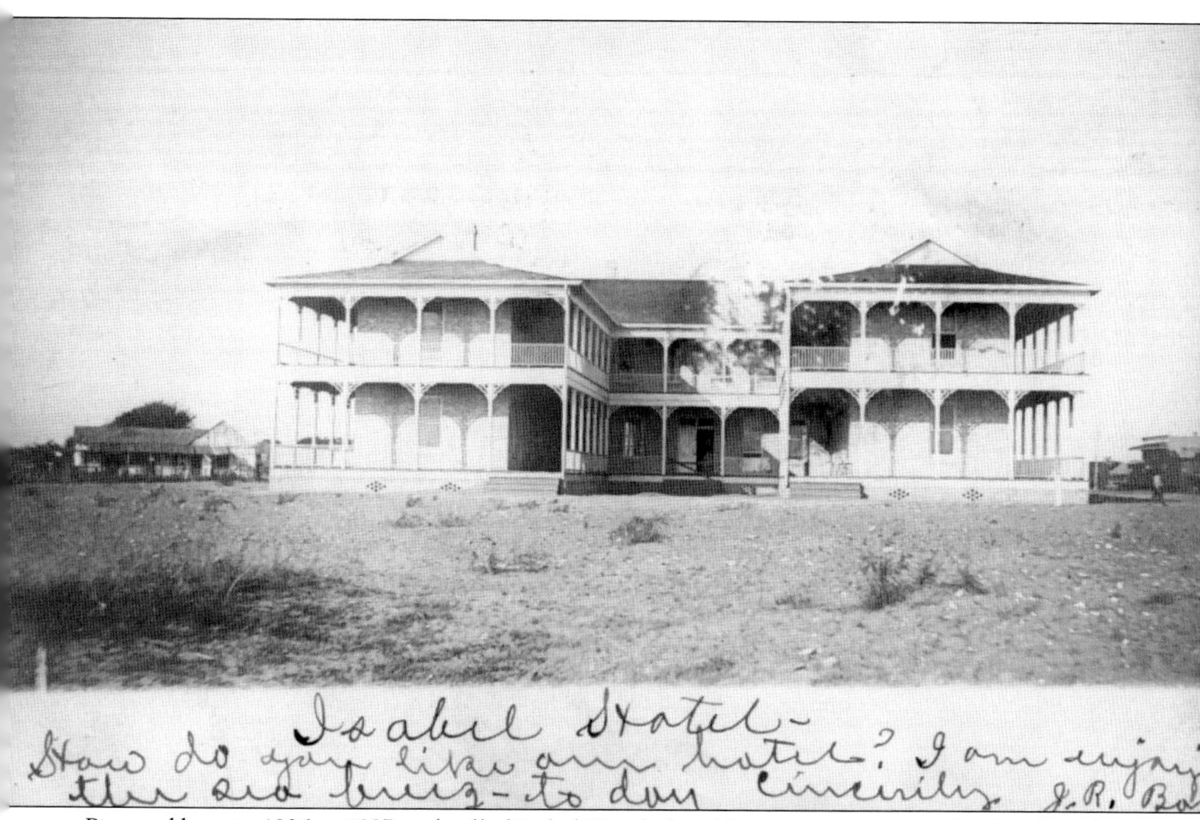

Pictured here in 1926 or 1927 and called Isabel Hotel, the oldest coastal resort in the Rio Grande Valley was constructed around 1905. Heavily damaged in the 1933 hurricane, the hotel's appearance changed and sported a more streamlined architecture without the verandas and peaked roofline. In 1936, it was home to the newly established Rotary Club. The hotel was also tournament headquarters for the Tarpon Rodeo. Over the years, it was known as Red Arrow Inn, Jefferson Inn, Coastal Inn, and Queen Isabel Inn. An excerpt from a 1950s brochure offered, "When the people of Port Isabel become acquainted with our guests—and a friendly people they are—they like to show the old well where Gen. Zachary Taylor's troops drew water back in 1846 and 1847, when 'Old Rough and Ready's' army made Point Isabel its headquarters and supply base for the Mexican War. The well is only a block or so from the Inn. Oldsters will tell you of President Taylor as their grandfathers knew him in those days, with his faded dungarees and oilcloth cap, or maybe an old wide-brimmed straw hat, riding horse or mule or even donkey."

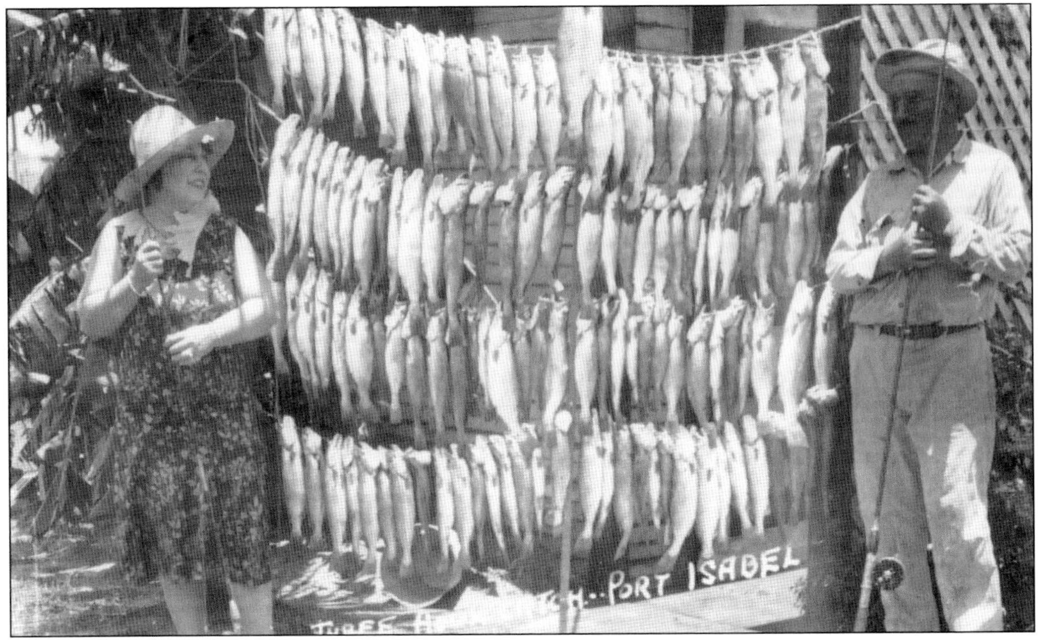

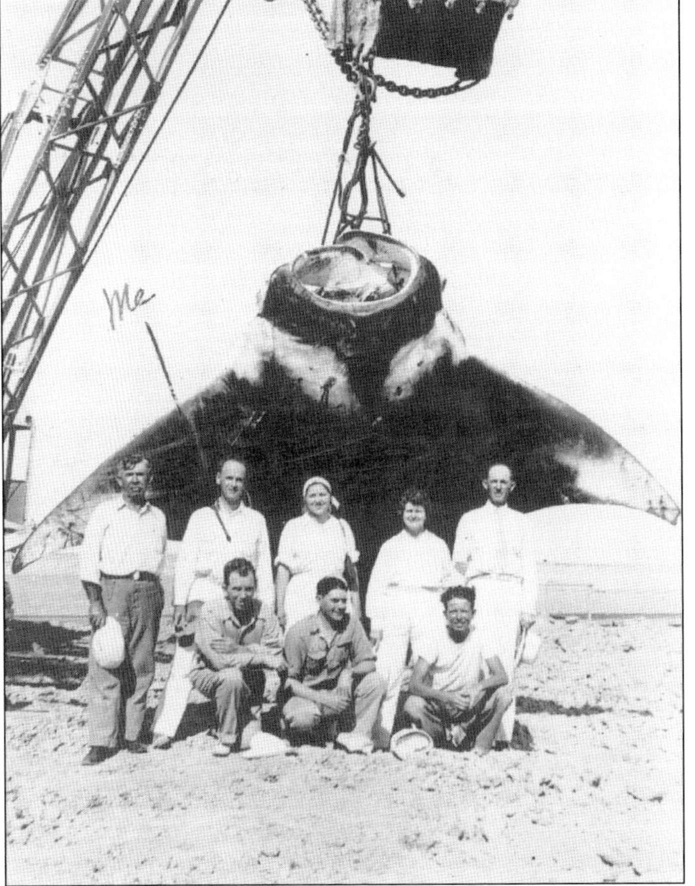

After a day of bay fishing, these two are beaming as they pose with their catch of dozens of speckled and sand trout. Renting a boat with or without a captain was possible from several docks along the shoreline. Full-day or half-day trips were available with almost guaranteed success.

Addressing his dad, Bill Beackmeyer wrote on the back of this postcard, "This is a very unusual fish, our party went prepared to harpoon one, but little did we realize the actual danger. Had we not had a very sea worthy boat I doubt very much whether I would be sending you this card."

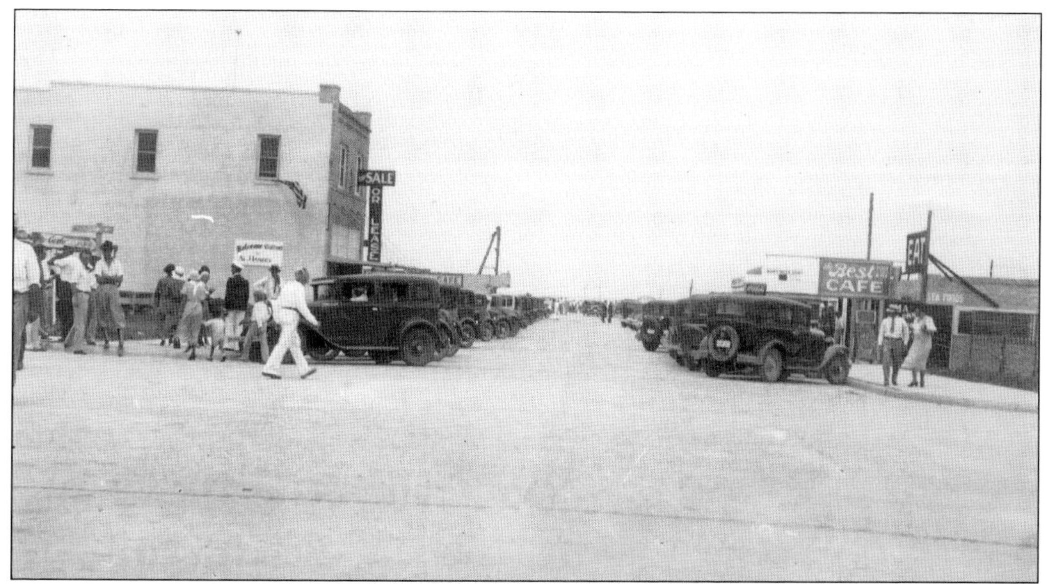

Here is the corner of Powers and Tarnava Streets on what appears to be a bustling day. Taken toward the east and less than six months before the terrible 1933 hurricane season, one would have found Colley's Ferry landing and the Laguna Madre Bay at the end of this street. The two-story building that is for sale or lease was constructed in the late 1920s as a drugstore. It was later used as a theater.

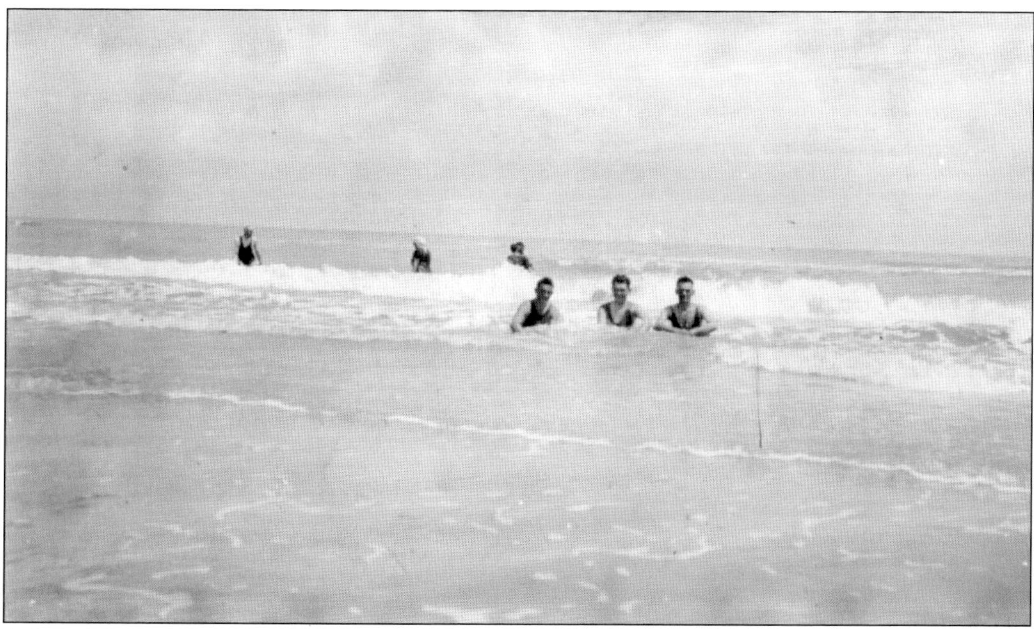

A January 1933 *Port Isabel Pilot* article headline ran about something these men discovered 17 years earlier when this photograph was taken, "Visitors Enjoy Surf Bathing at Christmas." Mild winters produced unusual opportunities to the traveler from the Midwest. Roy Remy, Earl Fort, and Bob Burns were from Iowa, having arrived in south Texas in 1916 at the end of the Mexican Revolution.

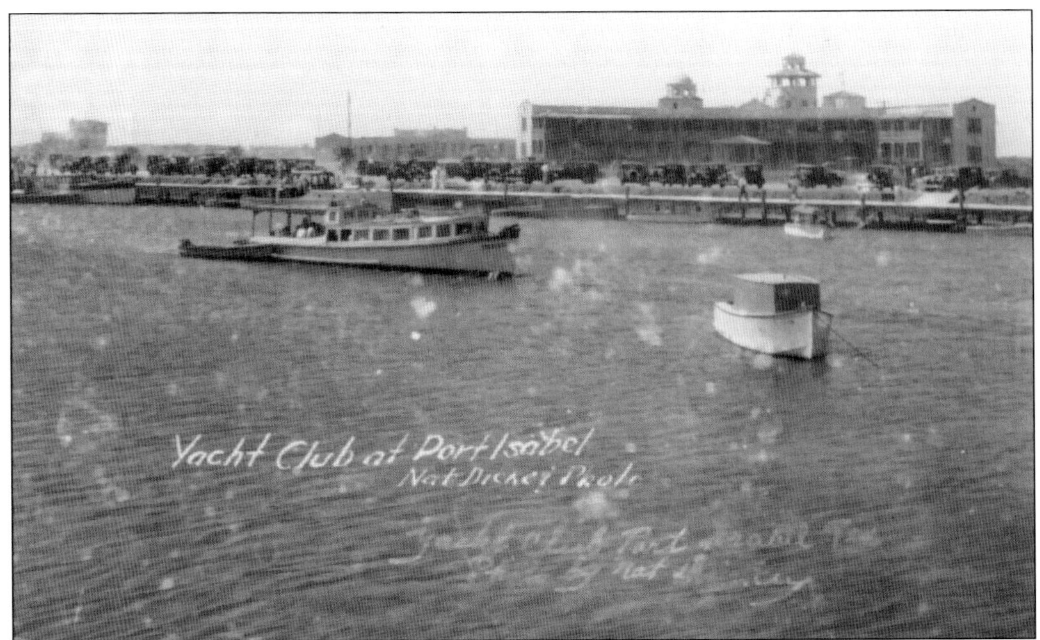

John Shary of Mission, Texas, built a private yacht club in 1926 on the banks of the newly dredged yacht basin. The Shary Yacht Club was used as home base for entertaining land parties, dignitaries, and fishing and yachting parties. In 1947, after Shary's death, the club became public.

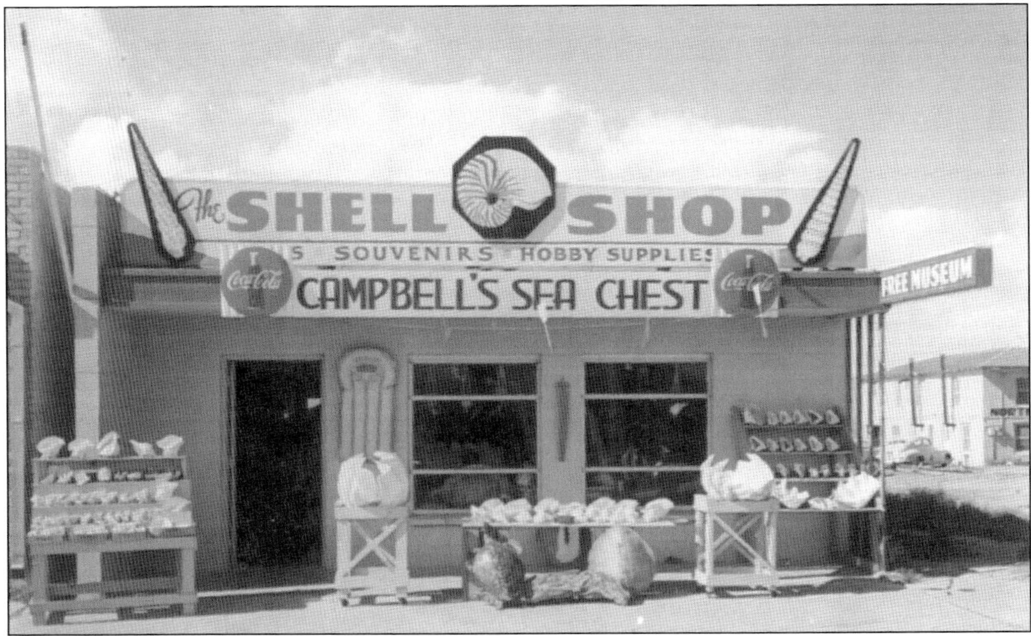

Over the course of 1932, a business owner observed nearly 1,500 automobiles from 42 states and three foreign countries that parked at his location, and this did not count those with Texas license plates. With favorable weather, great fishing, and attractions like the Shell Shop, visitors could take home lifetime memories.

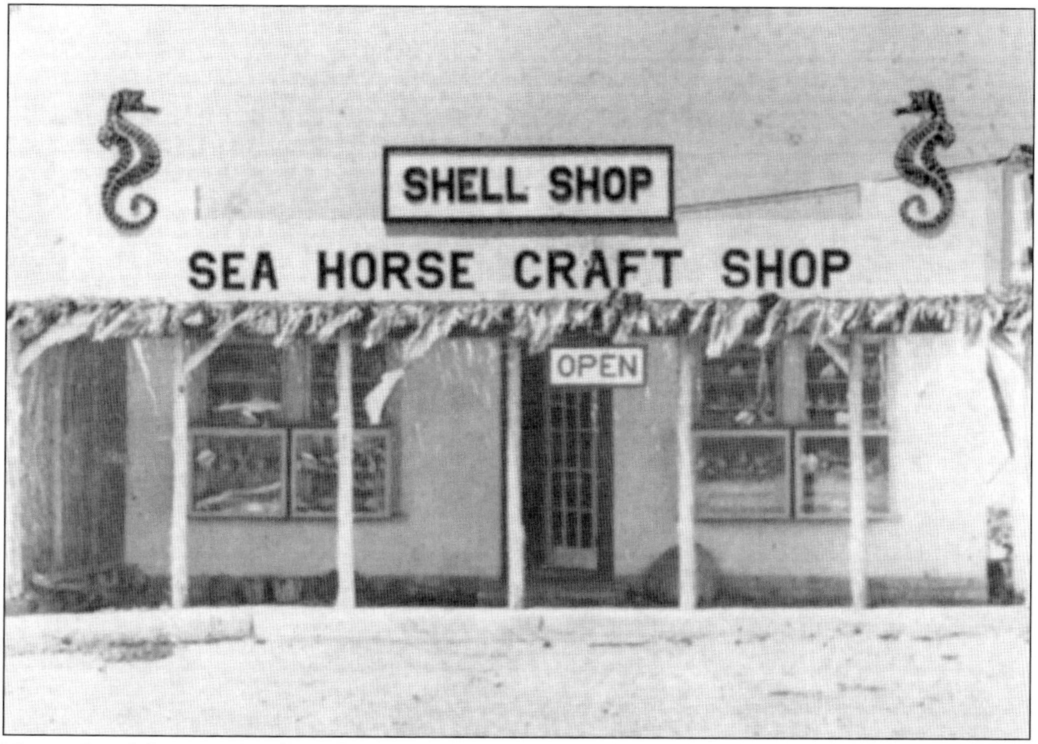

Unusual and distinctive gifts and souvenirs, handcrafted shell and costume jewelry, specimen shells, coral, driftwood, and other items were available at the Sea Horse Craft Shop, which helped feed a shell and shell-crafting frenzy. It was located on State Highway 100 in the west part of town.

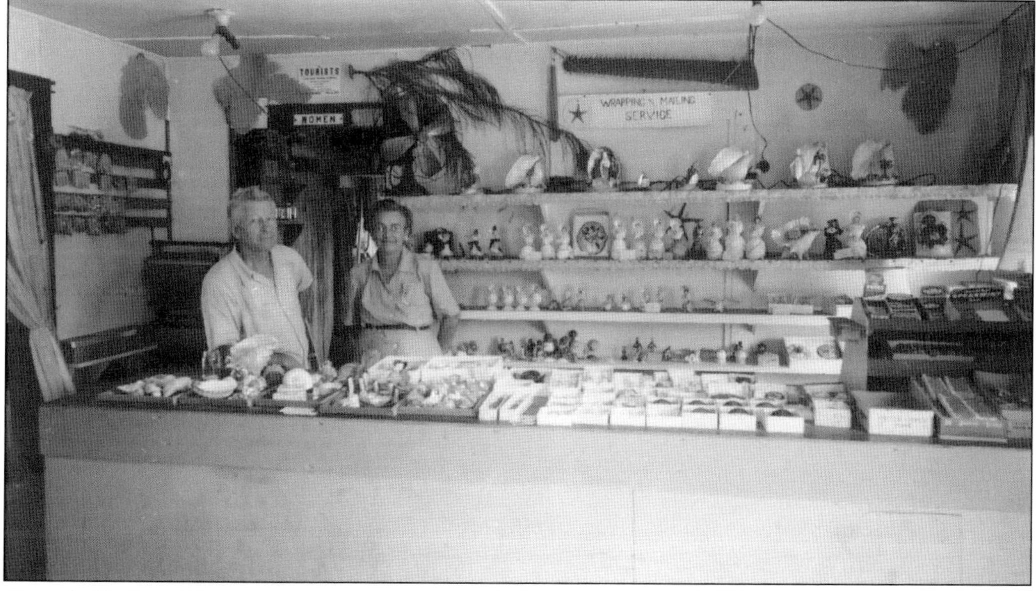

Campbell's Sea Chest was a treasure chest of all things nautical. Wrapping and shipping were available, and no suitcase was too small. Campbell's also had a small museum of locally found items of interest and seashells. These little shops were important ingredients in the recipe that is Port Isabel.

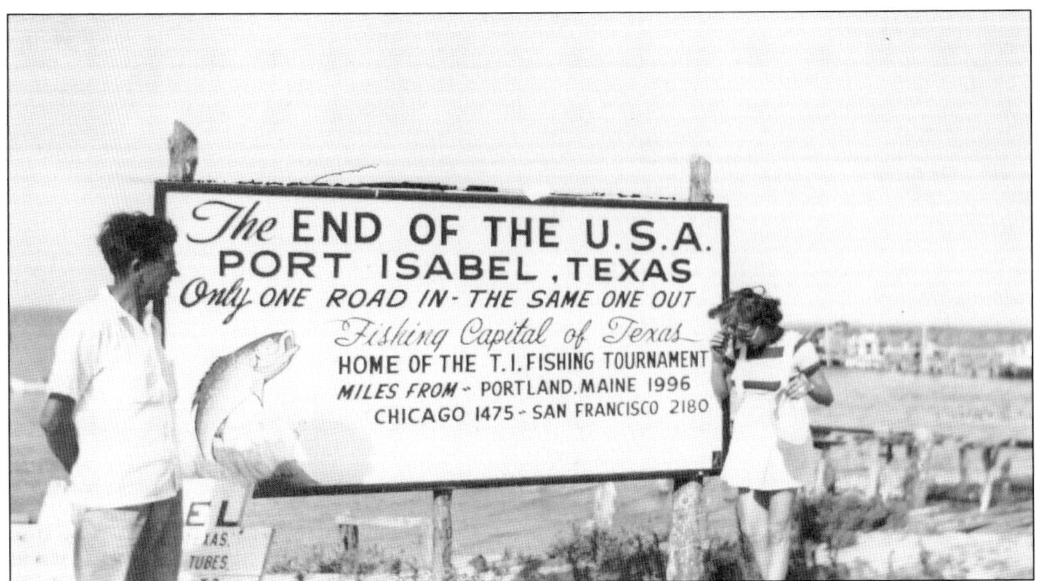

Located at the eastern end of Cameron County, Port Isabel was regarded as the end of the United States. It took a creative and observant copywriter to turn these facts into exciting news. This sign was one more landmark to memorialize for the folks back home. The Laguna Madre Bay laps the shoreline behind the posing travelers.

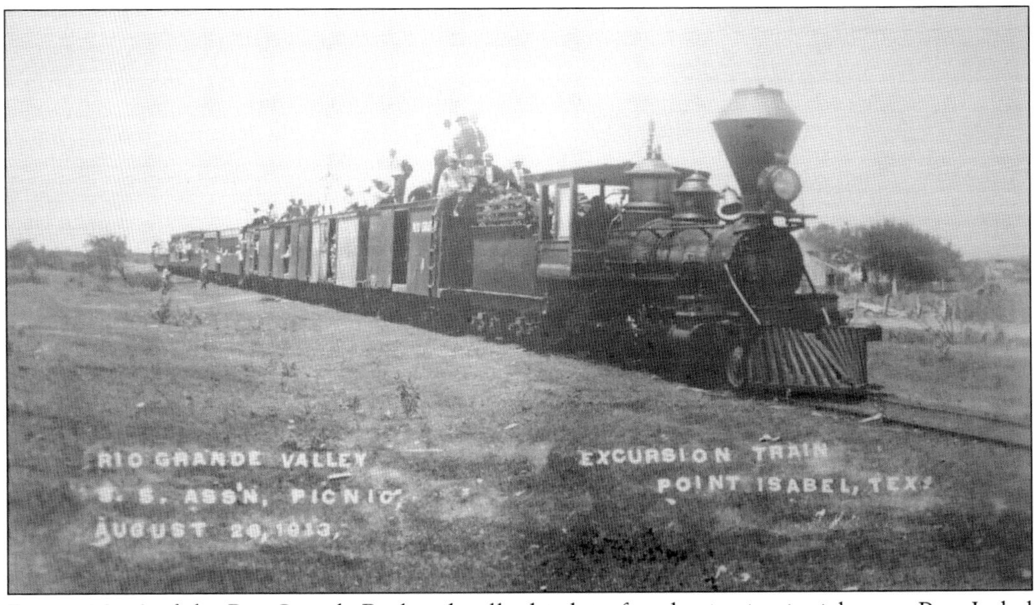

Engine No. 3 of the Rio Grande Railroad pulls this lot of enthusiastic picnickers to Port Isabel on August 26, 1913. A gentleman is removing his coat while standing atop the railcar, and others are running toward the train while traveling companions encourage them. A variety of activities must have been planned for the excursion, as the inscription on the reverse claims the writer had no time to even write a proper letter.

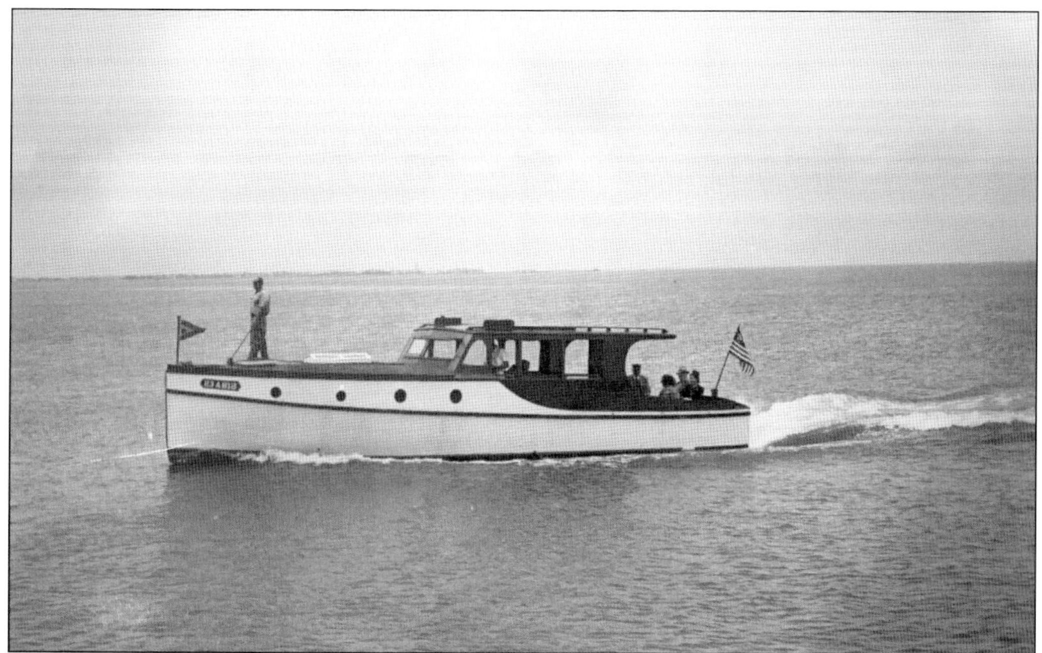

In this mid-1930s photograph, the Stuart family of Harlingen takes an afternoon outing on the Laguna Madre Bay. Visible in the background is the skyline of Port Isabel and the lighthouse. Many Rio Grande Valley residents who could do so kept a boat at the coast.

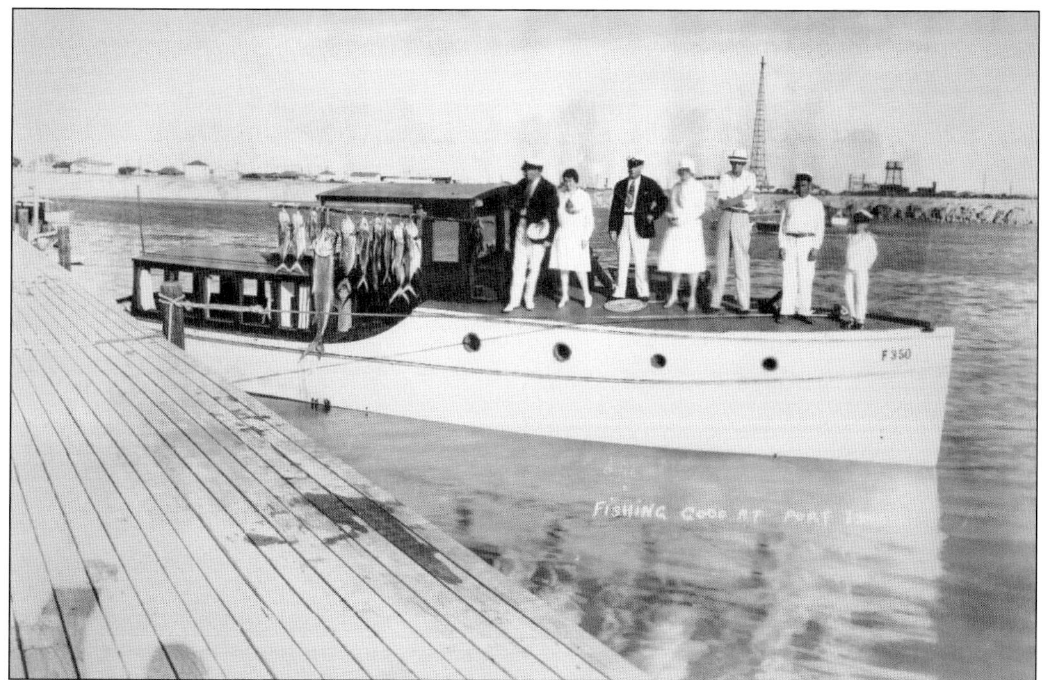

This card reads, "Good fishing is at Port Isabel!" The Robert Terry Stuart family and friends have returned from their outing with a very nice catch of fish, including a tarpon. They are docked at the turning basin. The remaining 330-foot wireless tower and cistern are visible on the shoreline behind them.

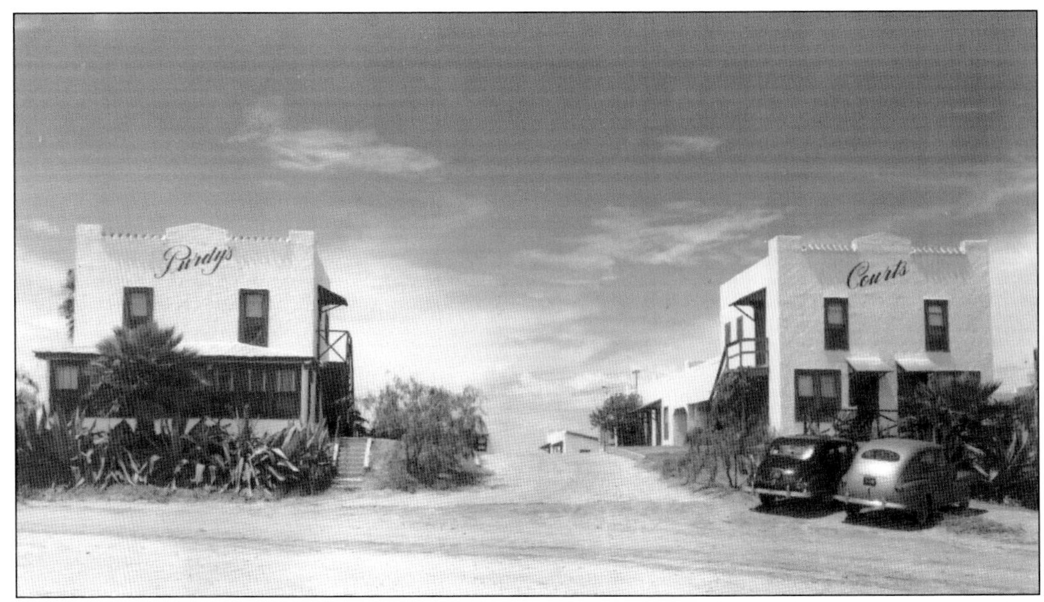

Purdy's Courts was an important accommodation addition. Complete with a private pier, a cabin for four people ran $6 or a single cabins for two at $4 and $5. Located just steps from Colley and Sullivan's ferry services and a number of restaurants and shops, Purdy's was a popular destination. The site was razed in 1984.

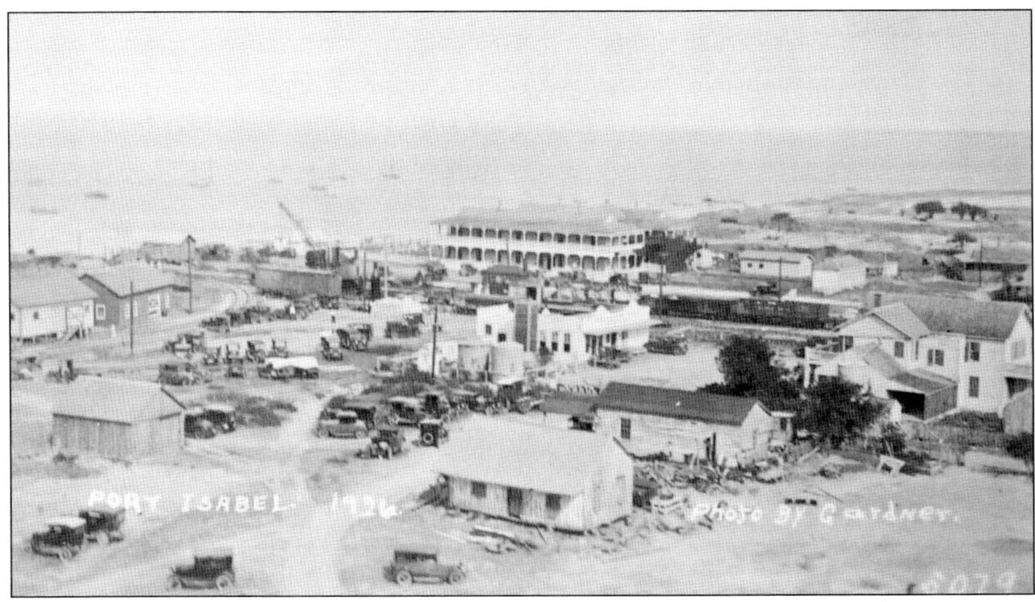

Many visiting automobiles are seen parked along Garcia Street in 1926. R.S. Coleman, a curio shop owner, noted that in just the month of December in 1932, license plates of 113 automobiles from 23 different states were found on his block, with Oklahoma being the most popular. In 1933, the final section of US Highway 77, the coast-hugging highway, was nearing completion in Kenedy County, making the drive to extreme south Texas more convenient.

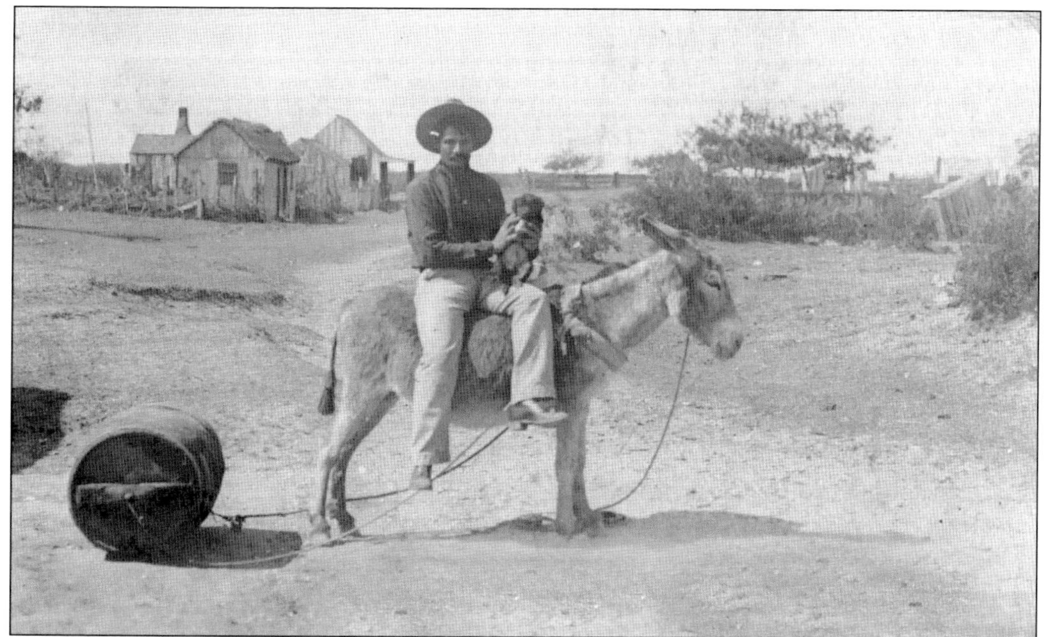

"Hubby" lovingly sends this postcard back to "Dear Sweetheart" in San Antonio in 1909. He adds that these are some of the residents of Point Isabel. This water hauler on his burro holds a puppy while posing for a photograph. Aguadores not only provided a service to the town, but they also served as ambassadors of tourism.

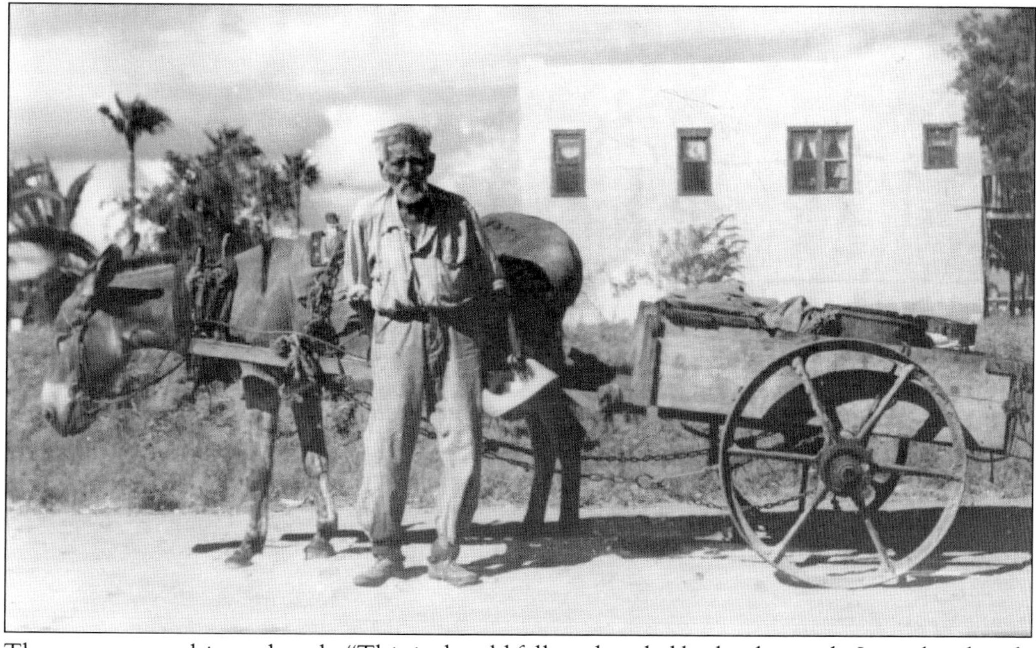

The message on this card reads, "This is the old fellow that dad had a chat with. It is taken beside the building where Hanna and me take our laundry." The 1947 postcard features Don Chencho; he was the oldest, and most photographed, man in the valley. Chencho helped build the first railroad dock and was another ambassador of Port Isabel tourism. He was about 112 years old in this image. He was rarely photographed without his hat.

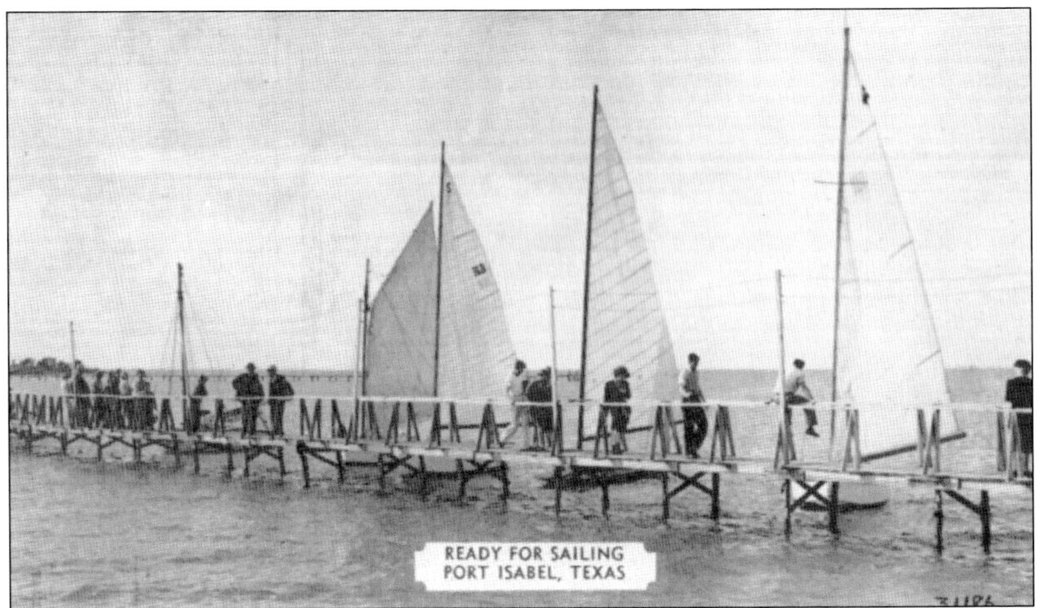

A 1948 postcard sends these sentiments home: "There are a lot of these sail boats here. I wouldn't want to be on any of them. The other day two young boys had a small skiff or boat. They had a motor on it and had it rigged up with a sail they had made. The were having a good time learning to sail. They were on the small canal. Gee, there is a pretty cabin boat going by now. They have some pretty ones, they cost, too."

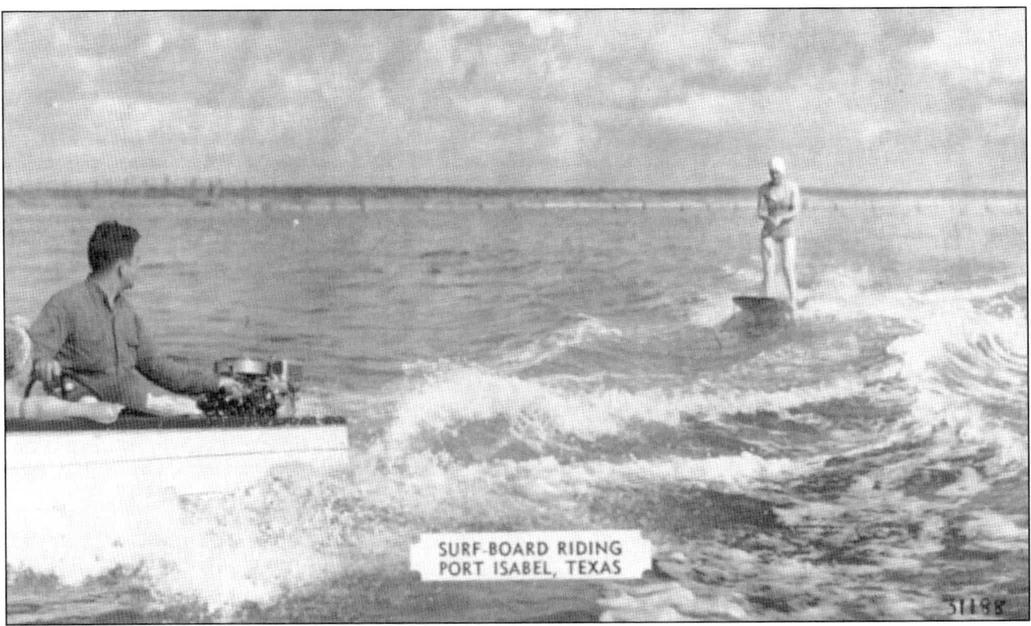

In the late 1940s, on the Laguna Madre Bay, the new sport of surfboard riding was introduced. The calm and relatively shallow water of the hyper-saline bay was home to a wide variety of sports, including water polo, sailing, yachting, and fishing. Marinas were constructed along the shoreline to accommodate the increasing number of boats that called Port Isabel home.

Seven

Building Bridges

Before the 1944 completion of the Gulf Intracoastal Waterway that cut a channel through the middle of the Laguna Madre Bay, when conditions were just right, it was possible to walk across the bay to South Padre Island. The hyper-saline bay had an average depth of three to four feet and was subject to the tide. Sailing vessels regularly crossed the bay, which gave way to gasoline-powered ferries and then ferries and barges that carried automobiles. A causeway across the mother lagoon that connects to the "father island," the longest barrier island in the world, changed everything.

A few pilings were driven at the foot of Maxan Street in the earliest attempt in the mid-1930s. Two decades later, the first Queen Isabella Causeway opened to a flow of excited tourists and residents. The span opened on February 14, 1954, and the first person to cross the swing bridge was Andrew King, a winter Texan from Manitoba, Canada. The bridge was dedicated on July 4, 1954. The length of the concrete causeway was 6,765.42 feet or 1.28 miles, and the width was 28 feet. Construction began on November 1, 1952, and was completed on June 1, 1954, at a cost of $2,238,952.02. By November 21, 1954, nine months, seven days, nine hours, and 15 minutes after its opening, the causeway received its 100,000th vehicle. The light green sedan bearing a Kansas license belonged to Mrs. and Mrs. Forrest E. Green.

The second Queen Isabella Causeway opened on September 28, 1974. The Hon. Juan Cabrero, consul general of Spain, was on hand for the ribbon cutting hosted by Cameron County judge Ray Ramon. Queen Isabella Days was organized, and the communities of Port Isabel and South Padre celebrated the new bridge. A walk over the bridge to South Padre Island started at 8:00 a.m.; additional activities included a turtle display, bingo, a street dance, the Queen Isabella Ball, historical displays, a fish fry, a Confederate Air Force flyby, sailing festival, barbecue, talent show, and fireworks. Many of these celebrations still continue, as does the connection to South Padre Island.

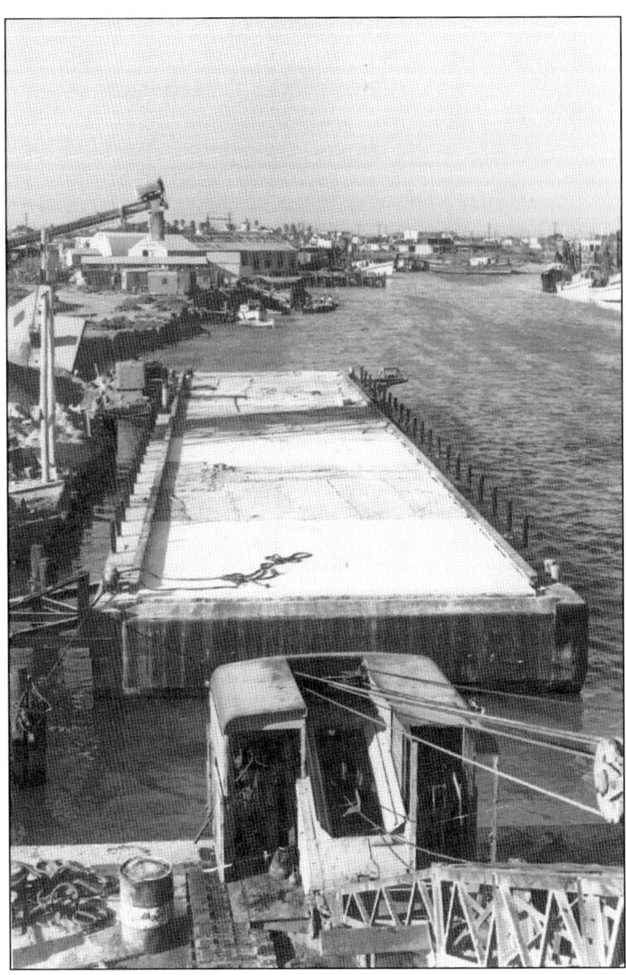

Abutments are carved out of the clay bank of this portion of the Gulf Intracoastal Waterway. A barge, which is essentially the swing bridge, is fitted with railings, machinery, winches, and hoists. The barge was floated down from Indiana, where the bridge was constructed. It is still in existence and is now privately owned.

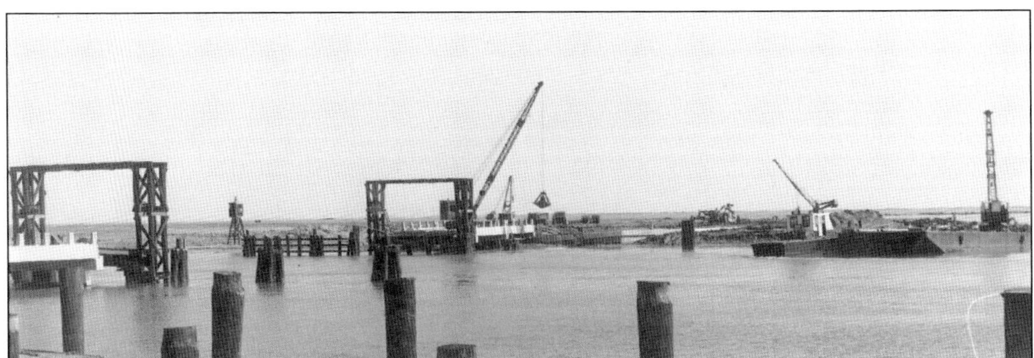

To accommodate Gulf Intracoastal Waterway traffic, a swing bridge was constructed as part of the Queen Isabella Causeway system. At 160 feet in length, 32 feet in width, and eight feet in height, the bridge was fitted with a pulley system, whereby it was swung out of the way to allow vessel passage on the Gulf Intracoastal Waterway. Residents of Long Island Village still use the swing bridge to access their properties.

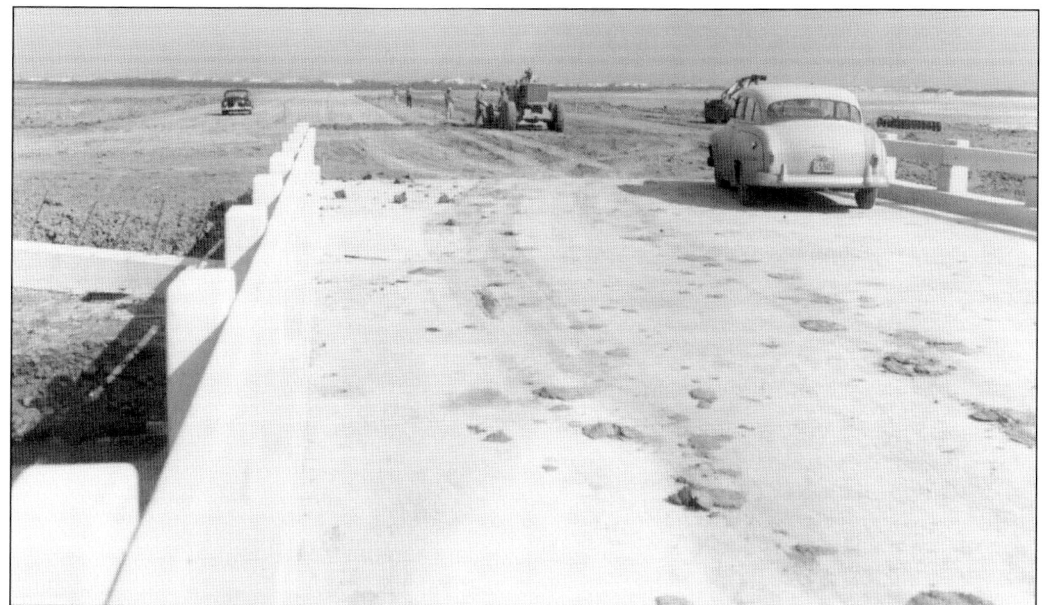

On the other side of the Brownsville Ship Channel after crossing the swing bridge, a section of roadway was created to meet the Queen Isabella Causeway. Long Island Village, then known as Outdoor Resorts, began a development on Long Island, complete with a golf course and all the amenities for both long- and short-term stays.

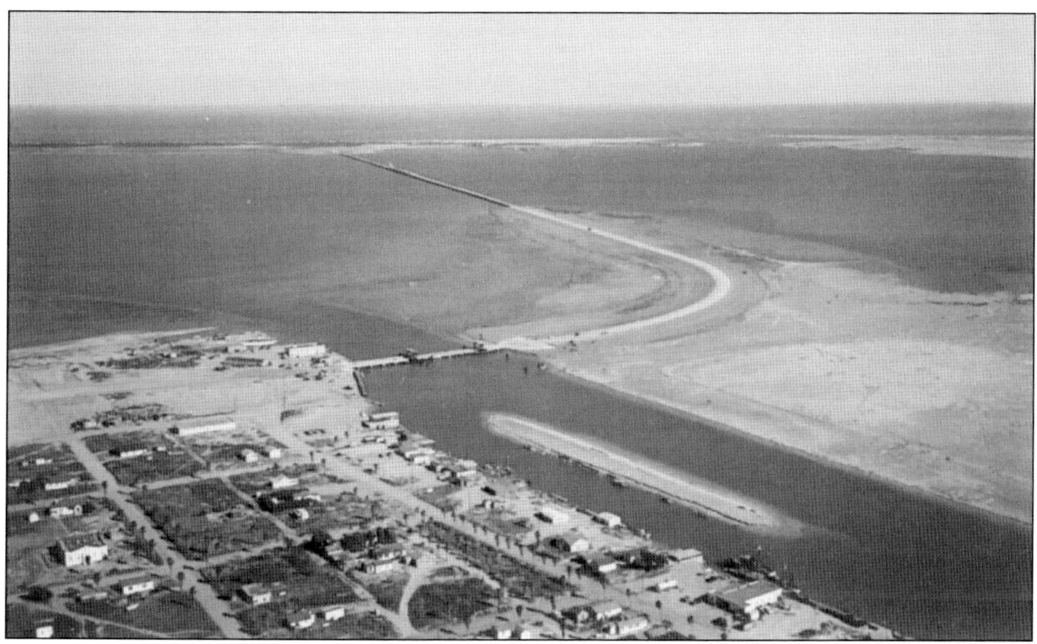

The $2,225,000 Queen Isabella Causeway was a masterpiece of steel and concrete, connecting Port Isabel, Texas, with the beaches of Padre Island. It extended 15,272 feet from downtown Port Isabel to the southern tip of Padre Island across the Intracoastal Canal and the waters of Laguna Madre.

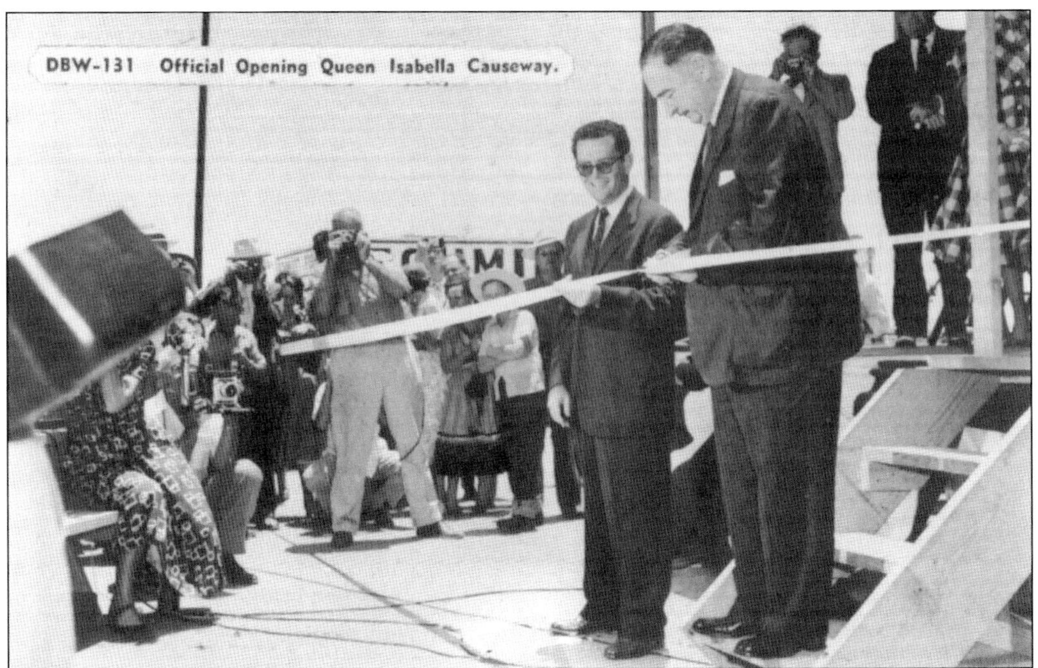

The ambassador from Spain cuts the ribbon, which officially opened the Queen Isabella Causeway. With the beginning of the celebration came some concerns. Additional security was requested, with reports of speeding on the island, and according to the *Port Isabel Press*, efforts to "step up law enforcement with more personnel now will forestall development of hippie colonies this summer."

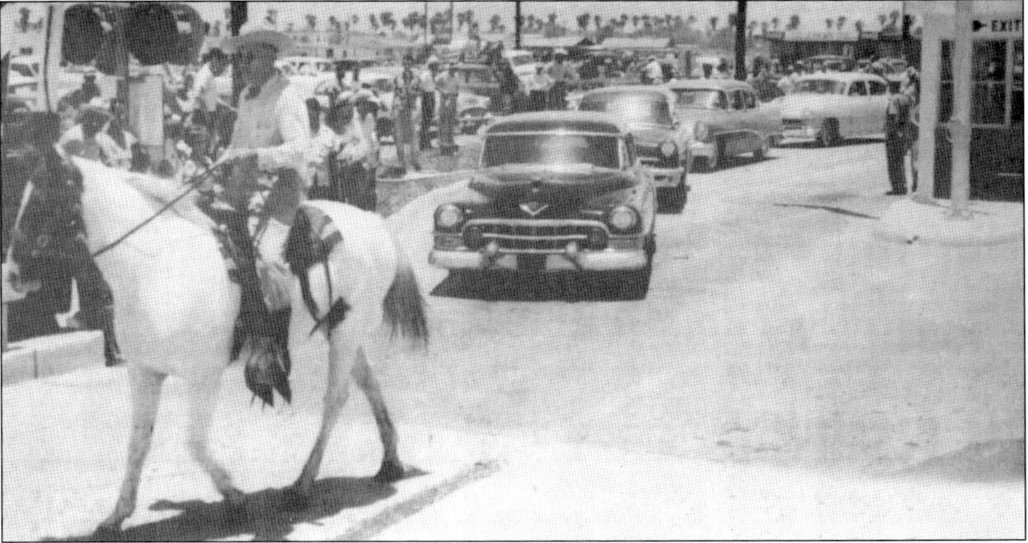

Headed by Bryan Long, of San Benito, on a white horse, the official party crossed the causeway following the dedication on July 4, 1954. Long made the crossing on horseback, followed by cars carrying the Spanish ambassador, the secretary of agriculture for Mexico, and the US secretary of agriculture Ezra Taft Benson. After the official party made the crossing, cars lined Garcia Street and roads back into Port Isabel for blocks as thousands made the first-day crossing onto the newly opened South Padre Island resort beaches into Isla Blanca Park.

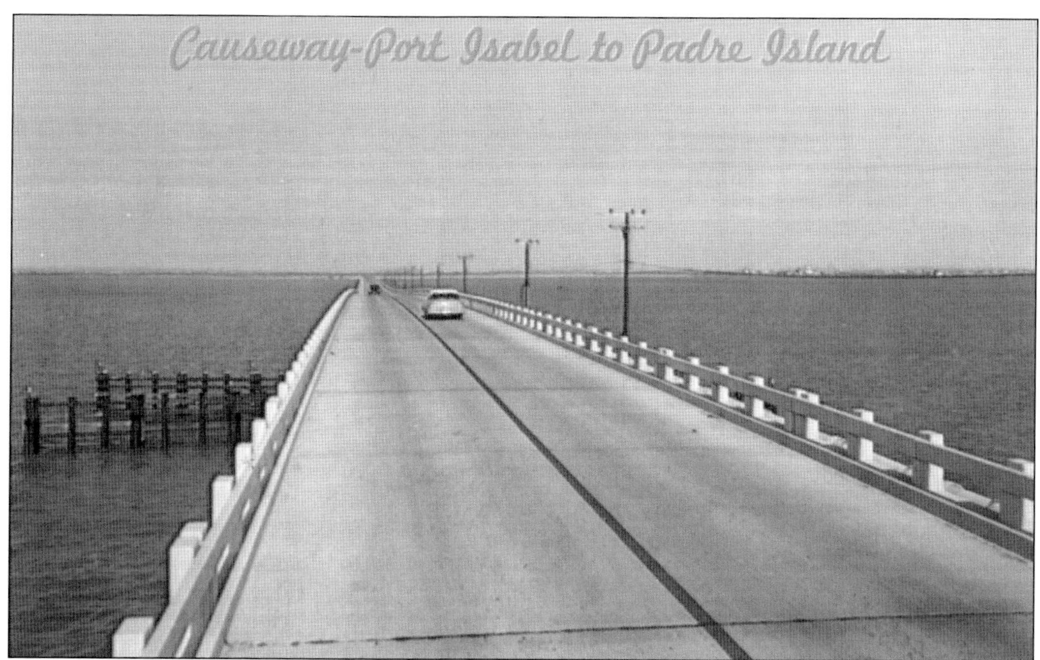

Locals and visitors were familiar with the clickety-clack sound made while crossing the 1.28-mile span. During its first 15 days of existence, there were 7,893 total crossings. A count of the last 15 days of toll taking 14 years later revealed 7,893 crossings. One resident on South Padre Island counted 16 cars a minute passing by on the first pretty Sunday after the toll was removed.

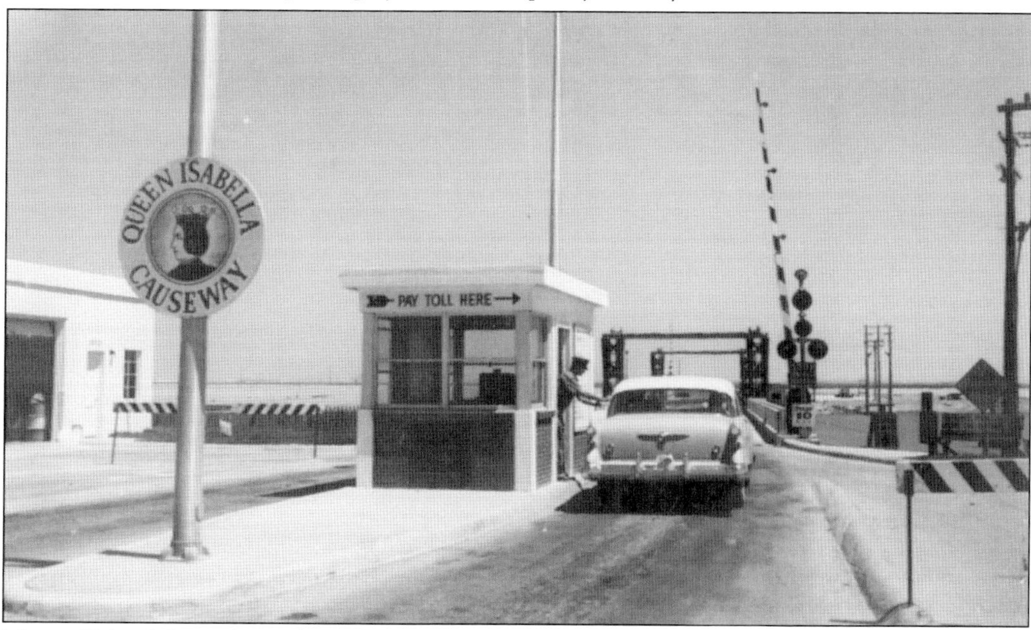

Mr. and Mrs. John White of South Padre Island were the last and first to make the crossing. John was the last to pay the toll at 11:59 p.m. on February 29, and his wife was the first to cross toll-free at 12:01 a.m. on March 1, 1968. The toll was removed at the midnight hour, and on the day of the removal of tolls, the tollhouse came down. The removal of toll collection came 14 years after the construction and 14 years ahead of schedule.

ACCT. #	VEH. #	DR. #	TOLL CLASS	AMOUNT
S 146	2	2	6	.50

QUEEN ISABELLA CAUSEWAY

This signed receipt represents one trip (2 axle) made by

Lee Bernd

(Driver's Authorized Signature)

On 7-16-64 (Date)   1 - 2 - 3 (Shift)

ORIG. — CUSTOMER

DUPL. — CAUSEWAY

L.R. (Toll att. init.)

This receipt shows a 50¢ toll in 1964. The planned schedule for bond payout set September 1, 1982, as the final redemption scheduled with $1.5 million being paid out to complete payment for the causeway. On April 24, 1968, the State of Texas officially assumed the responsibility for and ownership of the Queen Isabella Causeway.

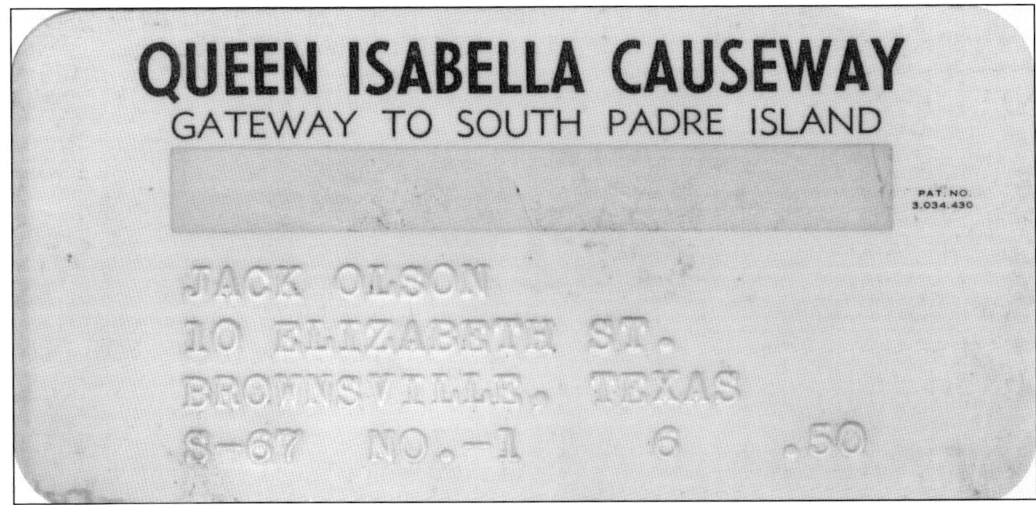

A billing system to accommodate residents, vendors, or frequent visitors making the trip over the bridge was implemented. This plastic charge plate was issued to a Brownsville resident who would be billed on a monthly basis; the toll was 50¢ to $1. Travel from Brownsville was on Channel Airline Highway, which was completed early in the summer of 1953. It is now known as State Highway 48.

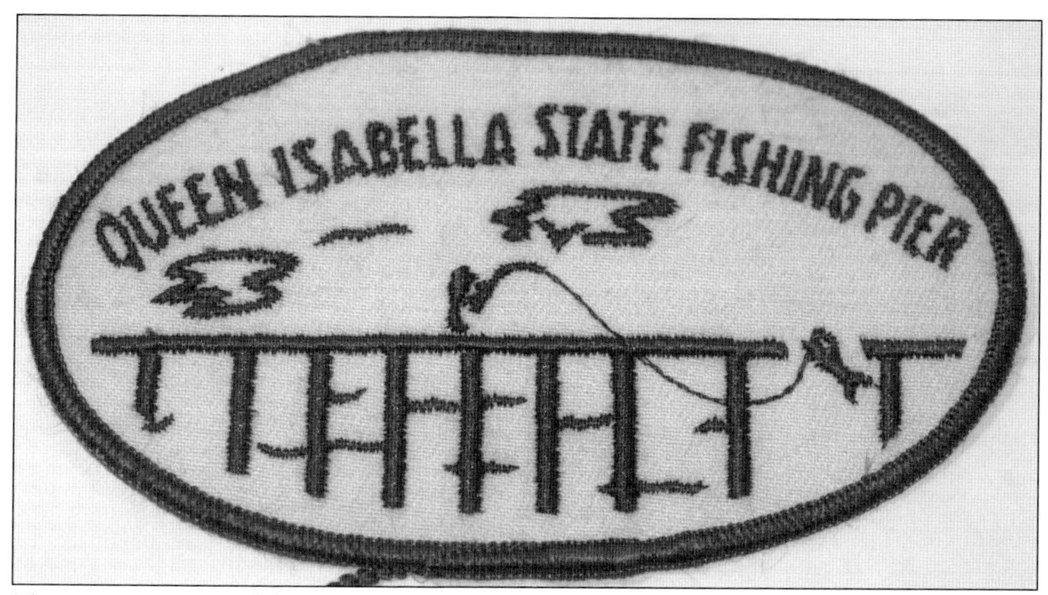

The eastern portion of the original Queen Isabella Causeway was converted into a fishing pier, the Queen Isabella State Fishing Pier, and now offers dock space to several fishing charter boats and also has a restaurant.

Plans for the second Queen Isabella Causeway included the removal of Powers Street to make way for the widening of State Highway 100 and the new bridge abutment. The dotted line shows the intended route. The alley on the south side of the lighthouse became the westbound lane.

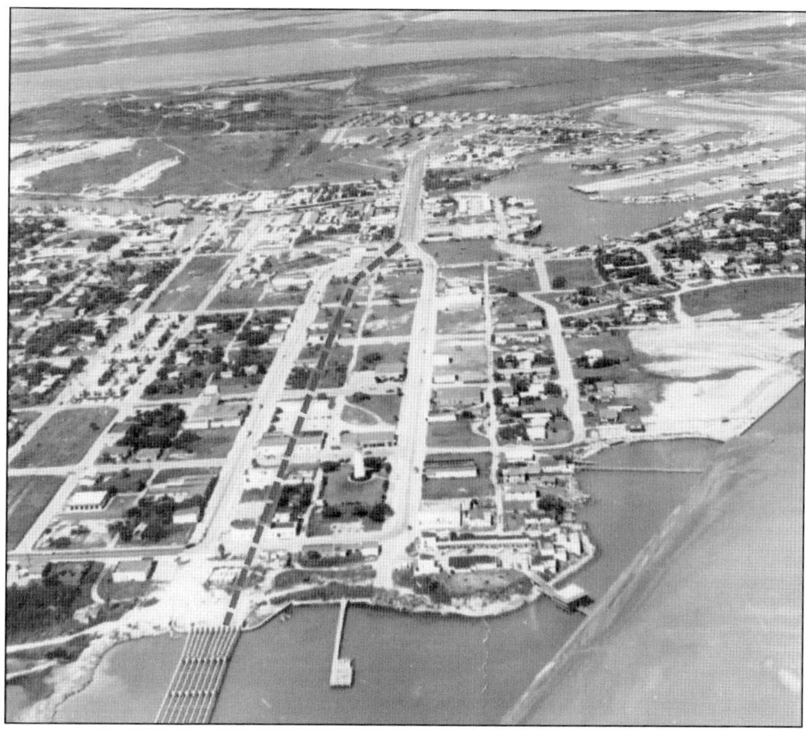

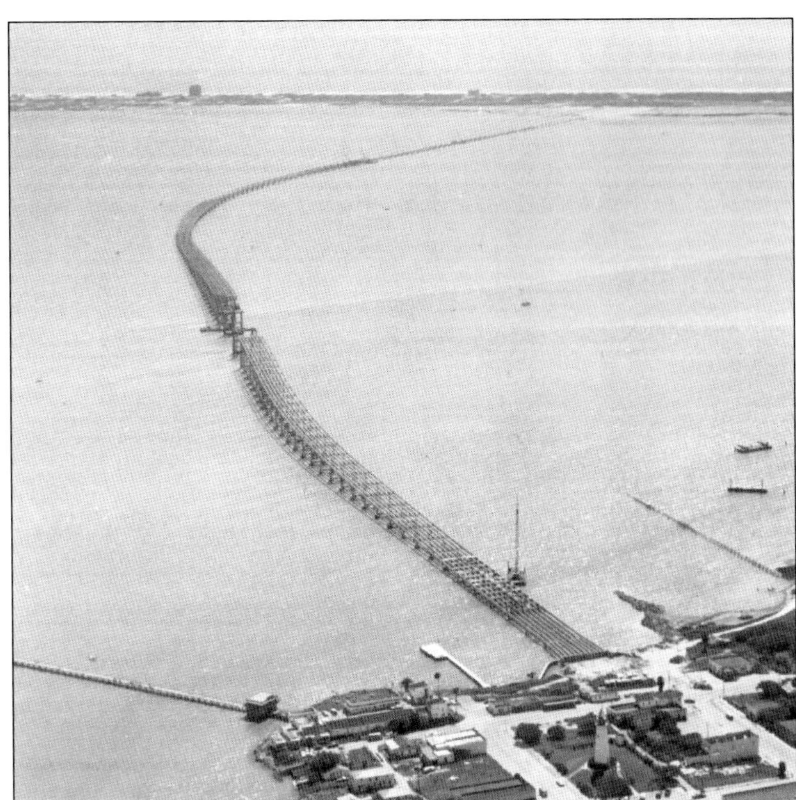

The structure of the 2.6-mile span is seen here nearing completion. Ship Café and the drugstore building, constructed in the early 1920s, were scheduled to be razed to make way for the easement required for bridge access. The railroad dock (right) is still visible a century later. Purdy's Courts (left) is still open for business at the time of this photograph.

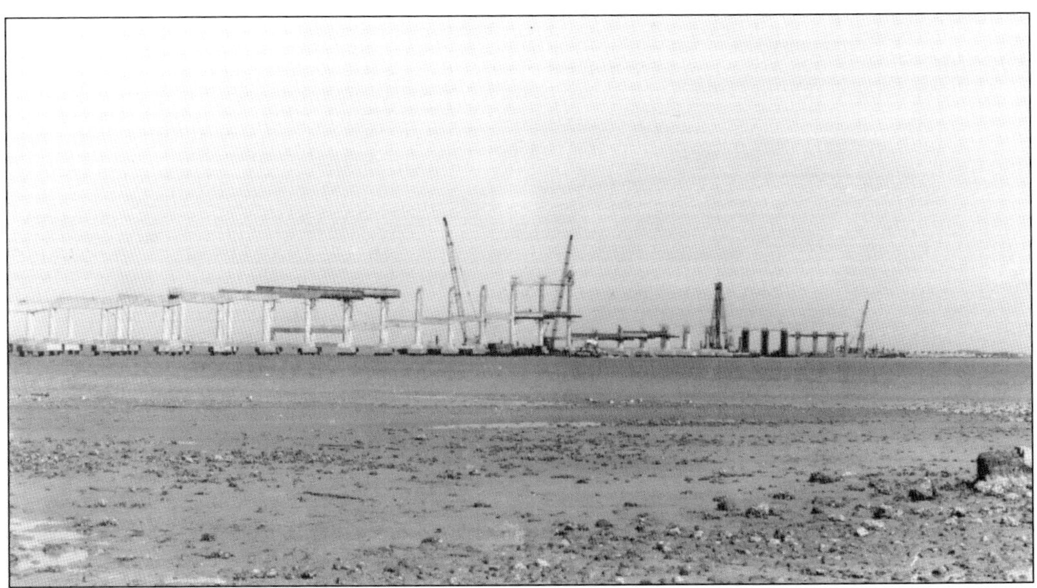

Spans 160 feet long are being lifted in place from barges atop pilings driven 65 feet into the bed of the Laguna Madre Bay. The center span of the bridge was 80 feet over the Gulf Intracoastal Waterway.

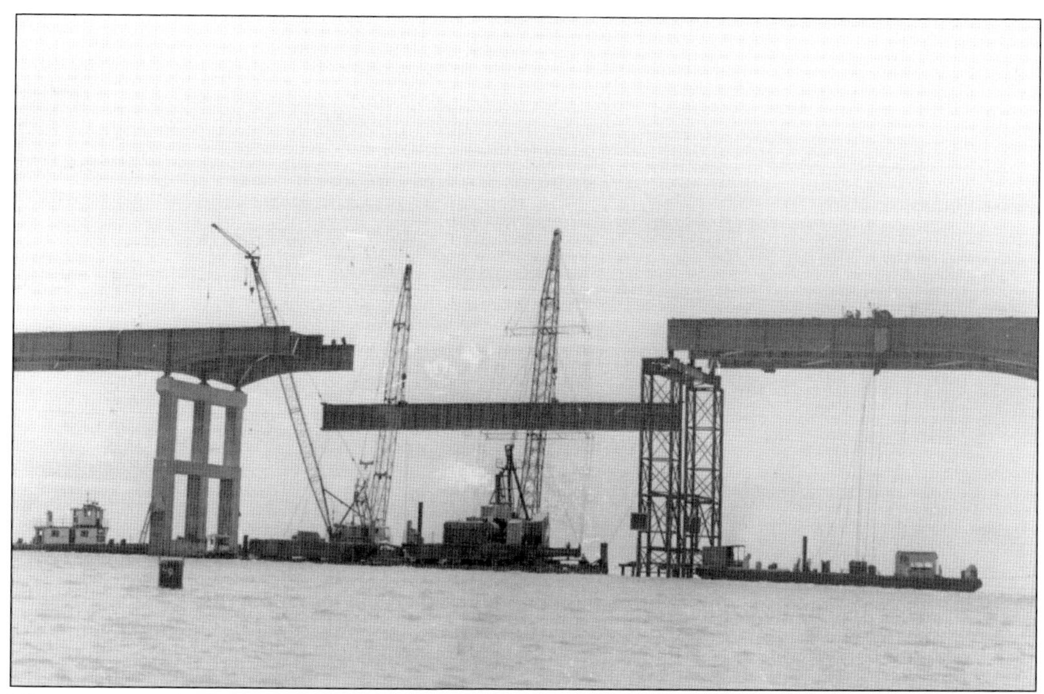

The capstone, the last span, is raised into place as the area is connected with South Padre Island with a new state-of-the-art bridge. The 2.6-mile span is the longest bridge in Texas. This is the approximate set of spans replaced in 2001 after the barge allision.

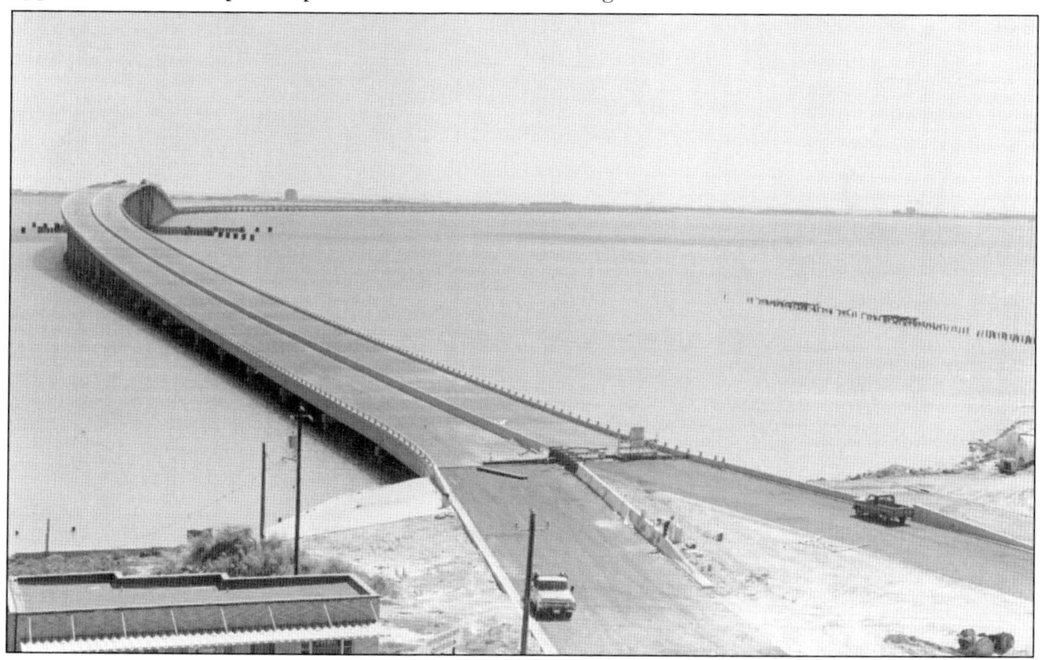

Very nearly completed, the Queen Isabella Causeway is getting some finishing touches, and State Highway 100 has just been paved with asphalt. Across the bay is the now distinctive South Padre Island skyline. Most visible is Sandy Retreat Hotel. On this clear day, the 1872 railroad dock (right) stands in sharp contrast to the new causeway.

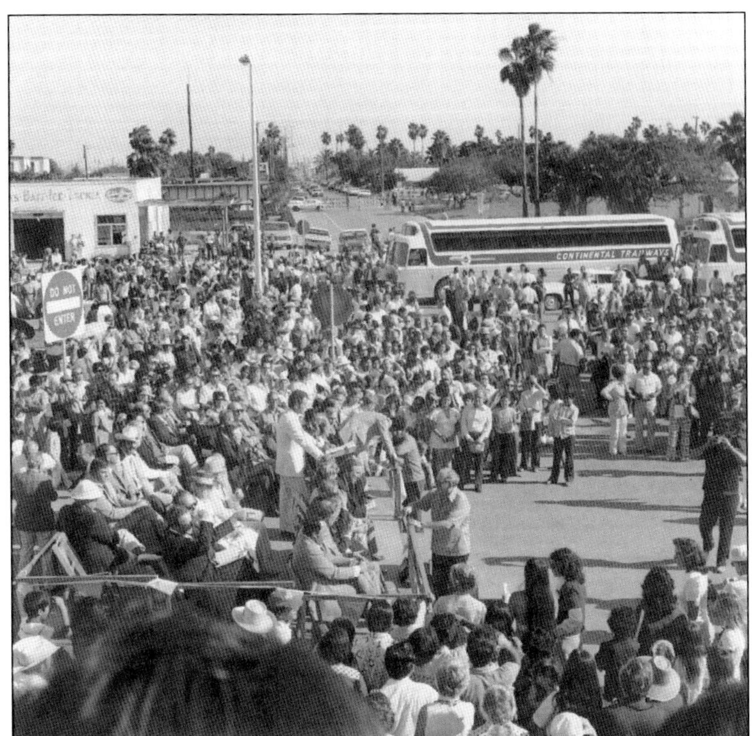

Pictured is the grand opening on September 29, 1974, with hundreds gathered to celebrate the Queen Isabella Causeway. Cameron County judge Ray Ramon and other dignitaries cut the ribbon. Buses crossed over the bridge for grand-opening festivities on South Padre Island.

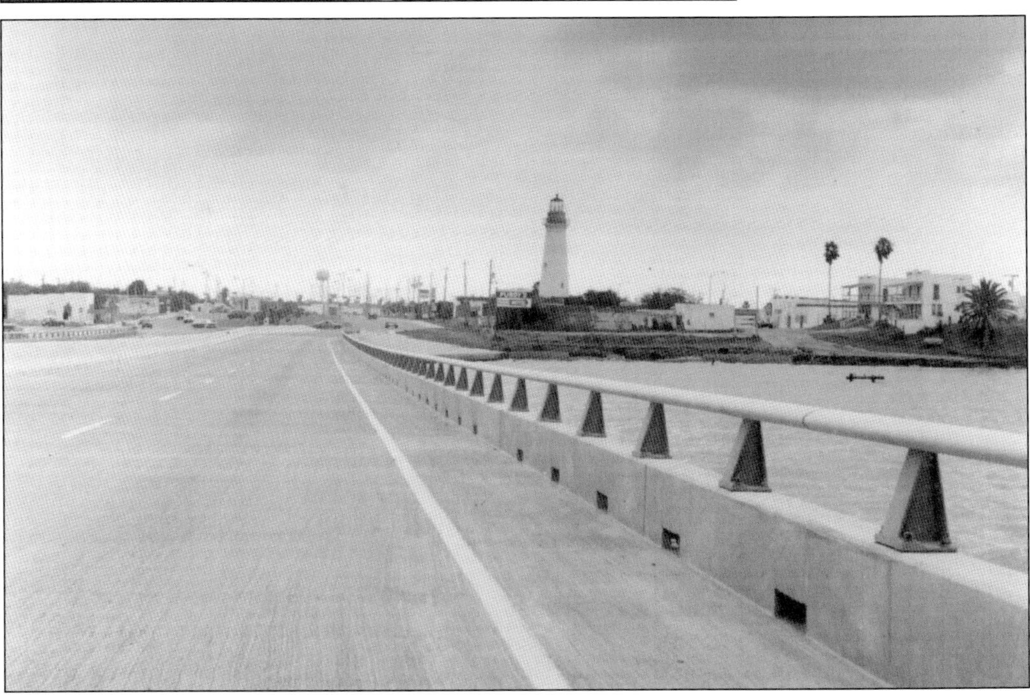

This is the view of the drive on the second Queen Isabella Causeway into Port Isabel. Purdy's Courts has added a sign near the highway. The site of Colley and Sullivan's ferry operations was now just an empty and dusty drive to the waterfront. A ferry operation would not be needed until 2001, twenty-seven years later.

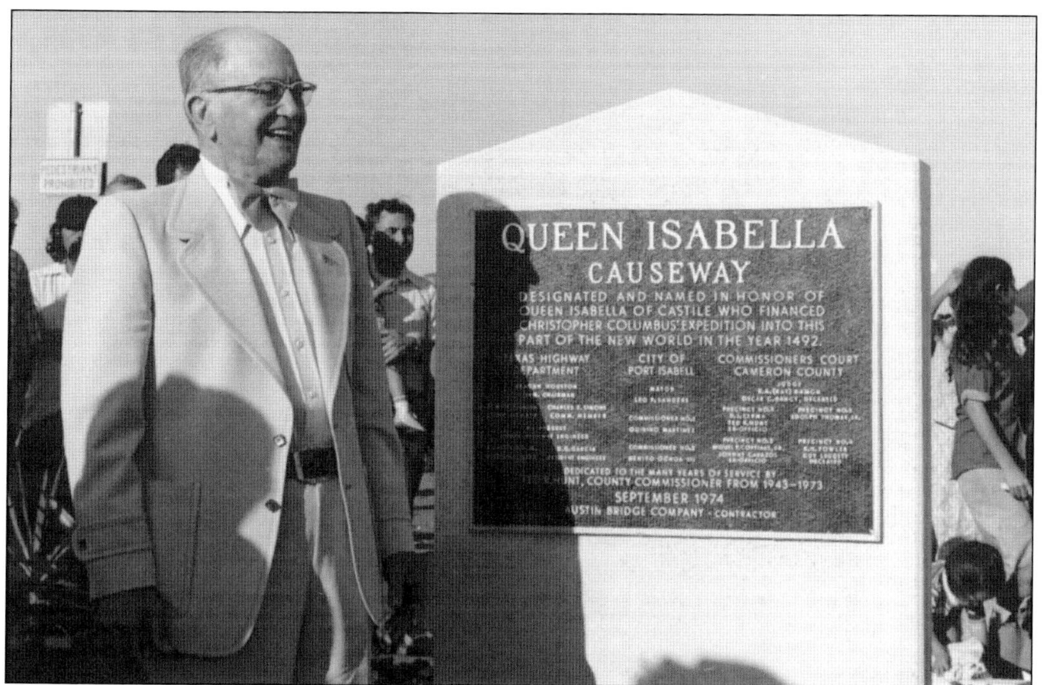

Former county commissioner Ted R. Hunt poses next to the marker on grand-opening day of the second Queen Isabella Causeway. The causeway and the historical plaque were dedicated to him at 3:30 p.m., September 28, 1974.

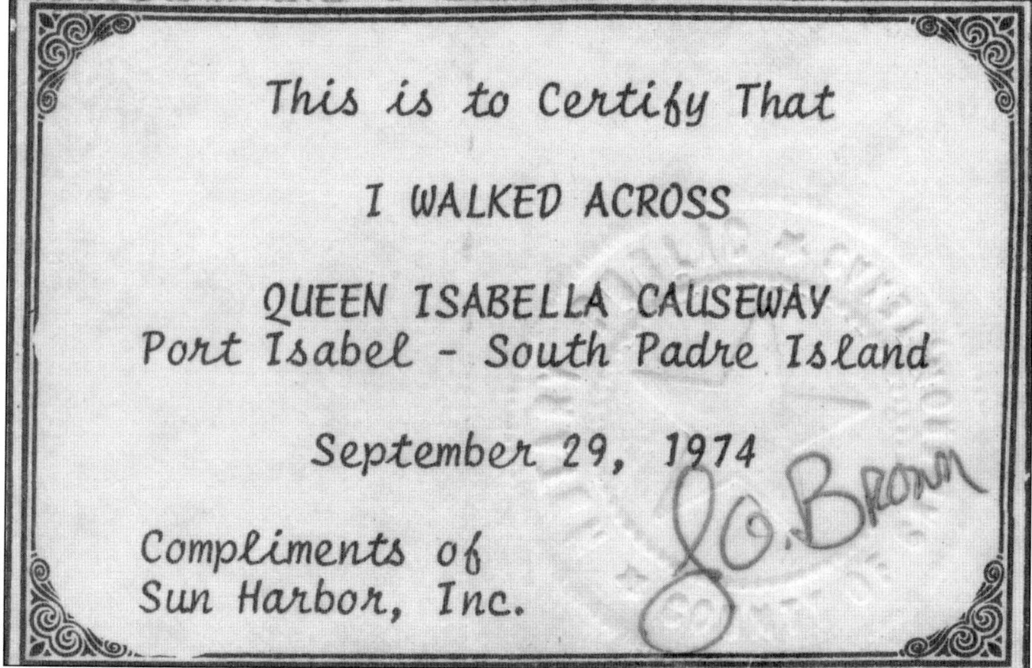

This is to Certify That

I WALKED ACROSS

QUEEN ISABELLA CAUSEWAY
Port Isabel - South Padre Island

September 29, 1974

Compliments of
Sun Harbor, Inc.

J.O. Brown

Cameron County, Texas, seal-embossed certificates were awarded to those who walked across the 2.6-mile bridge. The opening of the new bridge spawned a wide variety of events, including the Longest Causeway Run and Fitness Walk held annually in January.

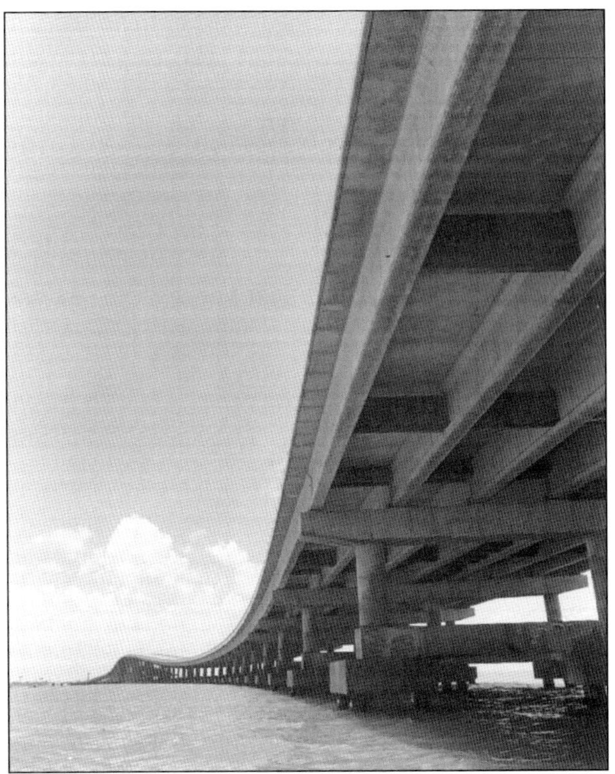

This westerly view of the new Queen Isabella Causeway was taken in 1974 on the occasion of its grand opening. Visible in the background is the Port Isabel skyline, complete with the Port Isabel Lighthouse just to the right side of the Queen Isabella Causeway.

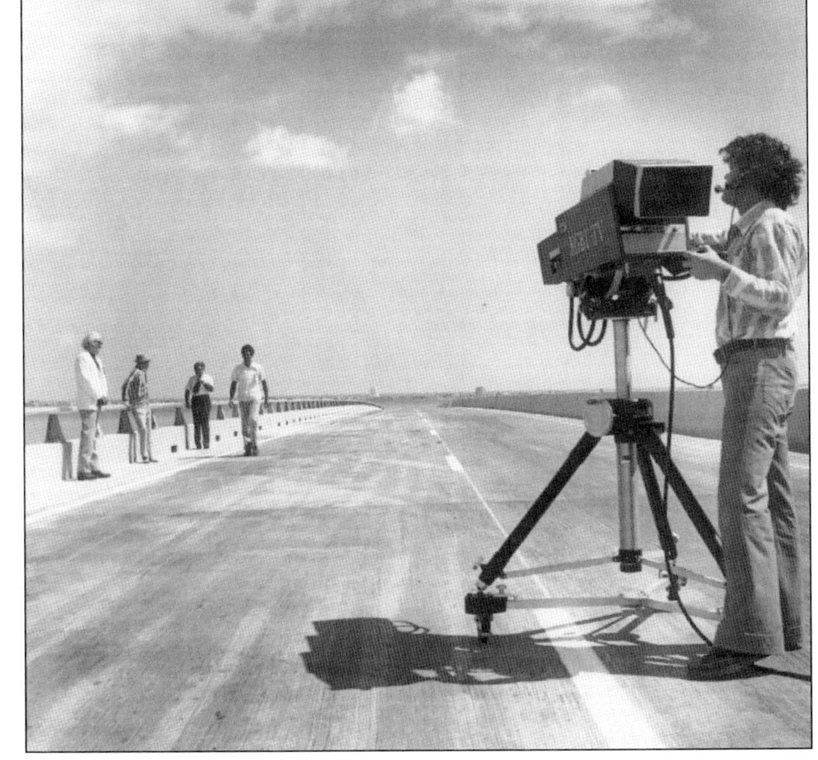

Local news media, such as KGBT of Harlingen, helped get the word out that the new Queen Isabella Causeway's grand opening was approaching. Queen Isabella Days was organized with events on both sides of the bridge.

Eight

A Causeway Collapse

In the early morning hours of September 15, 2001, a steel-laden barge collided with the Queen Isabella Causeway. This is called an allision, a term for a vessel running into a fixed object, not another vessel. It is also known as a disaster. The residents of the community of Port Isabel and its neighbor South Padre Island were stunned and confused. Occurring just four days after 9/11, the bridge collapse added to the already tenuous atmosphere that was shared by the rest of the nation.

In the early morning hours, a barge collided with the south side of the Queen Isabella Causeway while trying to execute the turn from the Brownsville Ship Channel into the Gulf Intracoastal Waterway. The contact caused two sections of the bridge to come dislodged from their supports and plunge some 80 feet below into the Laguna Madre Bay. In the darkness, six automobiles were unable to see the gap in the roadway, and eight lives were lost. Three survivors were rescued in the waters below by a group of fishermen.

Communities from across the Rio Grande Valley came together to support Port Isabel and South Padre Island. A contract was signed in record time, and work immediately began on debris removal and reconstruction.

Ferry operations were pressed into service much like the days before construction of the first Queen Isabella Causeway. Students going to school, employees going to work, delivery services, garbage collection, fuel, groceries, and supplies all made the trip back and forth by boat. Eighteen days after the collapse, the arrival of the first car ferry was met with much enthusiasm. Bank abutments were still being smoothed out as the first loads pushed up against the landings.

On November 21, 2001, just 50 days after the contract for reconstruction was signed, the bridge was reopened. A ribbon-cutting ceremony was held in Port Isabel, and once again, people were able to traverse over the Laguna Madre, a trip taken now with much more gratitude. The cost of the repair was a little over $5 million. In 2003, the structure was renamed Queen Isabella Memorial Bridge.

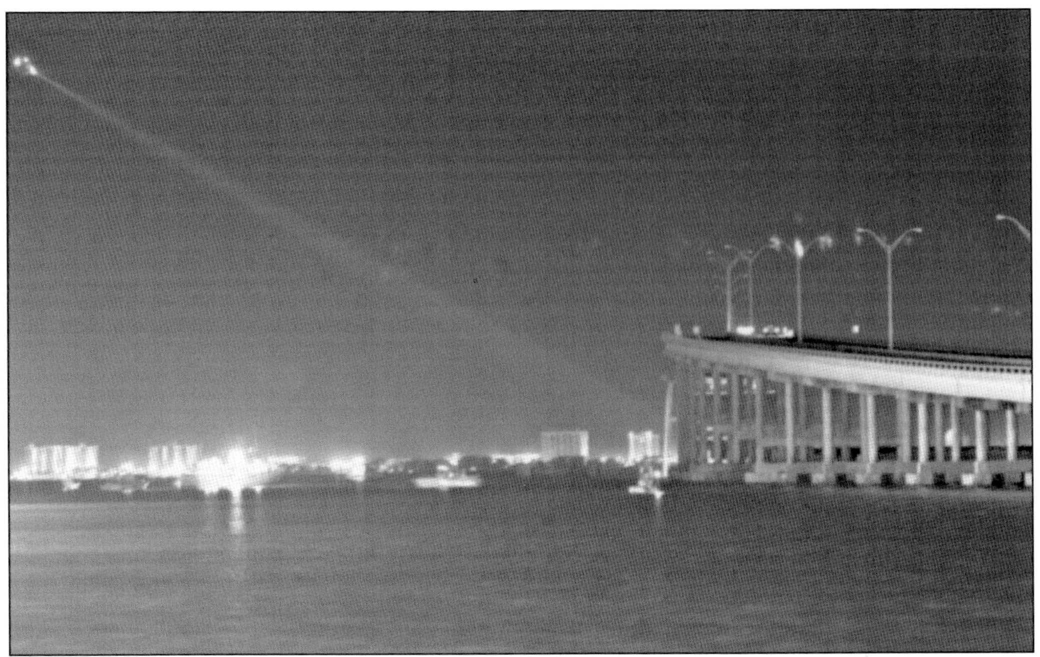

Peering into the darkness at about 4:30 a.m., a helicopter illuminates the area of the causeway that has been affected. The piling pushed north on its footing can be seen jutting out to the left of the causeway. Local private and commercial boat owners are already on the scene to assist in the rescue and recovery.

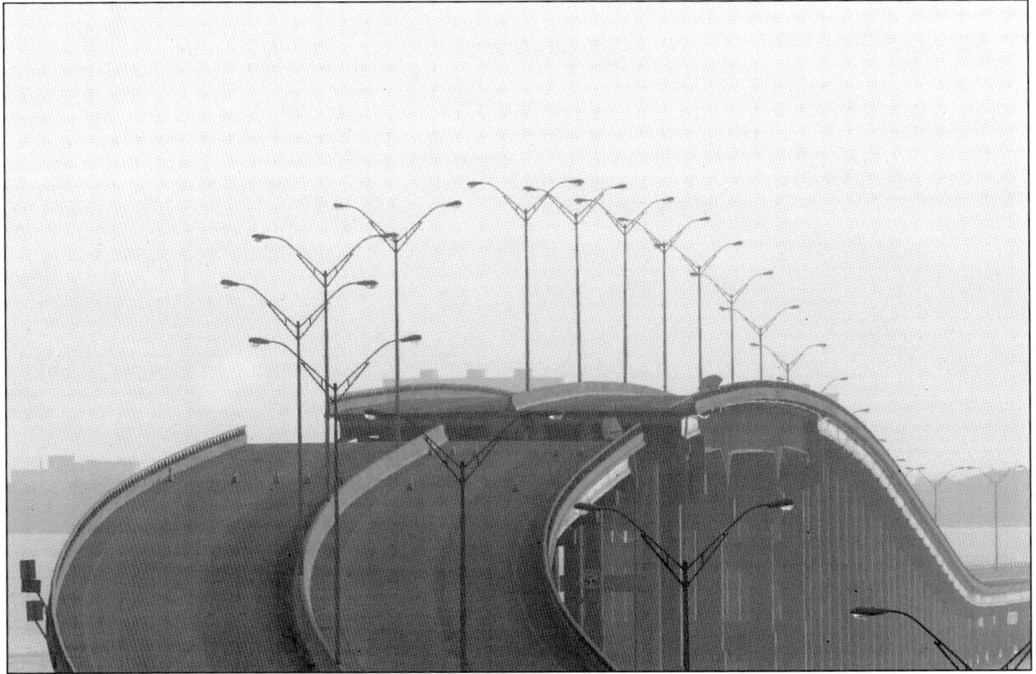

A few hours later, this view was taken from the top of the lighthouse, and the 160-foot gap is clearly visible as the sun rises. Crews were kept at a safe distance until the stability of the bridge could be determined, but recovery at the time was continuing.

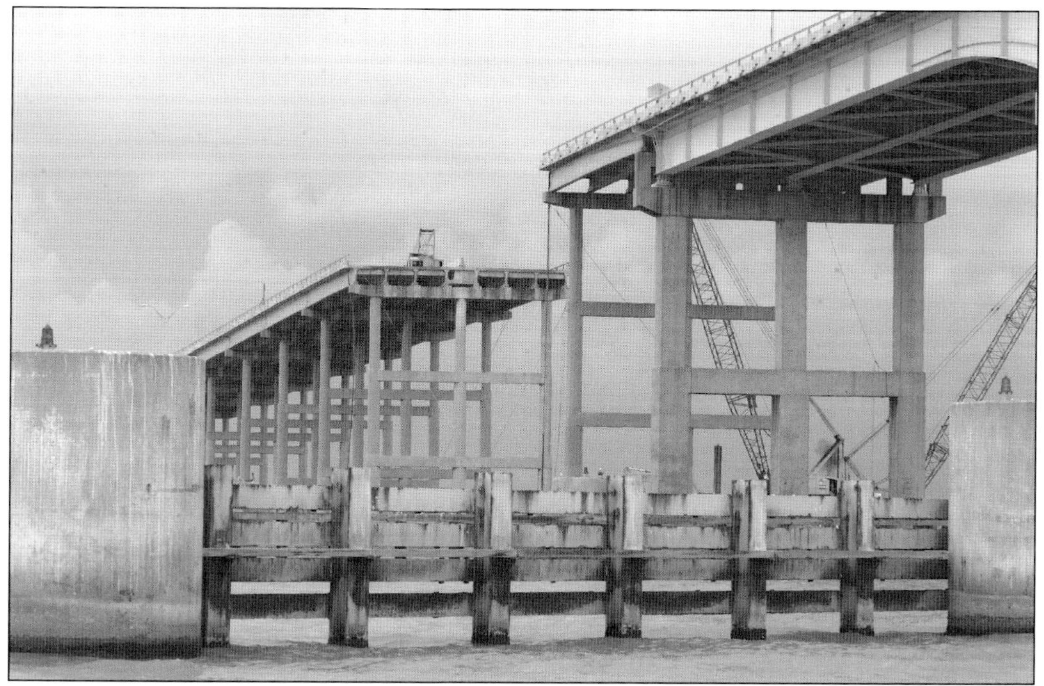

Entering the Gulf Intracoastal Waterway and heading north just after sunrise, this is the route the barge should have taken. In addition to first responders at the scene, engineers and officials are assessing the situation and beginning to put together a plan of action.

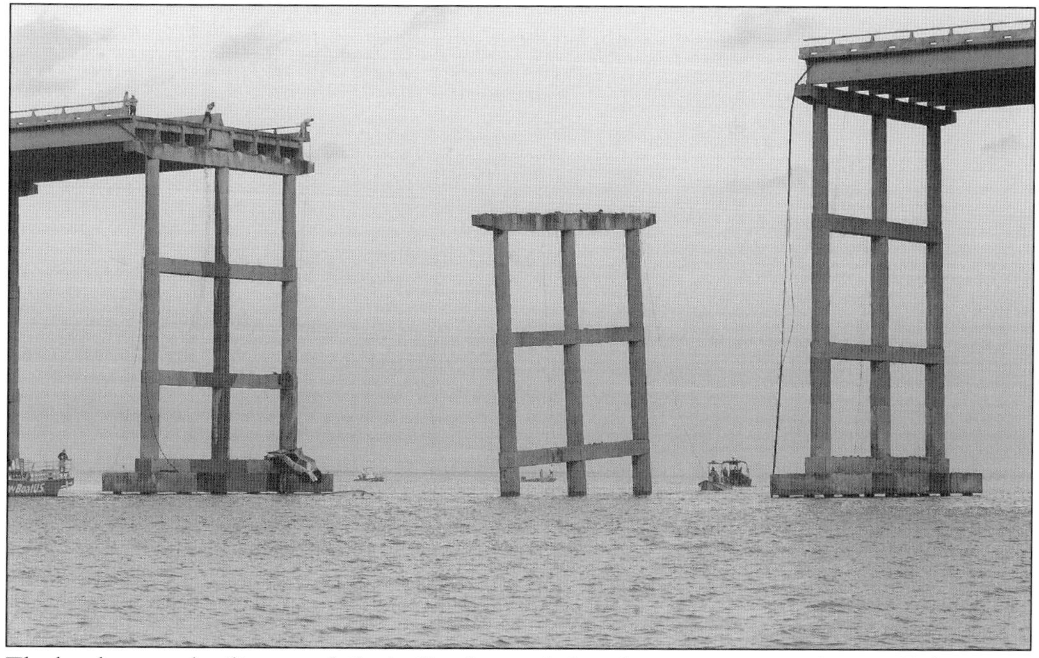

The hardest-struck piling was shifted off its footing below the water, causing the two 80-foot spans it supported to crash into the water. Communication with South Padre Island was effected as lines were severed. The Red Cross was on the scene almost immediately to assist in connecting friends and loved ones.

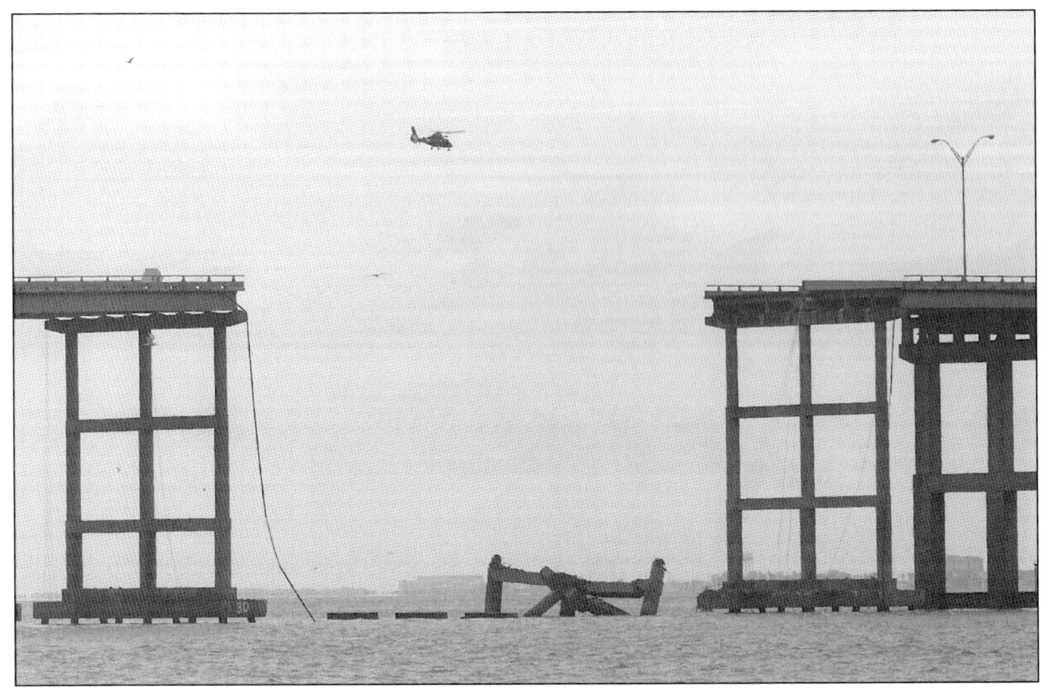

The afternoon after the collapse, at about 3:00 p.m., crews on the top of the bridge reported movement in the plumb line. All watercraft and personnel evacuated the immediate area just mere seconds before a second piling shifted, sending a third 80-foot span into the bay.

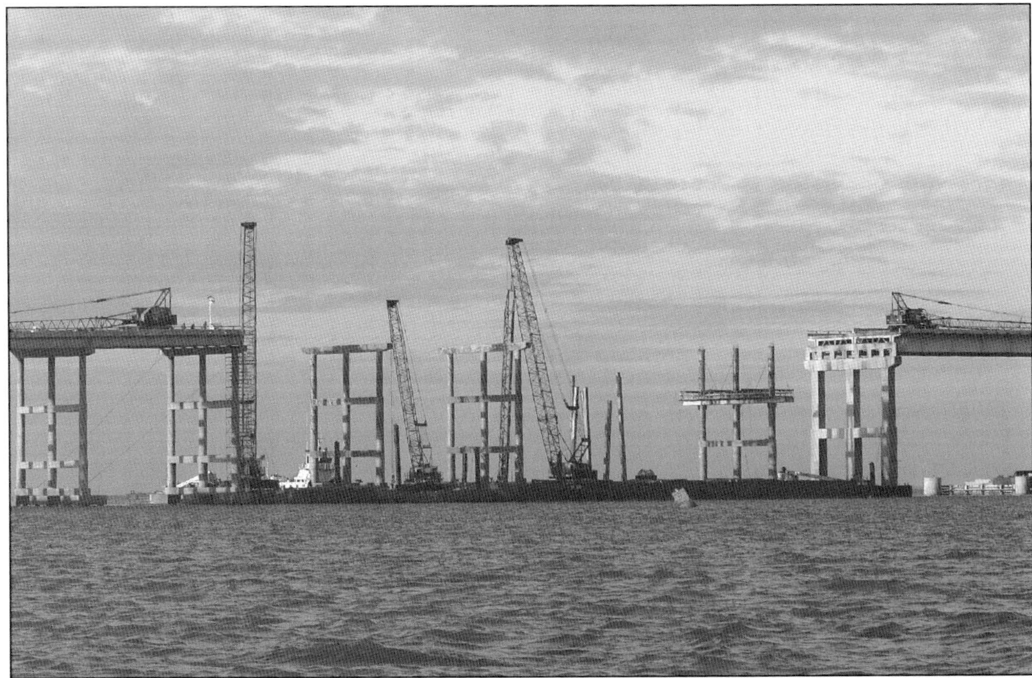

A total of 400 feet of Queen Isabella Causeway was replaced. Additional spans not originally collapsed were removed when they were deemed unsafe. Crews would at times work around the clock to complete the project in record time.

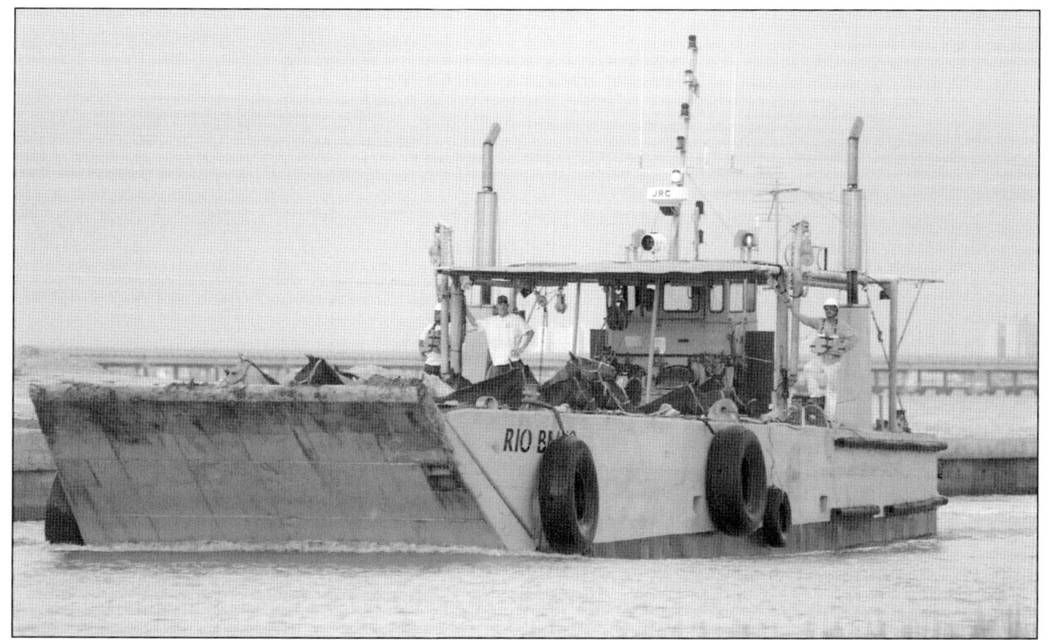

The *Rio Bravo*, a front-end landing craft owned by local Billy Kenon, was used to transport a wide variety of cargo, including livestock. South Padre Island business owner Doyle Wells moved his horses inland until the bridge reopened. The *Rio Bravo* also transported larger loads, such as collected garbage and fuel trucks.

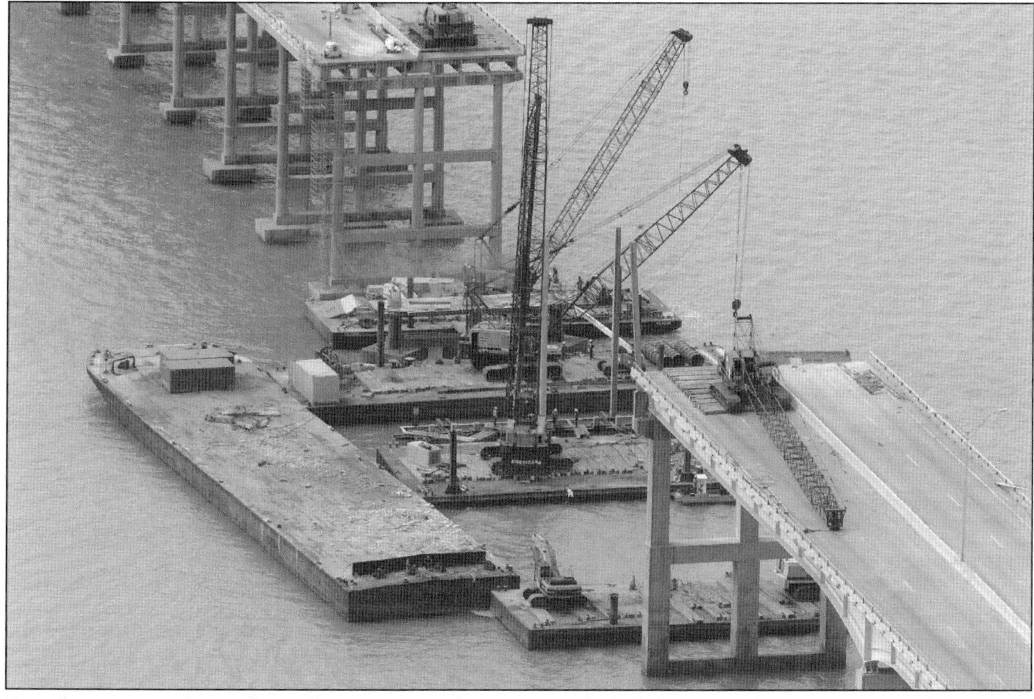

Simultaneous tasks at the collision site at this stage included driving pilings, removing debris, and pouring new footings. Workers called this "Barge City" and became adept at traversing between the barges on 2-foot-by-12-foot planks.

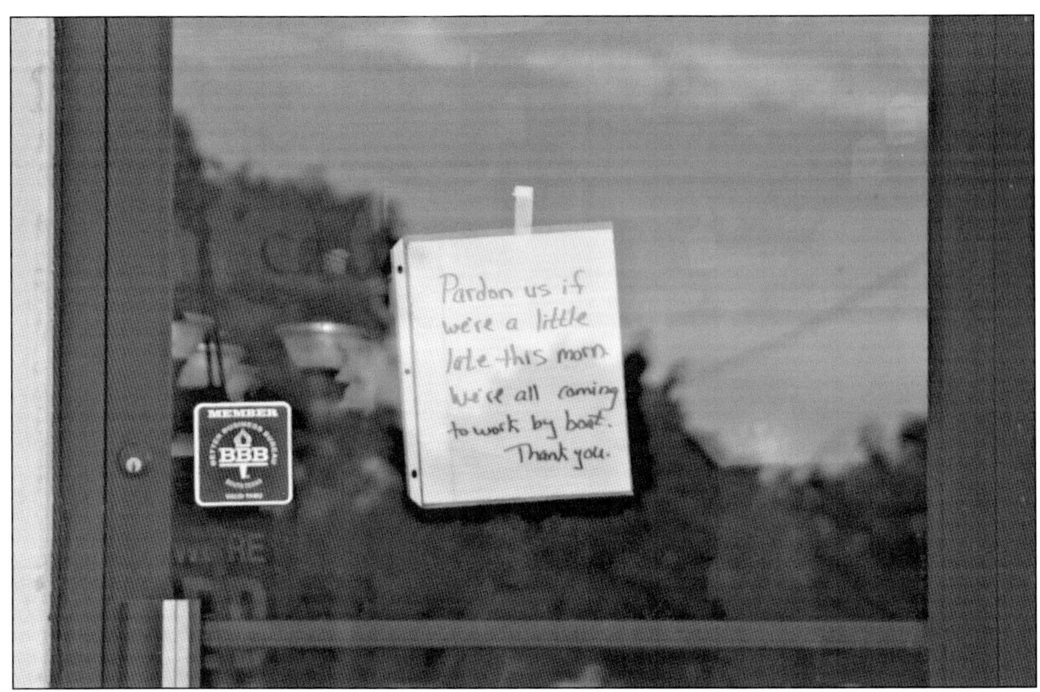

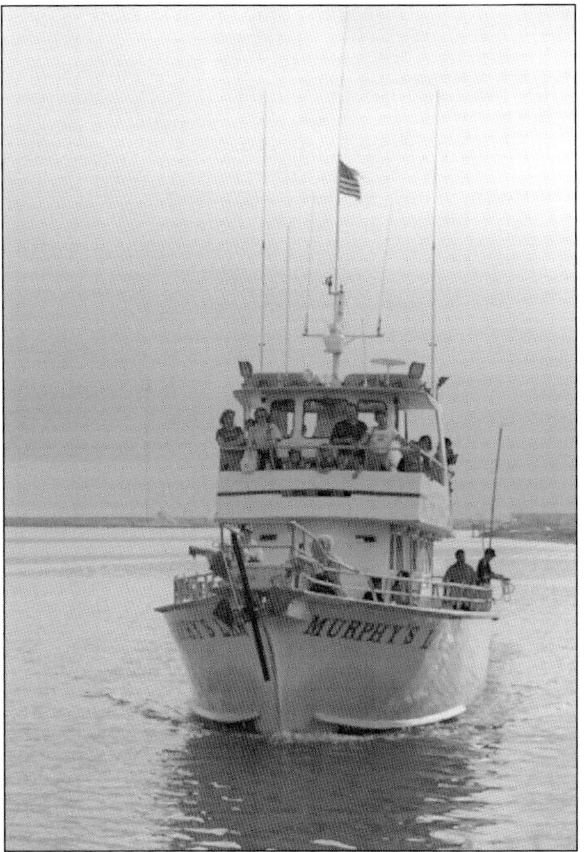

A Port Isabel business owner posted the following note: "Pardon us if we're a little late this morn. We're all coming to work by boat. Thank you." If it was not announced, it was understood. Workers living across the bay from their job arranged passage on one of the many boats in service. The H.E.B. grocery store parking lot served as a parking area where a shuttle service operated to the dock.

Murphy's Law served as one of the ferries between Port Isabel and South Padre Island. The Texas Department of Transportation, mindful of the concerns some travelers had about the bridge repair, extended the ferry service until November 25, 2001. This was the last ferry arriving in Port Isabel.

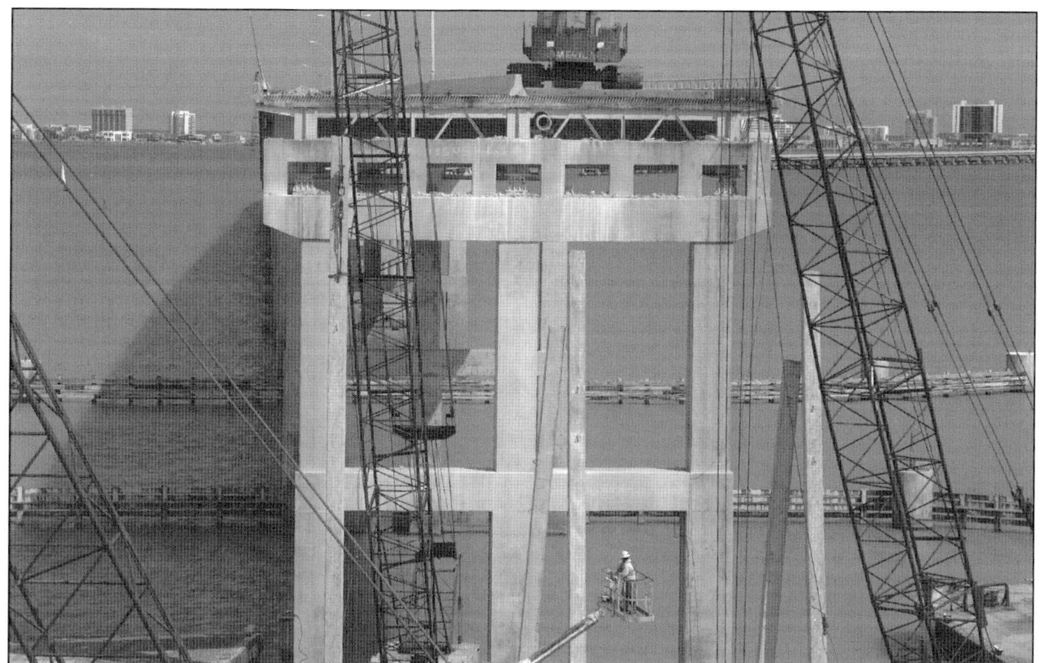

From the western side of the causeway looking eastward, the South Padre Island skyline is visible on the horizon. The Gulf Intracoastal Waterway, the intended target of the barge, is several hundred feet east of the missing roadway.

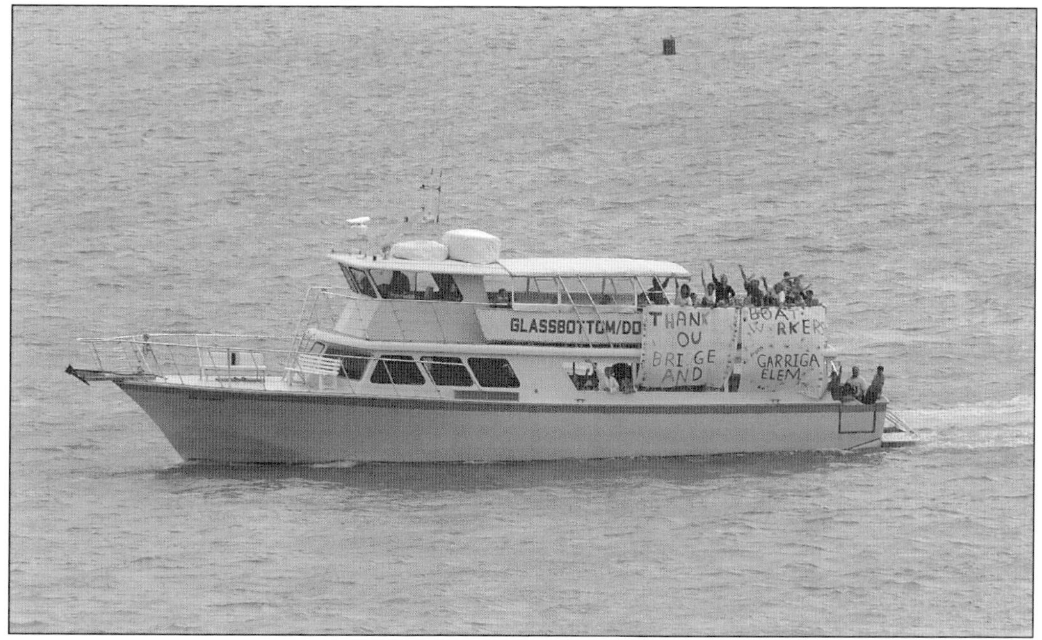

Students who lived on South Padre Island would catch this boat for the 2.5-mile boat ride to school in Port Isabel. The children painted large banners with the following message: "Thank you bridge and boat workers, from Garriga Elementary." The captain blew the horn, and all the students yelled and waved. This was one of their last trips to school by boat, just five days before the bridge reopened.

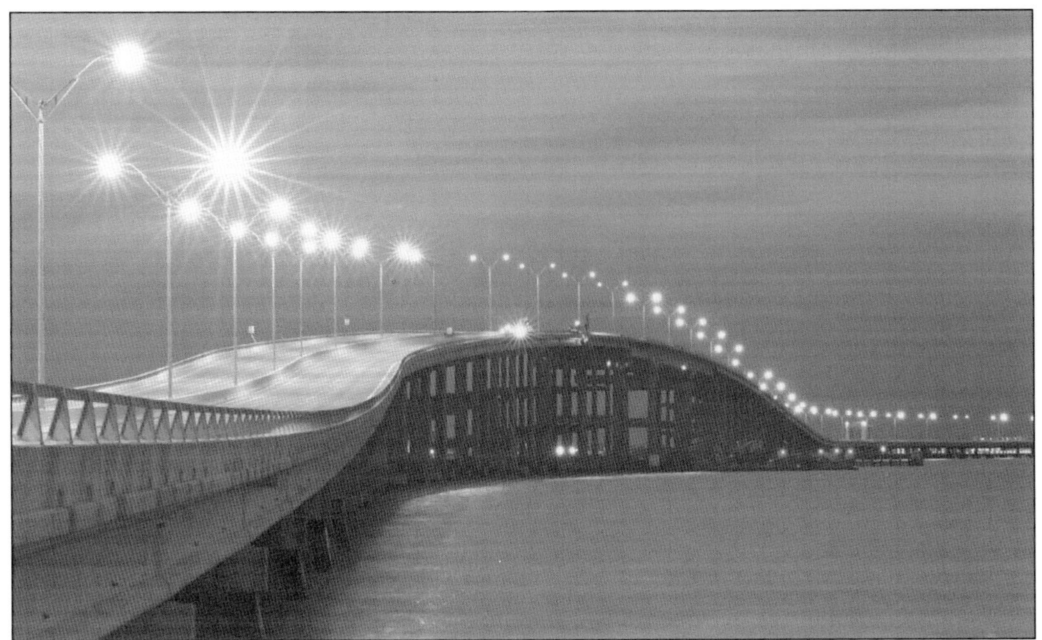

November 20, 2001, the evening before the reopening, last-minute tasks are being tackled. Earlier in the afternoon, crews swept the State Highway 100 route through Port Isabel. Locals and visitors alike were eagerly awaiting the reopening.

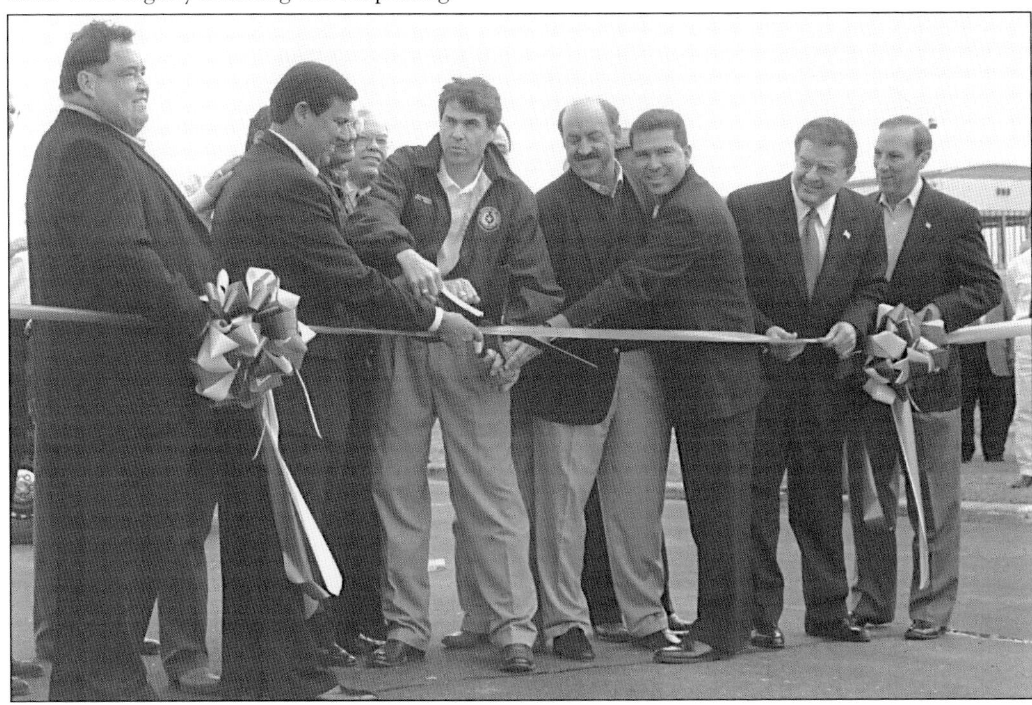

Gov. Rick Perry (third from the left), flanked by dignitaries (from left to right, starting on the far left) Pete Benevides, Sen. Eddie Lucio, South Padre Island mayor Ed Cyganiewicz, and Port Isabel mayor Patrick Marchan, cuts the ribbon on the morning of November 21, 2001. The bridge was now open to traffic.

Nine

Building a Life

It seems the coast requires a special breed to survive it, and Port Isabel is no exception. From the times when earliest Karanqua Indians were summering and fishing on the shores, to Don Rafael Garcia ranching and ushering in international trade and tourism and later shrimping, life could be challenging in the sea breezes. Earliest *Port Isabel Pilots* carried headlines reflecting the dust control problems. Annually, from June to November, the area is threatened by hurricane season. Several severe hurricanes and storms took their toll in the 1880s, 1933, and 1967. Port Isabel is home to where people build lives that occasionally have to be rebuilt.

With the arrival of the "building a city where a city belongs," many of Port Isabel's generational residents had to adjust to the hardship of displacement. Mexiquito and Palangana, areas of town not directly affected by the improvements of the 1920s, contributed to the workforce that began in rehabilitation and ended in tourism—a vital piece for both experiences.

In the 1950s, Port Isabel proudly flew the banner of "Shrimp Capital of the World." During the peak of the season, boats from as far away as Houston and Louisiana would join in with the Port Isabel fleets, numbering over 150. Supporting businesses employed locals to build and repair boats, nets, and engines. Shrimp was processed in houses along the South Shore Drive area where it was packed and shipped all over the world. The majority of the workforce in Port Isabel was directly or indirectly contributing to the industry.

Legislation brought about changes in the shrimping industry that saw the era come to a close, and the economy shifted to tourism, where it remains today. With the construction of the second Queen Isabella Causeway in 1974, tourism numbers continued to grow. Port Isabel is a community that can adjust and abide, though the difficulty to do so should not be underestimated.

Col. E.H. Downs made the following remarks during his address to the celebratory crowd at the official opening of the San Benito-Point Isabel Navigation District: "That we may have abundant measure of happiness and prosperity to which we are entitled it is necessary that we continue to have faith in the valley, our neighbors and ourselves."

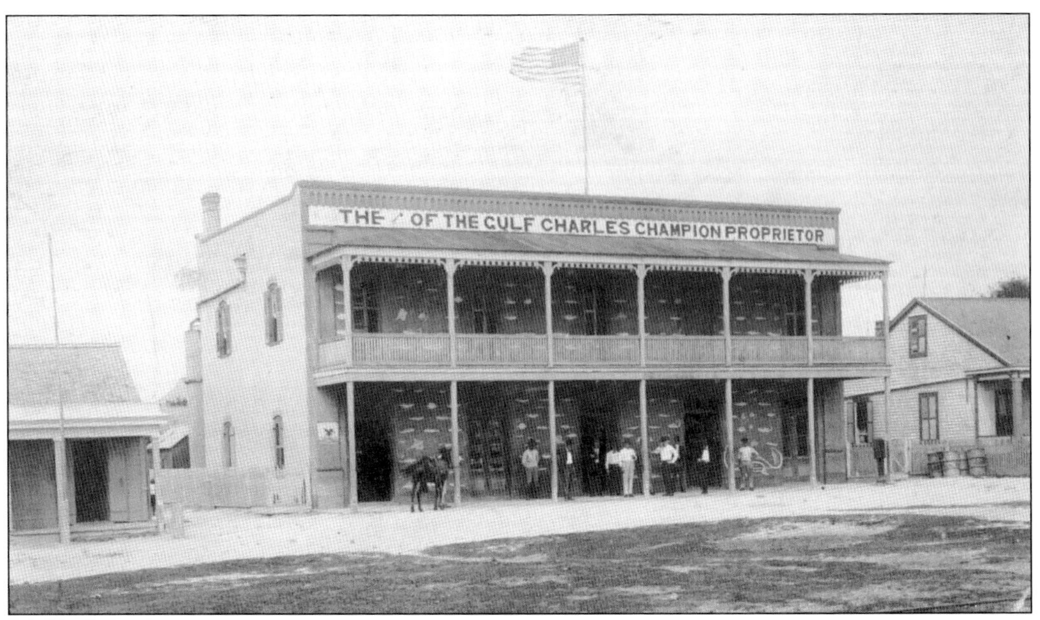

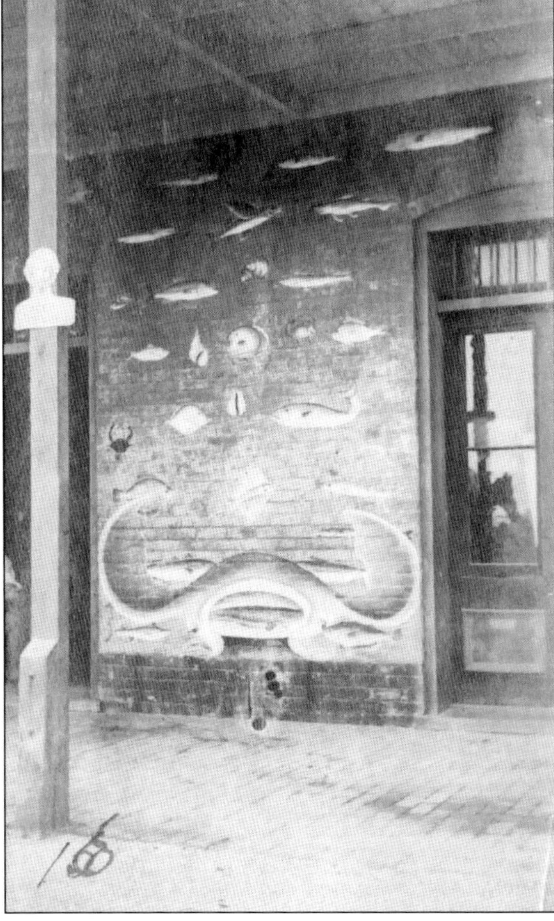

The Champion family was among the first settlers in Port Isabel. For a time, they were engaged in the business of transporting goods from ships off Brazos Santiago to the wharves of Port Isabel. In 1899, Charles Champion built this two-story structure, which served as general store, railroad depot, and post office.

The Champion family residence was on the top floor. A grocery store and meat market was in business until the mid-1940s. Painted by a local one-armed fisherman, the mural on the facade depicts dozens of species of native sea life. Throughout the years, the building fell into several hands and was used as a restaurant at one time. It now houses the Port Isabel Historical Museum.

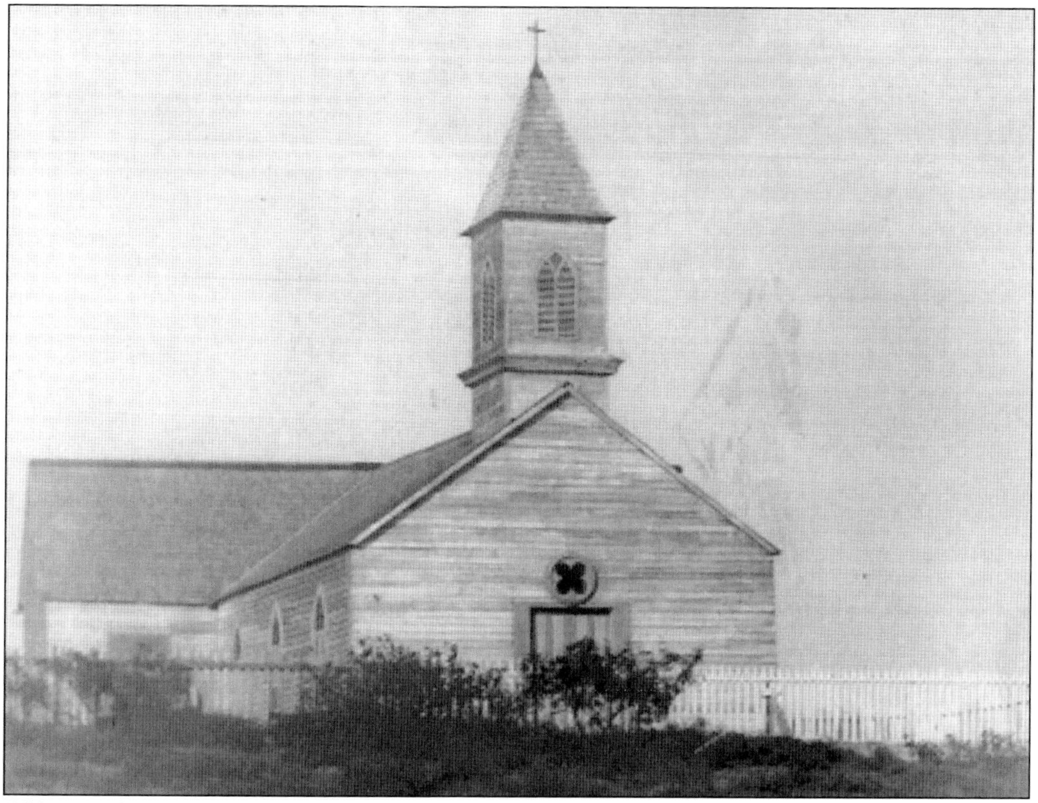

Oblate Fathers landing in December 1849 celebrated their first Mass on valley soil on their way to Brownsville, their intended destination. By 1854, the first framed chapel was built, which fell casualty to the US Civil War. In 1869 and 1877, second and third chapels were built, both succumbing to storms. A fourth church, constructed in 1881 (pictured here), was destroyed by the storms of the 1933 hurricane.

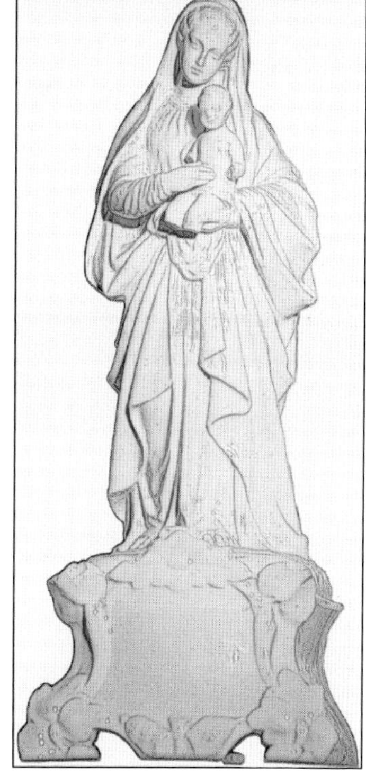

After the storm of 1884, US Coast Guard captain Encarnacion Delgado found this little statue in the sand on South Padre Island. How old it was or where it came from has remained a mystery. Delgado presented it to the Our Lady of the Sea Catholic Church. When the church building was demolished in the 1933 hurricane, only the little statue, the altar stone, and sacred vessels remained.

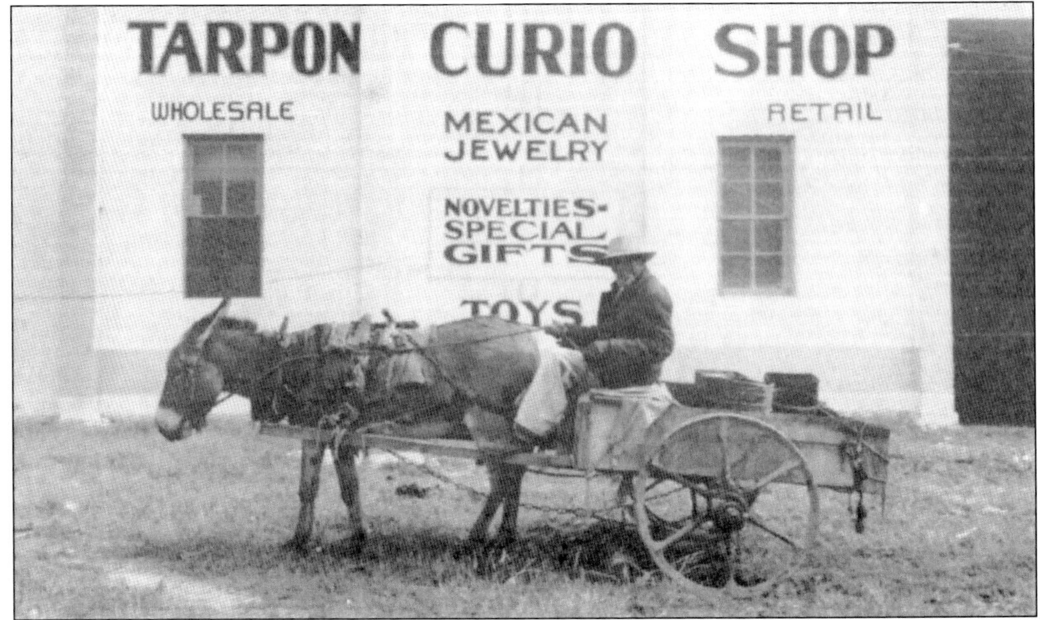

Don Chencho Rosales was an aguador among other professions. Long after the need for water delivery, he continued to ride his two-wheeled cart behind his faithful burro through the streets of town, collecting scraps for his pigs and posing for tourists.

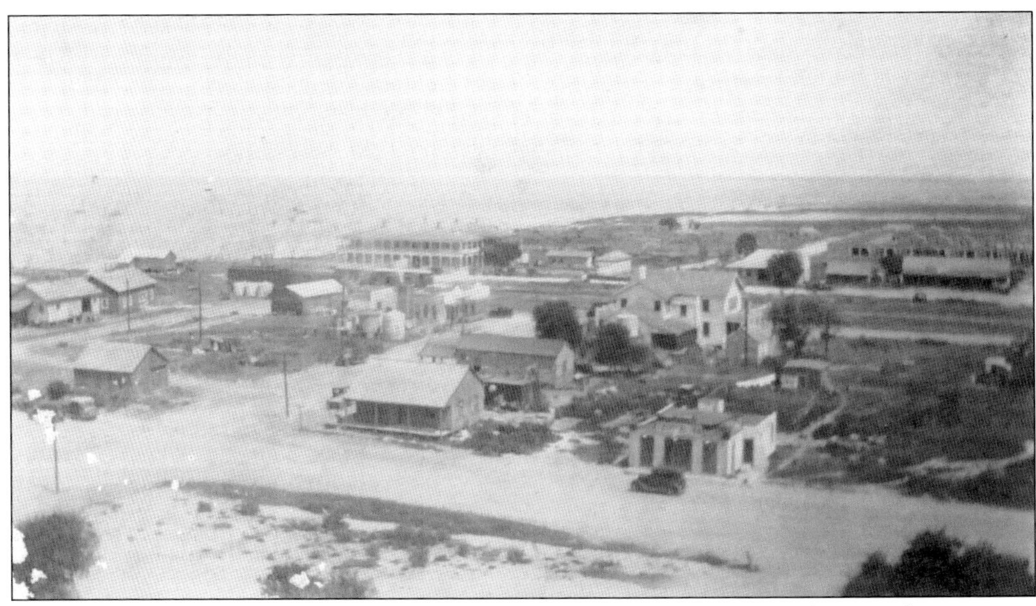

As Port Isabel's tourism industry grew, so did businesses to support it. Locals opened restaurants and cafés, souvenir shops, garages, hotels and courts, sweet shops, and laundries and employed other residents. Fishing was also an important industry. Port Isabel was first to ship out cleaned and gilled fish, which kept better after that preparation.

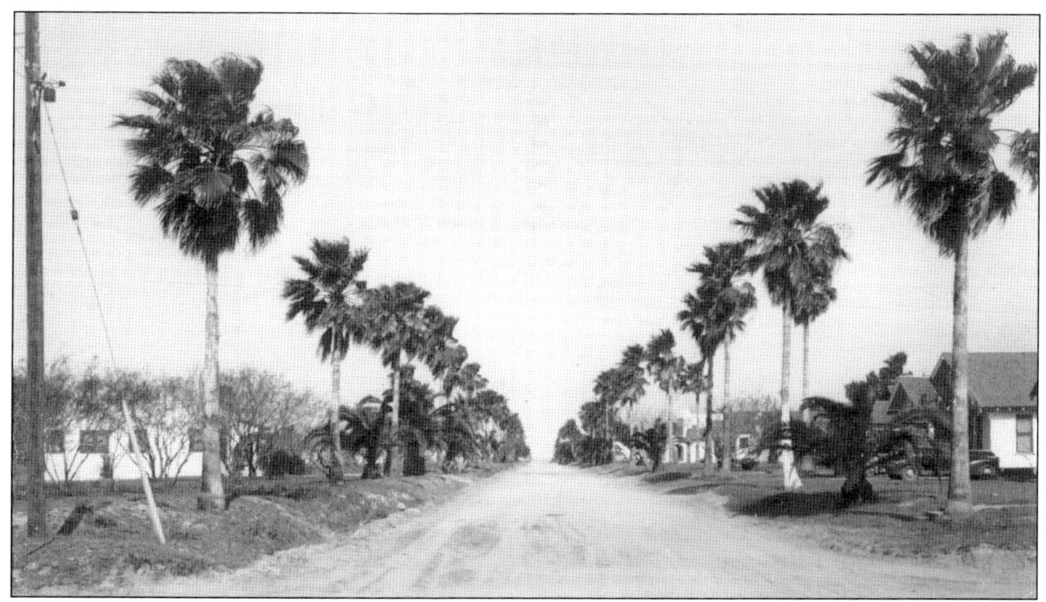

During the 1920s, while the city was developing, two palm trees were planted on every one of over 2,200 lots. Seen here nearly 20 years later, they have grown to postcard-worthy size and have served to further the tropical appeal of the coastal town.

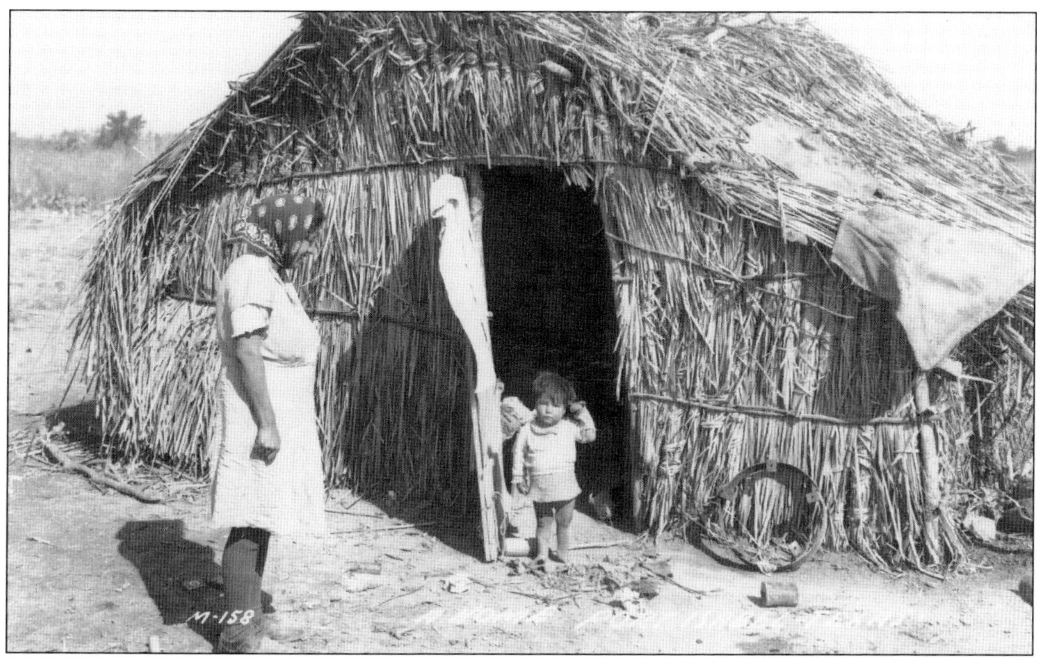

Some of the earliest residential and utilitarian structures were jacales. Using readily available materials, a jacale could be built fairly quickly and, with some maintenance, be quite durable. This one appears to have been constructed with Texas sabal palm fronds.

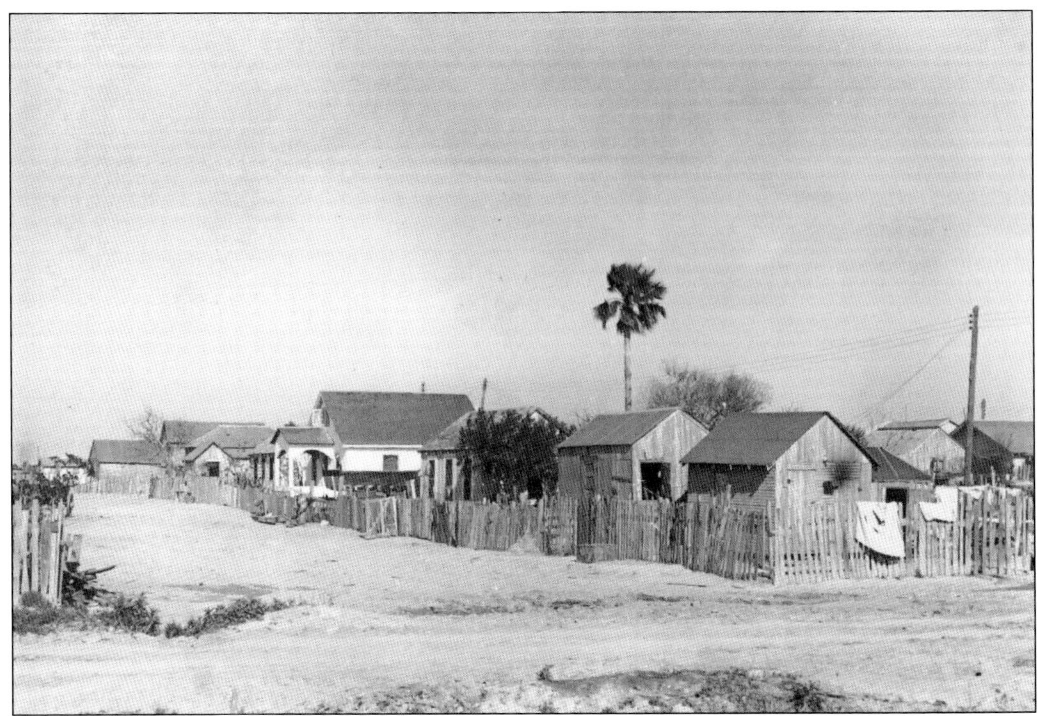

Jacales gave way to frame structures as materials became available. In 1949, before urban renewal, the Mexiquita area of town was a mixture of architectural styles. A great deal of resources had been used to develop other areas of town that left Mexiquito several decades behind the progress taking place just blocks away.

APPROVED January 26th 1895
E. H. Goodrich
County (........) Superintendent of Cameron County.

2310

No. 121 January 18th 1895.
$ 35.00
Public School No. one in District or Community No. one
Cameron County, Texas, January 19 1895
PAY TO Mrs. E. C. Best or order, the sum
of Thirty five DOLLARS
out of the Public School Fund apportioned to the Pt. Isabel Public School
District or Community No. one for services as Teacher in Public Free School No. one of said District or Community for the month ending the 18 day of January 1895

TO C. Garca
County Treasurer .... County, Texas.
NOTE.—Do *not* make the voucher in duplicate.

August Thomell
John G. Champion
Trustees of School District or Community No. ....
in .... County, Texas.

Public School No. 1 in District or Community No. 1 employed teacher Mrs. E.C. Best. This receipt shows payment in the amount of $35 for the month of December 17, 1894, to January 18, 1895, out of the Public School Fund apportioned to Point Isabel Public School.

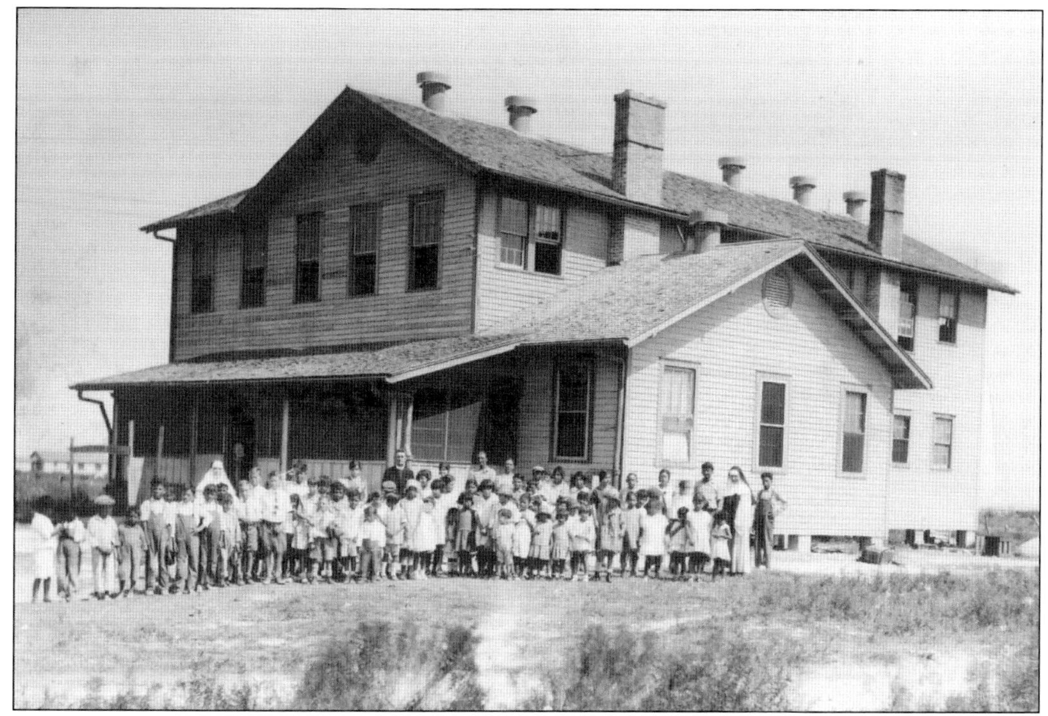

After the wireless station moved to Fort Brown in 1923, these buildings were repurposed. This structure was used as the Our Lady of the Sea Parochial School. Eventually, a public school was built and lessened the need for this school, and it was shut down. Here, students pose with the Sisters on a neighborhood cleanup day in the late 1940s.

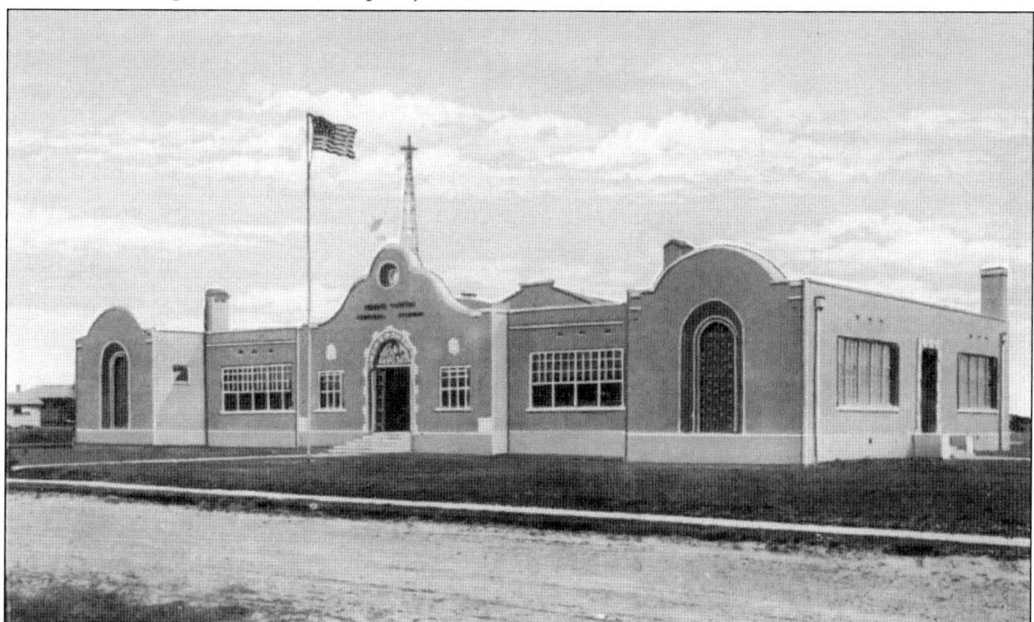

Port Isabel's public school, now Garriga Elementary, was named for the first native Texan to become a Catholic bishop. Mariano S. Garriga was born in Port Isabel in 1886. The completion of the public school in 1928 followed the service of the Catholic school, which closed soon after.

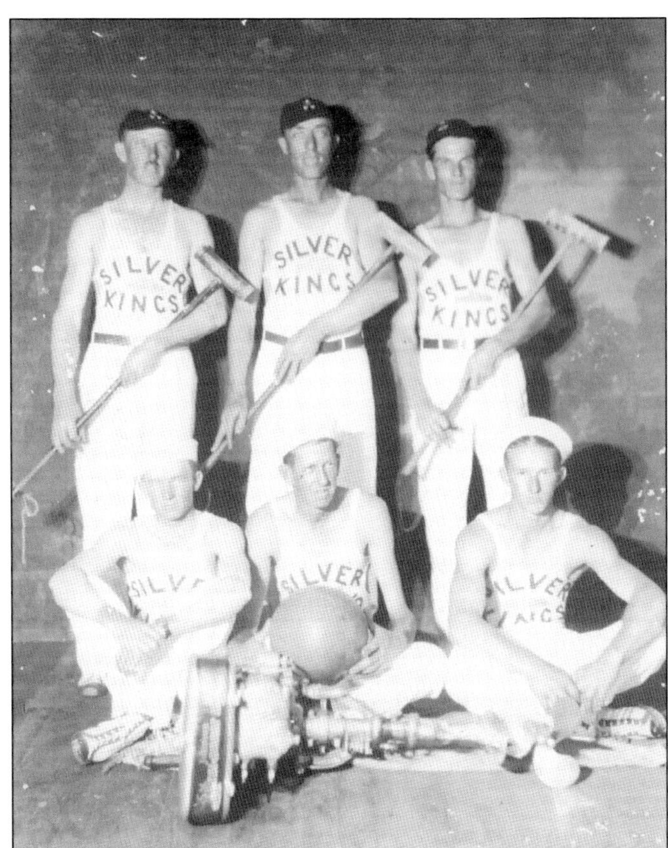

The Silver Kings was a water polo team introduced in Port Isabel by Dr. J.A. Hockaday in the 1930s as an addition to the activities offered at the newly formed Port Isabel Yacht Club. Buoys marked a rectangular 50-yard-by-200-yard course. Regulations called for a flat-bottomed four-foot-by-eight-foot boat fitted with a 12-horsepower motor whose construction cost was not to exceed $25.

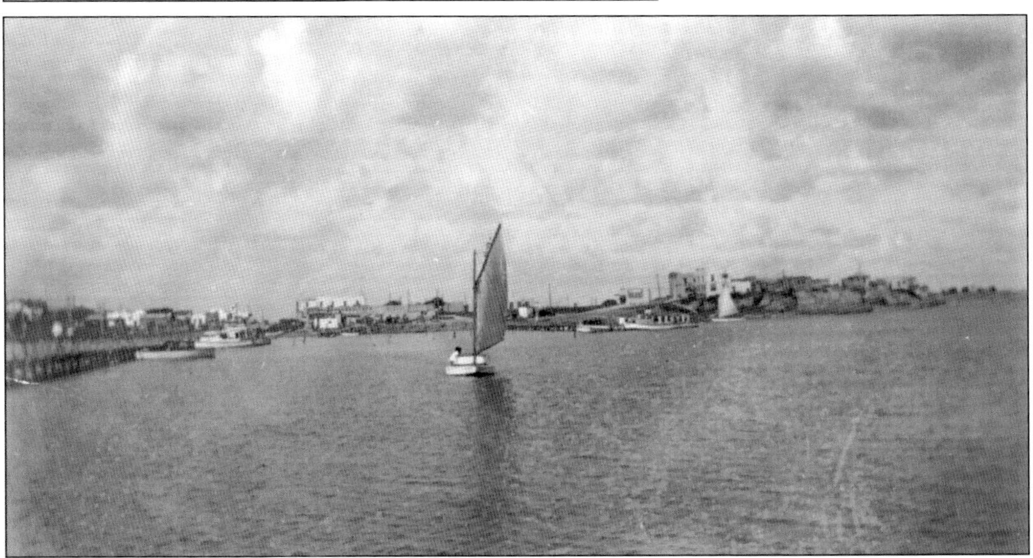

The *Alibi I*, owned and usually piloted by Ed Hinkley, sails on the Laguna Madre Bay off Port Isabel in the late 1930s. The Laguna Sailing Club held highly competitive sailing races on Sunday afternoons. Using the Moonlight Pier Pavilion as a temporary headquarters, the organization built a breakwater marina and clubhouse in 1940. During 1939, six world records for the fastest mile were set in the Brownsville Ship Channel.

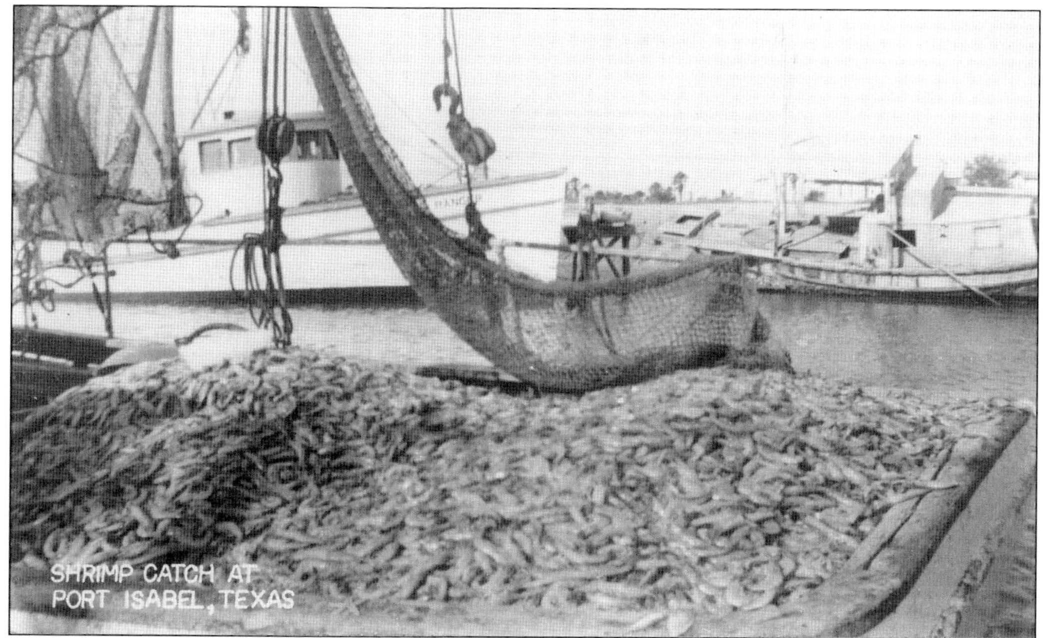

Prior to legislation changing regulations regarding shrimping, the industry was booming. Port Isabel's close proximity to the Gulf of Mexico meant that vessels had quick access to Gulf waters and abundant shrimp. By 1958, Port Isabel had 10 processing plants and 173 shrimp boats operating from local docks.

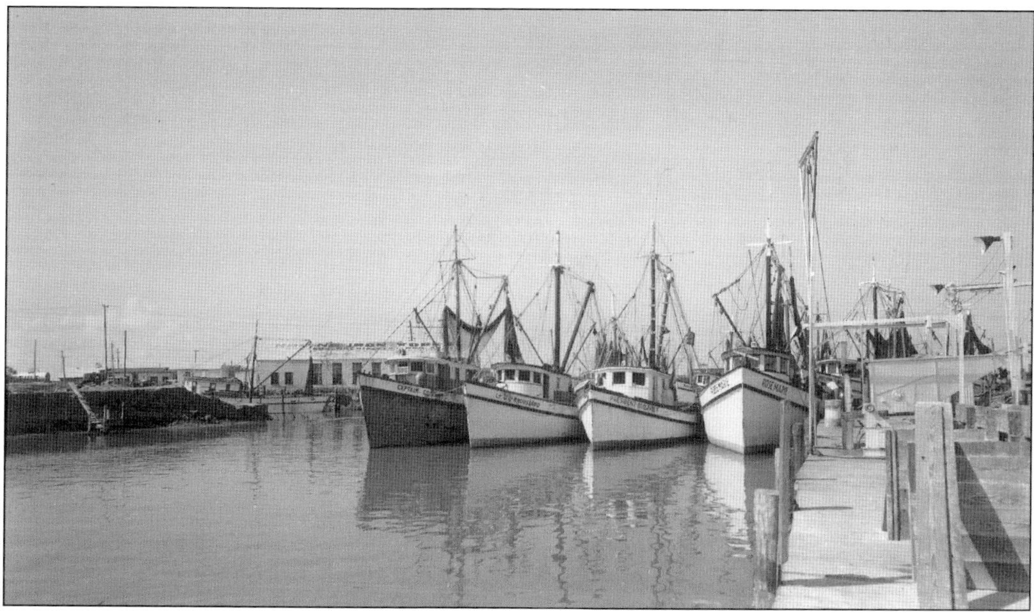

A 1968 article in *Tip-O-Texan*, the official publication of the Lower Rio Grande Valley Chamber of Commerce, titled, "They Farm the Sea," boasted that Port Isabel had the largest tonnage of shrimp in the United States with an annual harvest of 20 million pounds. In 1967, the industry was valued over $100 million, exceeding tuna and salmon. Restaurants proclaimed, "The shrimp you eat here slept in the Gulf of Mexico last night."

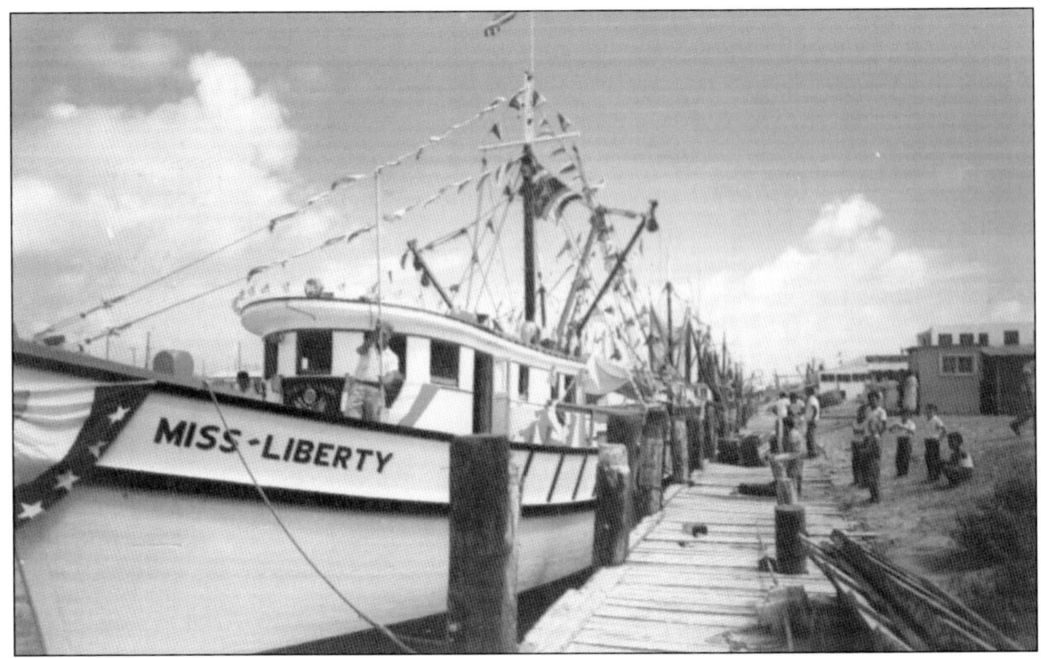

At dockside, *Miss Liberty* is decorated for the annual Blessing of the Fleet. At the opening of the shrimping season, decorated boats head into the channel as an officiating clergy would bless the passing vessels. It is also a popular spectator event.

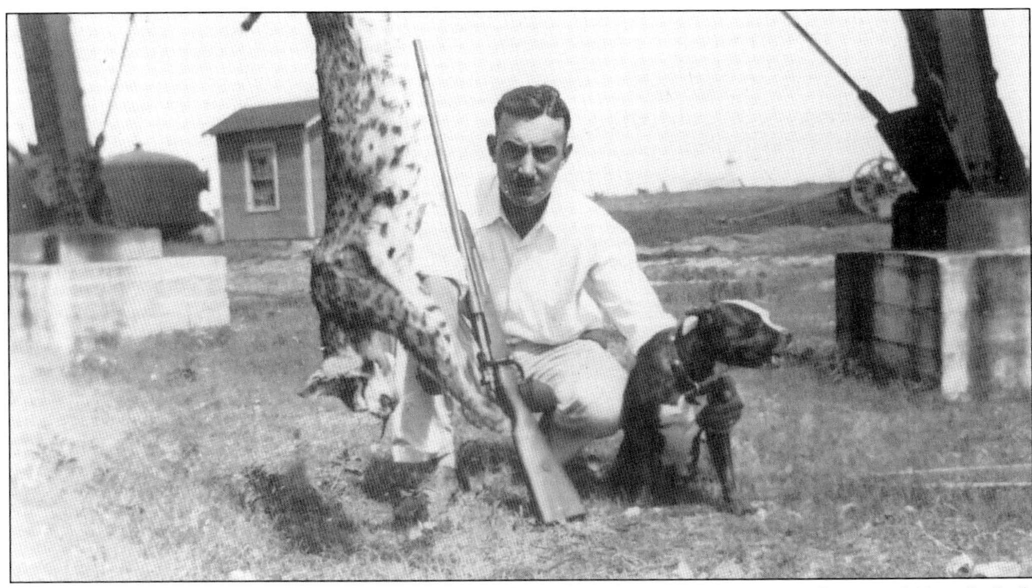

Locals and visitors alike took advantage of the hunting opportunities in and around Port Isabel. Here, a sportsman poses with his bobcat. Advertisements in the mid-1930s promised there was no place like Port Isabel for quail, wild duck, deer, and wild turkey, and within 50 miles the sportsman could hunt bear and mountain lion or almost any other type of game.

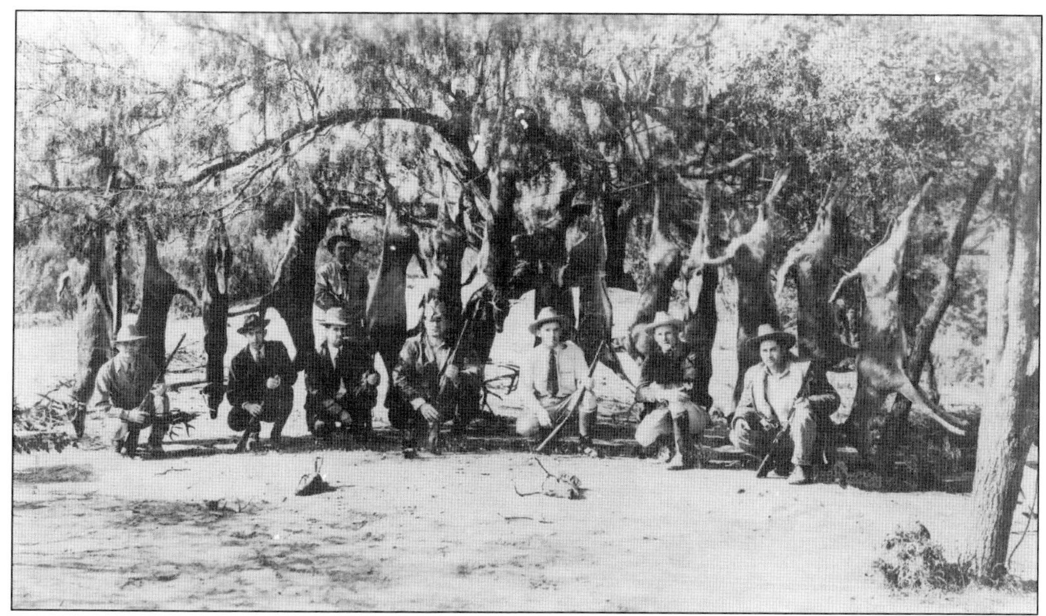

The bearer of this picture card was authorized to hunt in the Yturria Hunting Club Preserve from November 16, 1941, to January 16, 1942, and agreed to comply with all state and federal game laws, such as not hunting on land adjoining the preserve. The Yturria preserve was located just west of Port Isabel.

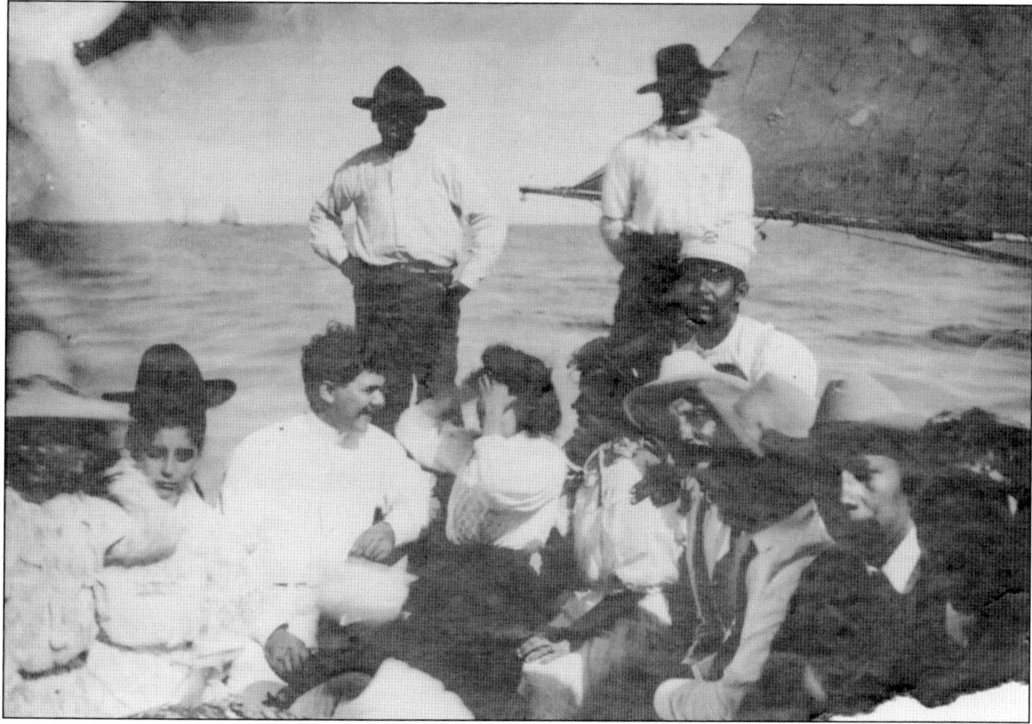

In the 1870s, the first ferries leaving Port Isabel for Brazos Santiago and South Padre Island left the Rio Grande Railroad docks. Locals would run the shallow draft sailboats across the Laguna Madre with tourists looking to spend the day on the beach.

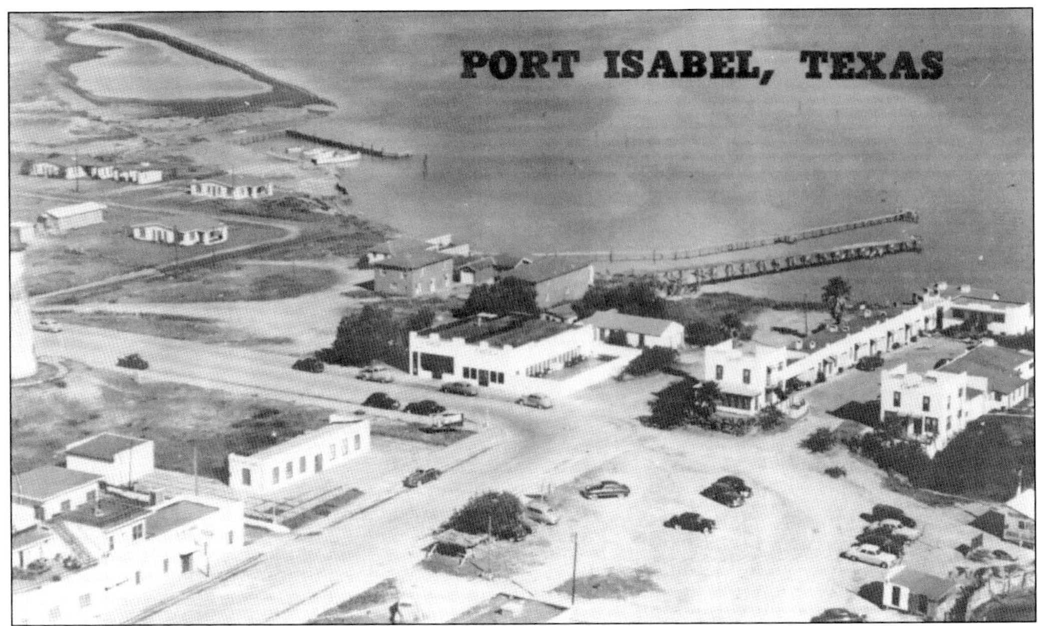

This 1951 diagonal aerial, looking northwest, shows a bustling coastal tourist town. Ship's Café (center) offered fresh seafood. Purdy's Courts (to the right of the Ship's Café) offered accommodations and pier fishing. Sullivan's (lower right) boasted a pier and boat rides to South Padre Island and snapper fishing trips. The Mexican Mart (bottom center, partly cropped) had a large selection of Mexican curios and local souvenirs.

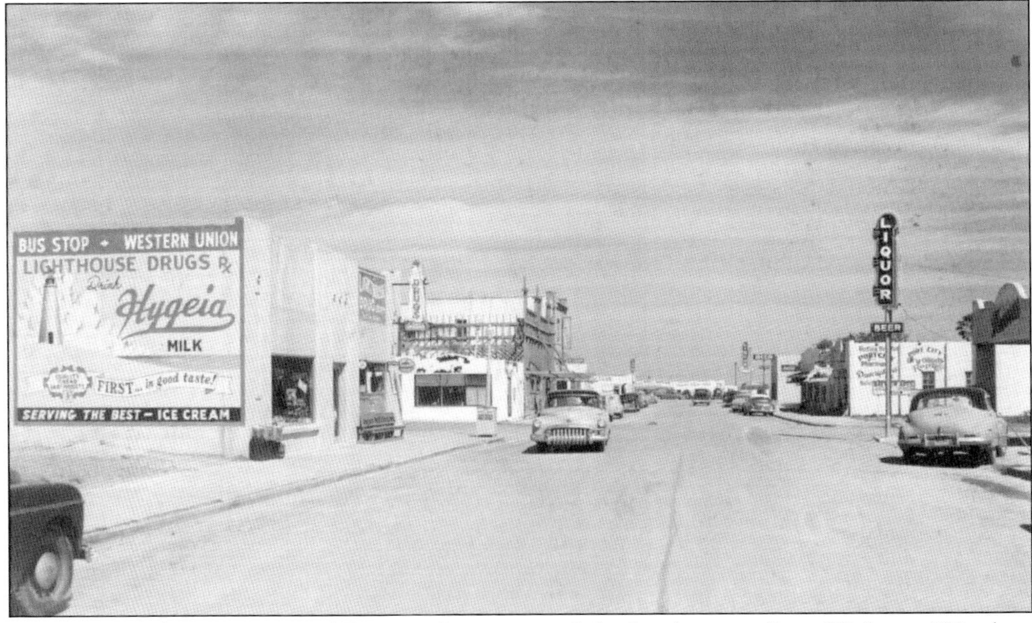

Powers Street from just west of Tarnava Street toward the bay became State Highway 100 when the new Queen Isabella Causeway was constructed in 1974. Bustling with commerce, Powers Street was the location of Lighthouse Drugstore, a Missouri Pacific Bus Line stop, a tackle shop, numerous cafés, clubs and liquor stores, television repair, Humble Gasoline, Port City Pharmacy and Dry Goods, and Colley's Boat Service.

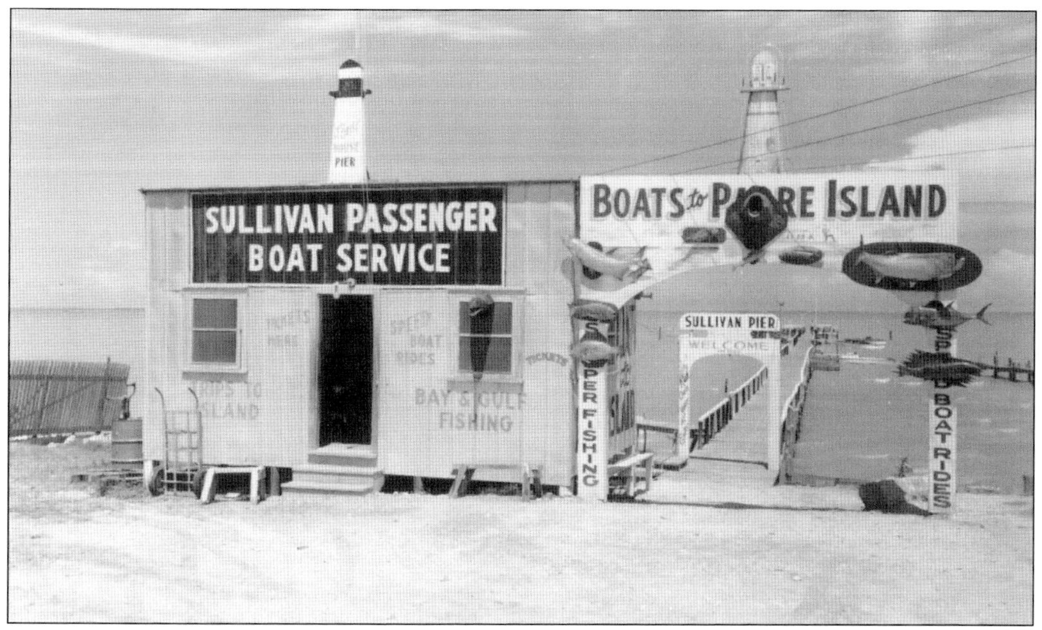

"Sullivan Pier, Port Isabel, Texas, Welcome on Dock," reads the smaller sign over the pier. And to the left, "enter at your own risk" cautions visitors as they walk down the pier to take a boat across the Laguna Madre Bay to South Padre Island. The small lighthouse, found on the top of the "Boats to Padre Island," was embellished by neon. Sullivan's was located just northeast of the lighthouse.

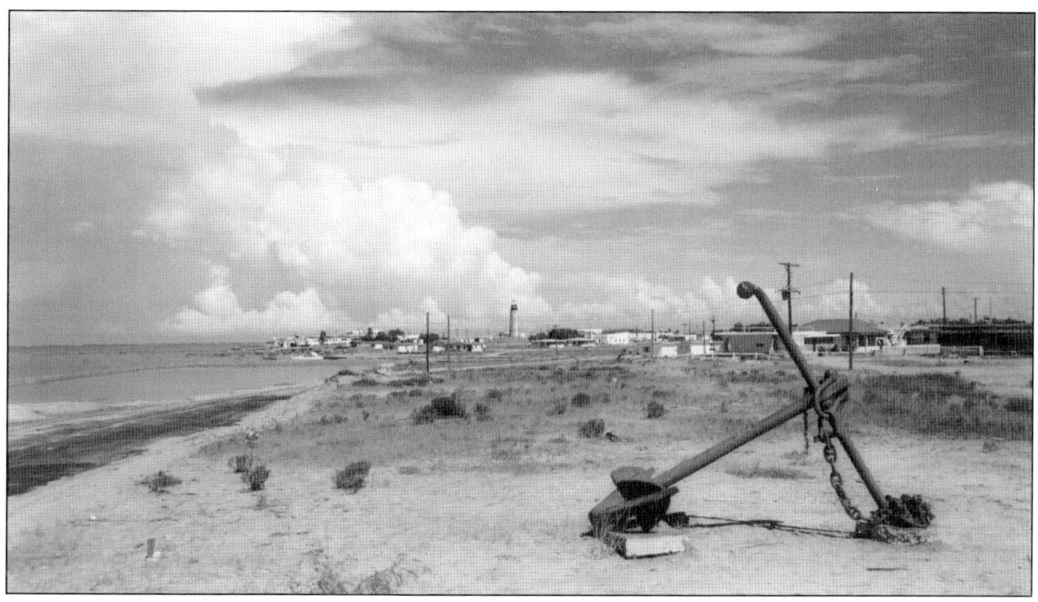

Anchors, floats, and other nautical items found their way back on land and were sprinkled throughout neighborhoods as yard ornaments. This view of the North Shore Drive area also boasts freshly oiled roads in the 1940s. To residents and visitors, the value of a paved, tarred, or oiled road could not be overlooked. Sand carried on strong southerly winds made it, as an account stated, "Impossible to keep a house clean."

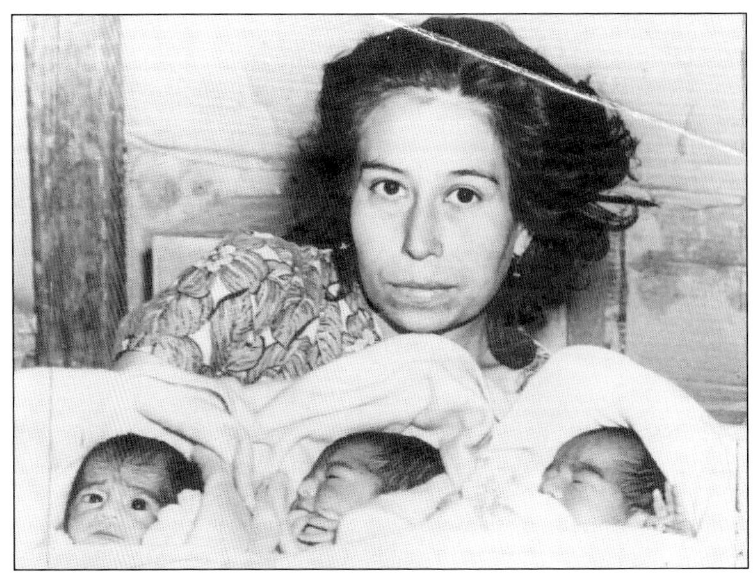

Port Isabel made the news in 1944 with the births of multiple children. Not since 1925 had triplets been born in Port Isabel, and within 20 hours, twins were born to one Mrs. Garza. Pictured are Mrs. Guadalupe Valdez and her three daughters. Mrs. Valdez was the daughter of Don Jesus Vega, proprietor of the Tarpon Beach Hotel, a popular South Padre Island beach resort in the 1920s.

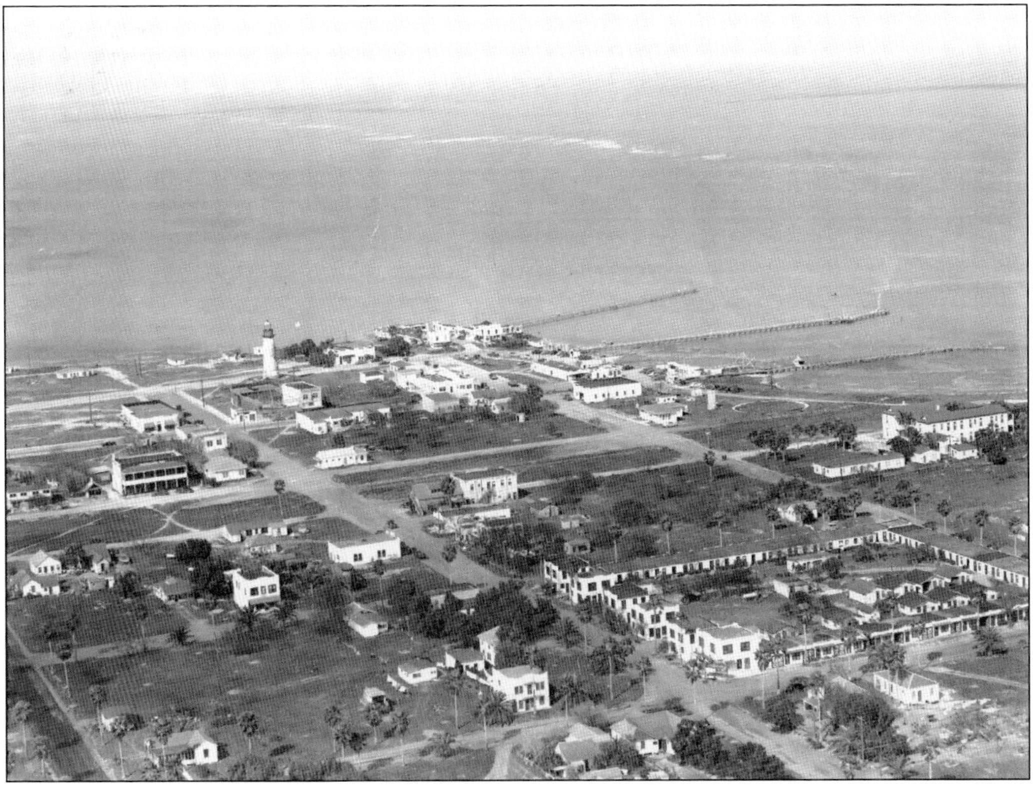

By the 1950s, Port Isabel was growing deeper roots. Architecture had changed from the vernacular to Spanish with a sprinkling of mid-century Moderne. Bay View Apartments and Courts took up an entire city block (right) and was a home base for many newcomers before settling into a permanent home. In 1944, one Mrs. Bellinghousen said in an article in the *Port Isabel Press*, "Here to make home, for the present we are domiciled in a Bay View Tourist apartment."

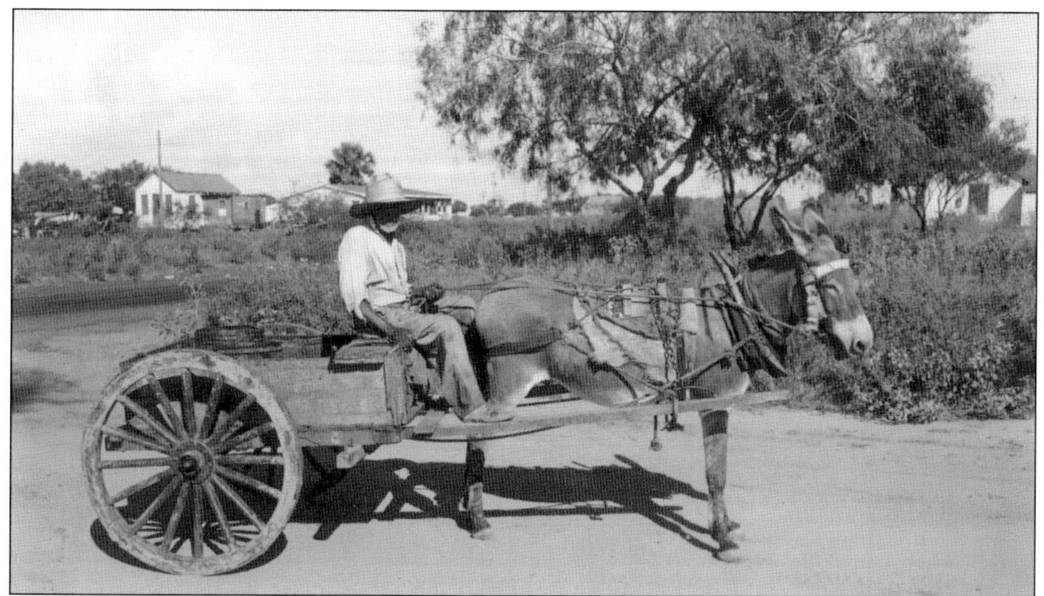

Don Chencho was remembered as a most ingenuous character. Being about the age of 16 when the lighthouse was under construction and having escaped the cholera epidemic that swept Port Isabel, Chencho was pressed into service. In a 1943 interview, he commented on the lighthouse as it "now stands forgotten in its glory except in memory and seems so lonesome in unfamiliar surroundings."

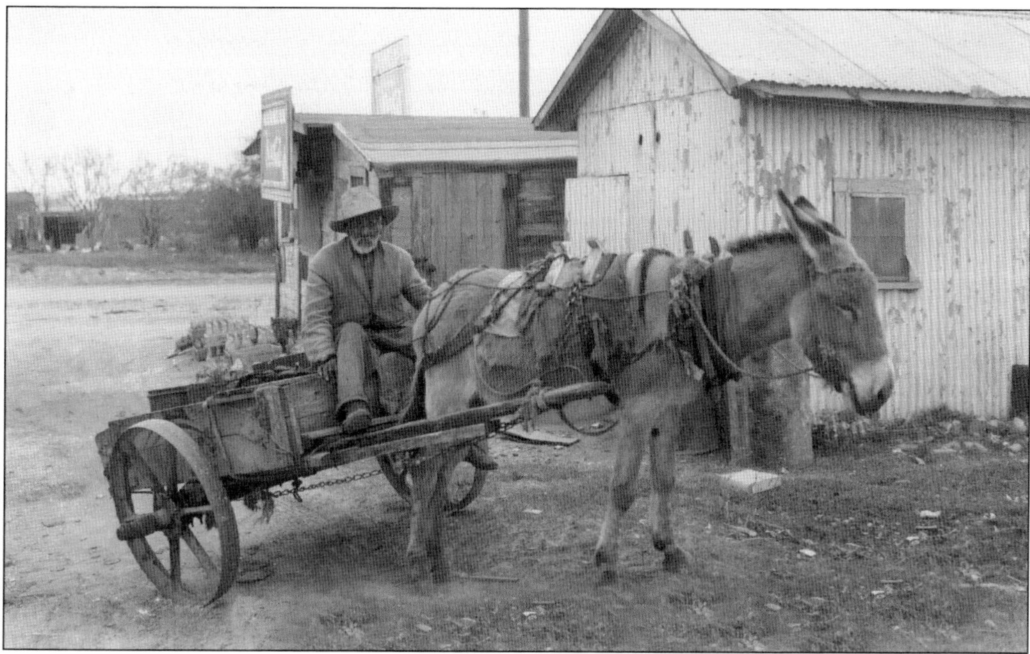

A question often asked, "What ever became of the little old man who rode up and down the streets in his two-wheel cart?" The query opens a 1952 newspaper article about the dedication of the lighthouse as a state park before the answer, "Old Don Chencho Rosalie is dead." He died in February 1950 at 115 years old. The spirit of Don Chencho is still in the little town on the bay that he helped to build.